DAIRY DIARY

FAVOURITE COUNTRYSIDE BIRDS

ACKNOWLEDGEMENTS

Executive editor *Nick Rowe*
Editor   *Debbie Robertson*
Designer   *Alyson Kyles*
Production   *Priti Kothary*
                  Teresa Wellborne

Printed & bound in the UK
by Butler and Tanner Ltd

This book was designed, edited and
produced by Eaglemoss Publications Ltd,
using material first published as the
partwork *The Country Bird Collection*.

Copyright © Eaglemoss Publications Ltd 2007

10 9 8 7 6 5 4 3 2 1

Published by
Eaglemoss Consumer Publications Ltd,
Electra House, Electra Way,
Crewe Business Park,
Crewe, Cheshire CW1 6WZ
Telephone 01270 270050
Website www.dairydiary.co.uk

ISBN 13 : 978-0-9554232-2-2

CONTENTS

CHAPTER 1 · FARMLAND & GRASSLAND

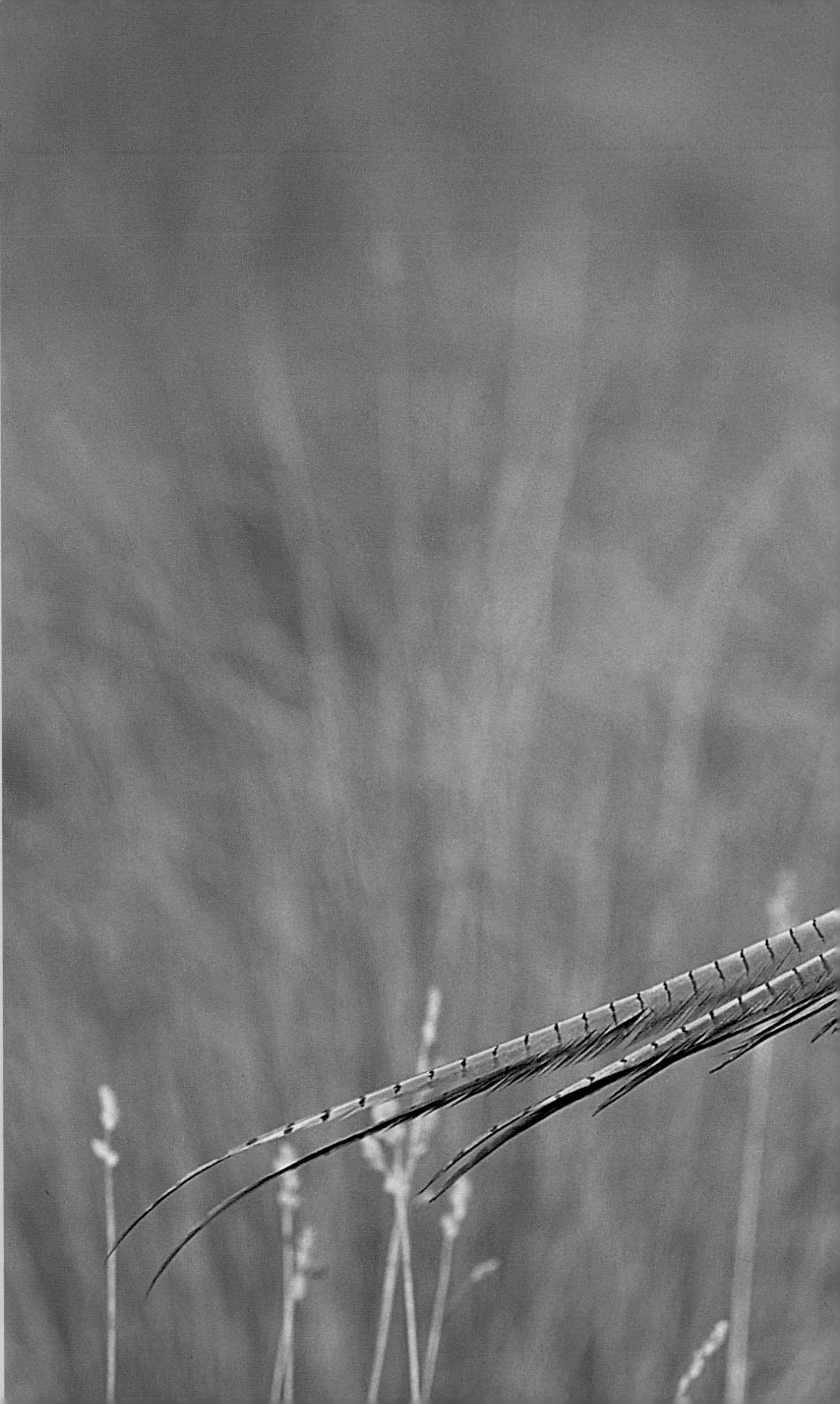

The Skylark

Far and wide, the male skylark is famous for fluttering to a lofty, invisible platform in the sky and raining down his sweet, cheerful lyrics on the fields and meadows below

Once, the skylark's musical voice was the loudest and clearest anthem to summer, ringing out from the skies above meadows, cornfields and heathland all over Britain. Sadly today it is rather a different story; although still widespread, numbers have declined dramatically in the past 30 years.

FLOATING IN THE AIR

The skylark is one of the few songbirds that thrives in open country without any cover, apart from tussocks of grass, or any tall trees and bushes from which to sing. He flies higher than any tree-top to deliver his sublime song while hovering over his territory below.

▶ **MUSICAL ARENAS**
The skylark was once almost exclusively a bird of open grassland, meadows and fields but today you are just as likely to see or hear one on heathland, sand dunes, saltmarshes and golf courses.

Up with the Lark

In spring, male skylarks sing passionately almost around the clock. Even the lengthening hours of daylight are not long enough for them. Famously anticipating sunrise by a couple of hours, they climb into the sky and sing while it is still dark. Early-rising larks were once a symbol of the fresh hope and joy of each new day.

'*And now the herald lark
Left his ground-nest, high tow'ring to descry
The morn's approach, and greet her with his song*'

from *Paradise Regained* by **John Milton** (1608-1674)

Heavenly Voice

DEPRIVED OF A HIGH vantage point in open country, the skylark creates his own flagpole by fluttering high into the sky and hanging in the air, while singing rapturously all the time.

Skylarks are exuberant singers. In *The Lark's Song*, Seumas O'Sullivan (1879-1958) describes the sparkling delivery of their song perfectly:

Falls suddenly and strangely sweet
The lark's song.
Bubbling, note on note
Rise fountainlike, o'erflow and float
Tide upon tide, and make more fair
The magic of the sunlit air.

According to Shakespeare in *The Winter's Tale*, the lark 'tirra-lirra chants'. To be fair, the male skylark does a bit more than *tirra-lirra*: he has about 300 notes at his disposal that he is constantly juggling into phrases of three to six notes, which form the basis of 50 song styles.

ENTHUSIASTIC SONGSTER

The skylark sings for 10 or 11 months of the year, falling silent only during August as he moults. When the male starts singing again in September or October, he sings nearer the ground and more briefly than he did during the early summer. On rare sunny days in November, December and January, sometimes he cannot resist a short, low-level trill. The great outburst of song starts in February when the birds are pairing up and gets more and more fervent during May and June until the chicks hatch.

▲ **SKY HIGH**
The sunlight shining through the white edges of its wings and tail creates a glowing aura around a singing skylark. The poet William Davies aptly described the skylark as 'day's black star'.

circling and hovering at the summit

the downward flightpath

the upward flightpath

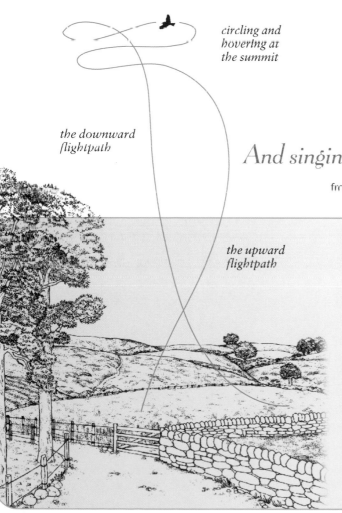

'*Higher still and higher*
From the earth thou springest
Like a cloud of fire;
The blue deep thou wingest,
And singing still dost soar, and soaring ever singest'

from *To a Skylark* by **Percy Bysshe Shelley** (1792-1822)

Breathless Solo

With a shake of his wings, a skylark takes off and rises steeply. He starts singing as soon as his feet leave the ground, matching the tempo of his song to his rapidly beating wings. Occasionally, the bird pauses in his ascent, as if resting on an invisible stairway. The warmer it is on the ground, the higher he climbs, reaching his ceiling anywhere between 50 and 100m (165 and 320ft) aloft. Still singing, the lark starts to hover and circle over his nest site. His aerial extravaganza usually lasts no longer than two to five minutes. Soon he is heading back to earth again, singing all the way. About 10m (30ft) from the ground, he closes his wings and goes into a dive, dropping like a stone. At the last minute, he spreads his wings once more to slow his breakneck fall and glides gently into land.

Musical Family

SKYLARKS ARE STILL about twice as common on arable land under cultivation as they are on pastures where there is livestock roaming about. Those nesting on grassland delay egg-laying until late April or early May, so that the hatching of their chicks coincides with the appearance of masses of creepy crawlies in mid to late May.

Some skylarks nest on the upper slopes of flower-strewn railway embankments. Others happily build along banks of estuaries, among the tufts of grass on saltmarshes or under a clump of heather on moorland. Wherever they nest, skylarks generally rear up to four broods each year, from April to July.

FAMILY HOME

The skylark's nest is a simple shallow depression in the ground lined with loosely woven dried grass, protected by an overhanging grassy tussock or clod of earth. Although its nest is well hidden, a skylark always knows where to find it. Building on the ground has its disadvantages though: many nests are destroyed by modern silage- and hay-cutting machines. When the grass used to be cropped by hand with a scythe, farm workers would often cut around them.

OPEN NURSERY

Into the grass-lined saucer, the female skylark lays from three to five small greyish white eggs, thickly speckled with greenish brown. Although there are no sides to the nest-cup, the pear-shaped eggs cannot roll far. They fit neatly together as a clutch under the hen skylark as she incubates them.

The chicks hatch in 10 or 11 days. Unlike most ground-nesting birds, the skylarks' hatchlings are totally naked and helpless, but grow up

▲ NOT EASILY MOVED
As ground dwellers, skylarks are vulnerable to attack from crows, hawks, stoats, weasels and foxes. When alarmed, a skylark crouches down and rises only reluctantly, issuing a purring note of alarm as it flies off low over the ground.

'*The bird that soars on highest wing Builds on the ground her lowly nest*'

from *Humility* by **James Montgomery** (1771-1854)

Times Have Changed

The numbers of skylarks breeding on lowland farms fell by three-quarters between 1972 and 1996. This worrying drop is due largely to changes in the arable farming calendar. In the past 60 years, there has been a shift to autumn sowing of cereal crops, leaving fewer fields fallow for the winter, which deprives skylarks of feeding and nesting opportunities. Also, the crops that are planted in the autumn have grown too tall to be of use to the skylarks by the time they start nesting in April.

Where once the skylarks could glean a reasonable living from the fields for at least nine months of the year, today their opportunity to feed is largely restricted to late summer and early autumn.

As the country poet John Clare presciently and rather ominously observed over 150 years ago:

*See the ploughshare bury all the plain,
And not a cowslip on its lap remain;
The rush-tuft gone that hid the skylark's nest.*

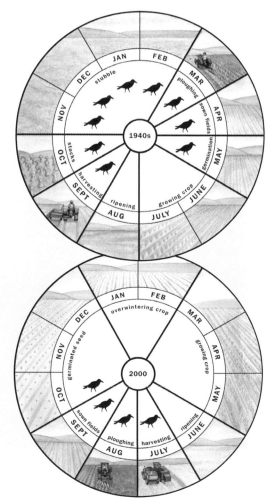

◀ HUNGRY CHOIR
A quartet of young skylarks greets a parent returning to its nest in the grass with a rousing chorus of 'Feed me! Feed me!' in Skylark.

▲ GRASS FLATTENER
A very long spur-like claw on the skylark's hind toes holds down clumps of grass, making it easier for the bird to run through pastures and meadows.

quickly. Both parents have their work cut out finding enough food to satisfy their hungry nestlings. For the first week they catch only insects, especially small beetles, and worms, then gradually introduce seeds and fresh shoots until the chicks are eating a mixed diet.

The youngsters leave the nest after nine to 10 days and start running around in the grass. They are fledged and ready to fly about 10 days later. At first, the juveniles' brown plumage appears scaly because each feather is outlined in white. They also lack the pale trailing edge to the wing of their parents. Young skylarks eventually develop their adult plumage during an autumn moult.

WINTER TIMES

In autumn, some skylarks migrate south to warmer parts in southern Europe. Those that stay in Britain are joined by a huge number of in-comers from northern Europe. They often join up with other birds, such as buntings and house sparrows, and

travel around in large flocks over the winter months. Their winter and spring diet consists mainly of seeds and tender young shoots of sprouting corn and clover which they find

growing in fields and meadows and along the waysides. The all-purpose beak is well suited to picking up and opening any tiny seeds it finds lying on the ground.

Grassy Bower

Sitting on her nest, a female skylark is almost invisible among the grasses and rushes. Her streaky cream, buff and brown plumage merges well into a backdrop of dried grass blades and earth. In a grassy field, it is possible to walk very close to a skylark and be completely unaware of its presence unless it moves.

To avoid giving away the location of the nest and to confuse would-be predators, a skylark always runs some distance away from it before taking off. It returns by a similarly circuitous, well-hidden route, stopping from time to time to look around and check that the coast is clear.

Exaltation of Larks

THE USE OF 'EXALTATION' as the collective noun for a flock of larks reflects how delighted people were to hear them singing so joyously from their choir stalls in the sky.

Some even claim that the skylark's scientific name, *Alauda arvensis*, stems from the Latin for to praise, *laudare*. Others contend that it is a combination of ancient Celtic words: *al*, which meant high, and *aud*, a word for song. The origins of *arvensis* are less contentious: it comes from *arvum* meaning field in Latin and *ensis*, a catch-all suffix that means belonging to.

The name lark itself seems to be a corruption of the Old English word *lāwerce* or *lāferce*, little songster.

◄ **HEAVEN ON EARTH**
Probably your best chance of seeing a skylark clearly is when he is singing ecstatically from the highest exposed perch available, such as a frond of bracken or the nearest fence post.

The Abuse of Skylarks

Considering how uplifting it is to hear skylarks singing, people have not always treated them very well:

● In England and all over Europe, there was an obscene trade in skylarks as caged birds and edible delicacies. Men called fowlers lured thousands of larks into their nets by dangling a small looking-glass and a scrap of red cloth known as a dare. To add insult to injury, captive larks were often blinded in the diabolical belief that blind larks sang better.

● When deprived of their liberty, skylarks frequently failed to sing as sweetly as they did in the wild:

> *But where is now the song I heard?*
> *For all my cunning art,*
> *I who would house a singing bird*
> *Have caged a broken heart*

from *The Fowler* by **Wilfred Gibson** (1878-1962)

● In the 1800s hundreds of thousands of skylarks were trapped along the South Downs. Most were exported to France to be cooked for the table. Many cookbooks contained recipes for skylark dishes. Today, huge numbers of migrating skylarks are still shot as they fly over southern Europe each autumn.

● In 19th-century Prussia, literally millions of skylarks were caught each autumn. A special shortcake biscuit marked with a pastry cross, called the Leipzig Skylark, is still baked to commemorate all the larks that were sacrificed. The trade in skylarks never recovered from a fierce hail storm which battered millions of songbirds to death in 1860.

● In the heyday of falconry, the merlin was trained for the sport of lark hawking. With their diving descent, skylarks were often able to elude the aerial hunters but were handicapped during their moult or if surprised near the ground.

Artistic Inspiration

Painters, poets and composers have all been enthralled by the skylark. Vincent Van Gogh painted a lark rising from a field of waving wheat in his *Wheatfield with Lark*. In his tribute to *The Lark Ascending*, the Victorian poet, George Meredith (1828-1909) depicted the lark as a link between heaven and earth:

> *He rises and begins to round,*
> *He drops the silver chain of sound,*
> *Of many links without a break,*
> *In chirrup whistle slur and shake.*

Fired by this lyrical verse, the English composer Ralph Vaughan Williams (1872-1958) composed his glorious homage to *The Lark Ascending*. The opening violin solo mimics the lark's song and its fluttering rise to a swooping descent. It lasts about two minutes – as long as the skylark's song on the wing.

In Scotland, the skylark was known as a laverock. In her version of *Will ye no' come back again?* Lady Carolina Oliphant (1766-1845) used the skylark's song to entice Bonnie Prince Charlie back to his homeland:

> *Sweet the laverock's note and lang,*
> *Liltin' wildly up the glen.*

LOST IN RAPTURE

The song of the lark was believed to have enchanting powers. According to one legend, a monk was walking through a field when a lark began to sing. He was enthralled because he had never heard the lark's song before. He stood and listened until the lark was a speck in the sky. Then he returned to his monastery and found a doorkeeper whom he didn't recognise and who didn't know him. In fact, no-one knew him, even by name. Eventually, they looked through the archives of the monastery and discovered that a Father Anselm had indeed lived there a hundred years before. Time had apparently stood still while he listened to the lark singing.

PRAISING THE LARK

Skylarks brought out the best in many of Britain's greatest poets.

> **' *Ethereal minstrel! Pilgrim of the sky!***
> ***Dost thou despise the earth where cares abound?***
> ***Or, while the wings aspire, are heart and eye***
> ***Both with thy nest upon the dewy ground?* '**

from *To a Skylark* by **William Wordsworth** (1770-1850)

Along with Shakespeare's, Milton's and Wordsworth's tributes to the skylark, Shelley's *To a Skylark*, has to be among the most famous:

> *Hail to thee, blithe Spirit!*
> *Bird thou never wert –*
> *That from Heaven or near it*
> *Pourest thy full heart*
> *In profuse strains of*
> *unpremeditated art.*

The only one who had a bad word to say about the skylark was Juliet in *Romeo and Juliet*:

> *It is the lark that sings so out of tune,*
> *Straining harsh discords and*
> *unpleasing sharps.*

She hated the lark because its voice heralded dawn and she wanted the night to last longer so that Romeo would not have to leave.

THE WOODLARK (*Lullula arborea*)
Confusion may arise between the skylark and woodlark, which is very rare now. It is restricted to patches of open woodland and heaths in southern England, East Anglia and local pockets in Wales. Both birds sing on the wing, but the skylark rises higher, faster and more steeply.

woodlark

The Cuckoo

A universally recognised summer visitor to these shores, the cuckoo advertises its arrival in mid April by calling out its name loud and clear – Cuc-koo! Cuc-koo!

When the cuckoo's double note floats through the air for the first time each year, there is general rejoicing that spring has arrived at last. Male cuckoos go on *cuc-koo*-ing their glad tidings from three in the morning until midnight, apparently never tiring of their unsophisticated lyric.

FAVOURITE HAUNTS

The males get back slightly ahead of the females, after a long flight from their winter quarters in sub-Saharan Africa. They settle in woodland, along hedgerows, on heath and moorland and in marshy areas. The best view you are likely to get of a cuckoo is as it flies fast, low and level from one lookout to another.

▶ **BEADY EYE**
From her spying-perch, a female cuckoo keeps watch on where prospective foster parents for her eggs are building their nests and when they start egg-laying.

Unusual Taste in Caterpillars

The eccentric cuckoo is a greedy eater of very hairy caterpillars, such as those of the drinker, ermine, tiger and gold tail moths, which most other birds refuse to touch. Their hairiness is usually a sign that they are poisonous, but apparently not to the cuckoo. The caterpillars' bristly hairs either stick to the lining of the cuckoo's stomach or the bird spits them out again in small pellets.

Cuckoos are also fond of magpie moths and gooseberry sawfly larvae, while fox moth caterpillars on bilberry and heather are a staple part of a moorland cuckoo's diet. When short of caterpillars, cuckoos eat beetles, grasshoppers, spiders and worms as well.

Arch Usurper

ON ARRIVING BACK in this country, the female cuckoo's first task is to establish a large territory, or reclaim one from a previous year. Then she defends her rights to lay in all the suitable foster nests in the area.

Rather than pairing off, cuckoos tend to be promiscuous, mating with several partners each season. To attract male cuckoos, the coquettish female sits in a tree and sings her bubbling call. While calling, she turns round very slowly on a branch, pressing her breast against it as though smoothing material into a nest cup. Excited males gathering in the same tree to compete for her attention set up a hubbub of *cuc-koos*, *cuc-cuc-cuc-koos* and *cack-cack-cacks* as they sway, bob and spin around, with their large tails raised and fanned out.

BROOD PARASITES

The female cuckoo is infamous for shirking her parental responsibilities. By dumping her eggs in the nests of other small birds, her hosts, she also foists the brooding and rearing of her chicks on to a pair of luckless foster parents, whose chances of raising their own family are sacrificed in the process.

Such behaviour is known as *brood parasitism*. The incentive for such a strategy is greater breeding success. One female cuckoo can distribute up to 25 eggs in as many different nests, reducing the risk of disaster befalling them all. And by leaving her chicks to be brought up by foster parents, she can spend less time in a cool northern climate.

▶ UNWELCOME VISITOR
Sometimes cuckoos get mobbed by irate would-be foster parents. Here two meadow pipits have spotted a cuckoo in a tree near their nest and are trying to drive it away.

Cuckoo Clans

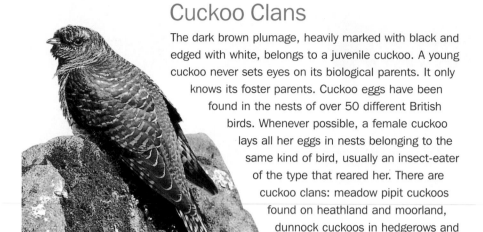

The dark brown plumage, heavily marked with black and edged with white, belongs to a juvenile cuckoo. A young cuckoo never sets eyes on its biological parents. It only knows its foster parents. Cuckoo eggs have been found in the nests of over 50 different British birds. Whenever possible, a female cuckoo lays all her eggs in nests belonging to the same kind of bird, usually an insect-eater of the type that reared her. There are cuckoo clans: meadow pipit cuckoos found on heathland and moorland, dunnock cuckoos in hedgerows and reed warbler cuckoos in reedbeds.

' The cuckoo, like a hawk in flight,
With narrow pointed wings
Whews o'er our heads – soon out of sight
And as she flies she sings '

from *The Cuckoo* by **John Clare** (1793-1864)

Cuckoo in the Nest

▲ QUICK GETAWAY
As soon as a female cuckoo has laid her egg in another bird's nest she beats a hasty retreat. In the air, her pointy wings are held well down and flap furiously.

AFTER DAYS OF careful reconnaissance, the female cuckoo chooses a nest with an incomplete clutch of eggs – often there is only one egg in the nest – where incubation has yet to start. She waits and watches for the owner of the target nest to lay her egg in the morning, then usually comes back and lays her own egg in the afternoon, while the occupants of the nest are likely to be away feeding. This strategy takes careful timing, because she only produces an egg every second day.

DEPOSITS AND WITHDRAWALS

To avoid drawing attention to herself, the female cuckoo makes a beeline for the nest. She removes one egg and holds it in her beak while she quickly lays one of her own in its place. Eventually she will either eat the egg she is holding or drop it somewhere. Amazingly, when the nest's rightful occupant returns, she is unphased by the presence of an odd egg in her nest and makes no attempt to remove it. She just goes on laying one egg every other day to complete her clutch before starting to incubate all the eggs.

FINE TUNING

To be a successful brood parasite, sure of duping its chosen foster parents, the cuckoo has had to fine tune the size and colour of its eggs and the rate of development and behaviour of its chick.

Once all her eggs are laid, the female cuckoo's task is complete and she plays no further part in her offspring's welfare. Nor do the males. They stop singing by the end of June and all the adult cuckoos are free to fly back to sunny Africa in July.

'From hedge to hedge she flies
And trusts her offspring
To another's care'

from *The Birds of Scotland* by **James Grahame** (1765-1811)

Nest Tampering

In a matter of seconds, a female cuckoo can sweep down on a host's nest and lay an egg. To minimise suspicion in the proxy parents, the female cuckoo removes one of their eggs from the nest before depositing her own.

The colour and markings of cuckoo eggs are so individualistic that it is possible to identify the female which laid each one. To fit in better with the host's egg, the cuckoo's egg is no bigger than a house sparrow's, which is small for a bird of its size. Sometimes, a cuckoo's egg looks vaguely like its host's eggs, but not in the case of the dunnock, where its eggs are plain sky blue and the cuckoo's egg is brown streaked.

Murder in the Nest

The cuckoo's egg is incubated with the host's eggs but generally hatches first. (The meadow pipit's eggs normally hatch in 14 days, the cuckoo's egg hatches in 12.)

Though tiny, blind and naked, when the cuckoo chick is only about eight hours old, it sets about getting rid of any nest-mates. For the next six days it has very irritable skin. When it brushes against an egg or a chick, the young cuckoo squirms under it, manoeuvring it into a temporary hollow in its back. By pressing its head into the bottom of the nest and using its muscular legs and strong wings, the cuckoo chick heaves itself backwards up the side, arches its back and dumps its burden over the rim. It repeats this Herculean feat until it is alone in the nest, with the undivided attention of its foster parents.

INFATUATED FOSTER PARENTS

Meanwhile, the host families are left to incubate and rear their strangely compelling guests. The foster parents do nothing to prevent their precocious guest kicking their eggs or chicks out of the nest, nor do they make any attempts to retrieve the eggs or feed the ejected chicks.

Instead, they lavish all their parental care on one cantankerous cuckoo chick. The rapidly growing nestling's huge orange gape and wheezy hunger calls, *chiz-chiz-chiz*, seem to exert a mesmeric power over its foster parents. It seduces not only them but other passing birds to drop food into its gaping beak.

A reed warbler that would usually rear its own chicks in 10 to 14 days is prepared to go on feeding a cuckoo for twice as long. In 20 to 23 days, the young cuckoo is twice as big as its exhausted foster parents. At about four weeks old, the juvenile cuckoo reaches independence.

▼ GIANT FOSTER CHICK
The reed warbler is the cuckoo's favourite host in marshy habitats. The little birds work overtime caring for the monstrous alien with the voracious appetite that has hijacked their neat nest in the reeds.

The Wandering Voice

CUCKOO FOLKLORE AND superstitions abound, along with many old rhymes and proverbs. They are a reflection of how eagerly the messenger of spring's return was awaited each year. In his poem, *An Angler's Rambles*, Thomas Tod Stoddart (1888-1915) conveyed a sense of that excitement and keen anticipation very clearly.

> *Is the cuckoo come?*
> *Is the cuckoo come?*
> *Hear you its happy voice*
> *Bidding the hills rejoice?*

Traditionally, the cuckoo sings from St Tibertius' Day on 14 April until St John's Day on 24 June. First Cuckoo Day was always celebrated on 14 April with the Cuckoo Fair at Heathfield in East Sussex. An old woman at the fair would release a cuckoo from her apron where it had supposedly spent the winter.

FIRST CUCKOO

There has always been plenty of good-natured rivalry in letters to the national press over when and where the first cuckoo of the season was heard. Since the collared dove first arrived in Britain in the 1950s, people have frequently confused its buzzing coo with the cuckoo's call. This is one reason why letters reporting the first cuckoo are less reliable than they used to be. Great significance was attached to the position or timing of the first cuckoo call heard each year. If the call came from the right, it was lucky; from the left brought bad luck; if you were in bed, it warned of illness; the number of calls signified how many years before you married.

WELCOME BACK

An early anonymous English poem, rejoiced at the cuckoo's return:

> *Sumer is icumen in*
> *Lhude sing cuccu!*

' Sweet bird! thy bow'r is ever green,
Thy sky is ever clear;
Thou hast no sorrow in thy song,
No winter in thy year! '

from *Ode to the Cuckoo* by **Michael Bruce** (1746-1767)

Myths and Folklore

- As cuckoos disappeared in late summer, it used to be thought that they either turned into hawks for the winter or lost all their feathers and hibernated in a tree-hole or burrow until the following spring.

- According to John Bunyan (1628-1688), cuckoos were foolish birds:

Thou booby, say'st thou nothing but cuckoo?

These days, *to be cuckoo* is to be silly. In the United States a *cuckoo's nest* or *academy* is slang for a psychiatric hospital, which is how the famous 1970's film *One Flew Over the Cuckoo's Nest,* starring Jack Nicholson, got its title.

- Globs of white froth on plant stems in early summer (containing young insects called froghoppers) are known as *cuckoo spit* because country folk used to believe that grasshoppers developed from cuckoo spittle.

- Jingle the coins in your pocket when you hear the first cuckoo and you will have plenty of money in your purse all year.

- The *cuckoo's fool, cuckoo's footman, cuckoo's messenger* and *cuckoo's mate* are all folk names for another bird, the wryneck, which usually gets back to this country just before the cuckoo each spring.

▼ *The Wise Men of Gotham, a village south of Nottingham, earned themselves a reputation for being batty by building a fence around a bush harbouring a calling cuckoo to stop it flying away so they could enjoy eternal spring. Needless to say, the cuckoo escaped. One local wag said at the time: If only we'd built it one storey higher!*

Having hunted for cuckoos as a boy, but never seen one, to the poet William Wordsworth (1770-1850) the cuckoo was a mysterious voice:

Thrice welcome darling of the spring
Even yet thou are to me
No bird, but an invisible thing
A voice, a mystery.

Not everyone was as charitable about the cuckoo's behaviour or voice. In his poem *Ingratitude*, Francis Thynne (1545-1608) penned a fierce indictment of the cuckoo's tactics:

The stamm'ring cuckoo, whose lewd voice doth grieve,
Sucking the eggs which that haysugge (dunnock) hath laid,
In lieu whereof, her own egg she doth leave.

◀ **TIME TO GO**
Having been abandoned by its real parents and outgrown its foster parents, in August or September a fat young cuckoo is left to navigate its own way to Africa for the winter.

' *In Aprill the kookoo can sing her song by rote;*
In June - of tune - she cannot sing a note;
At first koo-coo, koo-coo, sing still can she do;
At last, kooke, kooke, kooke; six kookes to one koo '

from *Of Use* by **John Heywood** (1497-1580)

Musically Copied

Thanks to its simple but familiar call, the cuckoo is a favourite with composers:

- In *Le Coucou*, a lively harpsichord piece composed by Louis-Claude Daquin (1694-1772), the cuckoo's two-note call is clearly heard against the gentle tinkling melody.

- Beethoven slipped a cuckoo into his *Pastoral Symphony (Number 6)*; Mahler has one in his *First Symphony*.

- One of Frederick Delius's best known short pieces for a small orchestra is *On Hearing the First Cuckoo in Spring* from 1912.

The Swallow

Each year, the sight of the first swallow swooping and wheeling its way across a clear blue sky symbolises the welcome arrival of spring

By the time the earliest swallows reach southern England in late March or early April, they are flying on weary wings. It is hardly surprising, as these little birds, which weigh no more than 20g (⅔oz), have spent the last five weeks flying over 6250 miles from southern Africa.

REST AND RECOVERY

For the first few days after they get back, flocks of swallows swoop over water meadows, marshes and sewage farms, catching masses of insects. They hunt all day and roost together in nearby reedbeds at night. When the exhausted swallows have regained their strength, they disperse to their traditional family nesting sites all over Britain.

▶ **AERIAL DOMAIN**
Resting briefly on a telephone wire, this swallow shows off the streamlined shape and tail streamers that help to make it such an accomplished flier.

Great Globetrotters

As summer fades, hundreds of thousands of twittering swallows congregate on telephone wires and in noisy roosts in reedbeds and withies. Ahead lies the long journey back to southern Africa, where it should be summer by the time they arrive.

Weather permitting, flocks of swallows embark on their voyage at dawn. They fly southwards in daylight, feeding in flight and stopping to roost each night. They cruise at about 20mph and cover between 60 and 190 miles a day. Some young birds take up to four months to complete the arduous trip.

Those that make it will have flown over the English Channel, run the gauntlet of storms and gunshot across France and the Pyrenees, crossed the Straits of Gibraltar, evaded hungry falcons in North Africa, endured the Sahara Desert and monsoons through central Africa. After enduring all these perils, they may still reach southern Africa before the risks of spring frosts and starvation are over.

Swallowing Flies

IN CLEAR WEATHER, you can see and hear flocks of twittering swallows swirling over meadows and fields, parks and playing fields or skimming through farmyards and across the surface of rivers and pools, catching flying insects. At times, swallows swoop so low you can hear the click of their bills as they close around another luckless insect.

A swallow may streak along with its beak open, sucking up mouthfuls of insects from swarms. Its short bills are rimmed with bristles that funnel insects into its gaping mouth. Or it can jink, hover and dive to snatch individual insects from the air. If not eaten at once, the catch is stored in the throat to be carried to the nest.

FAVOURITE FOODS

Among the swallow's most sought after prey are bluebottle-sized flies – greenbottles, horseflies, blowflies and dungflies – but it chases aphids, butterflies and moths too. Patrolling above sewage works, reservoirs and canals, they pick off scores of dragonflies, mayflies, alderflies and mosquitoes which breed there. Low-flying swallows also gather tiny caterpillars abseiling on fine silk

threads from the branches of trees on the fringes of woods in early summer. First-brood swallow nestlings are often fed on caterpillars as well as flying insects.

In cold, wet or windy weather, swallows congregate downwind of large bodies of water, where insects are blown, or in the lee of a wood or hedge where there is some shelter.

▲ DRINKING IN FLIGHT
Flying low, a swallow dips its beak into the water to take a drink. Sometimes, it may momentarily dive under the surface to refresh its plumage too.

When preparing to migrate, swallows fatten up on clouds of gawky daddy-longlegs (craneflies) emerging from grasslands in August or September.

male

fledglings

Mid-air Refuelling

A swallow is such a master of flight that its feet do not have to touch the ground or land on a perch for it to be able to feed its fledglings. These two youngsters are calling to be fed, opening their beaks to expose the orange lining of their mouths. Their father is hovering in front of them to deliver some insects he has collected before whizzing off to catch more.

When the juveniles are more skilful flyers, parents and young are able to offer and accept food on the wing. As you watch swallows whirling about the sky, you may see two meet, twitter excitedly and seemingly halt in mid-air, as though they are kissing. The duller, paler one, without any tail streamers, is a youngster exercising its flight muscles and enjoying its freedom after the confines of a cramped nest; the other is its parent, transferring a ball of insects into its offspring's mouth.

Master Plasterers

male *female*

EACH SPRING, MALE swallows arrive back in Britain slightly before the females and quickly reclaim their old nesting sites or, as first-time breeders, pick out new ones near where they were hatched. Although swallows nest communally, each pair fiercely defends the area within pecking distance of its nest.

GETTING TOGETHER

Pairing takes place after males perform aerial displays and sing their twittering song for the females. A newly-formed pair gets to know each other better with a bout of mutual preening and by exploring the nest site before mating, which may take place on the wing in mid-air.

By constructing their nests in the rafters of barns, outhouses, porches and garages, swallows become some of our closest neighbours. Each pair either renovates an established nest, by replacing the old lining with fresh dried grass and feathers, or constructs a new one in which to lay the eggs.

COPING WITH A FAMILY

The hard work really begins when the eggs hatch. A nestful of begging chicks keeps both parents on the go, insect-catching from dawn 'til dusk. On still, sunny days, each parent swallow brings food to the nest 15 to 20 times an hour. A pair has to

'The swallow, oft, beneath my thatch Shall twitter from her clay-built nest'

from *A Wish* by **Samuel Rogers** (1763-1855)

▲ **GENDER DIFFERENCES**
Male and female swallows look very much alike, although to the experienced eye the male has longer, finer tail streamers, glossier plumage and ruddier underparts.

▶ **MAKING MUD PELLETS**
A nest-building swallow is making a rare visit to the ground to collect mud from a drying puddle or churned-up river-bank. Despite its short legs, this bird is managing to keep its tail clear of the mud so that its flight will not be impaired by dirty feathers.

catch roughly 150,000 insects to rear a single fledgling. Prolonged spells of wet, cool weather, when insects lie low, are disastrous for the chicks.

All being well, after 18 to 21 days, the nest is full to overflowing with newly-fledged swallow chicks, which have to be coaxed into the air for the first time by their parents. Once airborne, they must keep flying until one of their parents finds a telephone wire or wire fence and shows them how to land and perch on it.

Their parents feed the fledglings for another week, before starting to rear a second, and later maybe a third brood. After that the young swallows spend their days honing their flying and hunting skills, taking note of local landmarks and preening

▲ SHARP TURN

The swallow's long, narrow wings and forked tail afford it great speed and manoeuvrability as it swoops out of a barn door on its way to find more insects.

their feathers on telephone wires. At night they sleep in communal roosts, where they are joined by thousands of adults when breeding is over.

Life in the Nest

A swallow's nest is made from pellets of wet mud, reinforced with straw and mixed with saliva, then pressed together to form a shallow half cup, which is lined with hair, feathers and dry grass. Once it is completed, the female lays one egg a day until her clutch of four to six elongated white eggs with reddish markings is complete. While she incubates the eggs, the male feeds her until the chicks hatch 13 to 15 days later.

Unfortunately, the nestlings are likely to find that they are sharing their nest with lots of irritating mites, fleas and feather lice, which were already in residence when their parents opted to reuse an old nest. These parasites suck the chicks' blood, possibly slowing their growth, damaging their health and forcing them to leave the nest early while still weak.

Fork of the Wind

TO THE ROMANS, the swallow was *hirundo*, which now forms part of its scientific name *Hirundo rustica* – the country swallow. The English name swallow stems from the ancient Anglo-Saxon *swalewe*. In early German, *swalwo* meant cleft stick like the swallow's forked tail. The Gaelic for swallow, *gobhlan-gaoithe*, translates as fork of the wind, a phrase that is highly evocative of its tail in flight.

In Jewish folklore, the swallow is said to have got its forked tail after a dispute with a snake, from which it escaped with ripped tail feathers. According to a Swedish legend, swallows circled Jesus on the cross calling out *Svala! Svala!* (Cheer up! Cheer up!). Swedes now call them *ladusvala,* or barn swallow, marking their habit of nesting in barns.

THE CHIMNEY SWALLOW?

Puzzlingly, in the mid-19th century, respected British ornithologists wrote of the chimney swallow, claiming that swallows frequently nested '*a few feet down an unused chimney*', which today's swallows rarely if ever do. Writing as early as 1744, the famous English naturalist, Gilbert White, had his doubts: *though called the chimney swallow, it often builds*

▲ ROOSTING AMONG THE REEDS

Each evening juvenile swallows gather in chattering flocks over reedbeds before descending to find a stiff stem of Phragmites reed to cling on to all night.

within barns. Maybe before brick chimneys, when smoke simply escaped via a hole in the roof, swallows flew through this to reach the nests they built in the roof space.

'*Then the clouds part,*
Swallows soaring between;
The spring is alive,
And the meadows are green'

from *Old Song* by **Edward Fitzgerald** (1809-1883)

Legends and Folklore

● Over 2000 years ago, the Greek philosopher, Aristotle, coined the proverb *One swallow does not make a summer*.

● Children on the Greek island of Rhodes used to sing a song to welcome the first swallow of spring:

The Swallow is here and a new year he brings,
As he lengthens the days with the beat of his wings.
Throw open your coffers and give for the Swallow!

● Swallows are said to have won divine favour and their red head markings by helping the wren bring fire from Hell.

● As swallows were thought to represent the spirits of dead children it was bad luck to kill them. It was also considered unlucky if a swallow flew under a cow.

● Swallows nesting in the eaves of a house were believed to be a blessing and to protect against fire and lightning strikes.

● In Cornwall it was customary to jump on seeing the first swallow in spring.

● Because swallows nested in buildings rather than trees and rarely landed on the ground, they were often depicted in heraldry and art with legs ending in feathers rather than feet.

● Supposedly, every swallow carried two precious stones: a red one to cure insanity, a black one for prosperity. Anyone who put one of them under their tongue would be able to talk persuasively.

● In Ireland, the swallow was regarded as the Devil's Bird. Every swallow was said to carry three drops of the devil's blood. If a swallow plucked a certain hair from a human head, that person was condemned to eternal Hell.

● An old West Country saying predicted the weather:

Swallows fly high, no rain in the sky;
Swallows fly low, 'tis likely to blow.

● Traditionally, swallows started leaving for Africa on 4 October, St Francis's Day, and returned on 15 April, Swallow Day.

WHERE DID THEY GO?

Shrewd old Aristotle suggested that swallows might migrate to warmer places for the winter. But fanciful ideas about swallows hibernating held sway for another 1500 years or more.

Support for Aristotle's theory came in about 1250, when the abbot of a Cistercian abbey in Germany reported how a strip of parchment bearing the question '*Oh swallow, where do you live in winter?*' was tied to a swallow's leg before it disappeared one autumn. Apparently the bird reappeared the following spring with an answer: '*In Asia, in the home of Petrus*'!

TIME TO SAY GOODBYE

From late summer to early autumn, masses of swallows start congregating on telephone wires, stretching their wings and preening their feathers in readiness for the grand exodus. One day there is a regiment of swallows, twittering with excitement; the next they are gone for another year.

Mythical Wintering Grounds

● For a long time it was believed that naked comatose swallows hibernated in caves or holes in the ground for the winter, rather like bats.

● In the 16th century, Olaus Magnus, Bishop of Uppsala, Sweden, observed swallows gathering in reedbeds in autumn and then disappearing. He proposed that the chattering birds conglobulated, '*joining bill to bill, wing to wing, foot to foot*' to form a ball and '*after sweet singing*' sank into the mud where they spent the winter sleeping. On waking the following spring, they emerged from the swamp and reappeared in the reeds. He illustrated his theory with a woodcut showing men hauling up swallows and fish in their nets from under the ice. To test this notion, dyed threads were tied to swallows' legs to see if they would fade after a winter under water but the birds returned with bright threads in spring, disproving the theory.

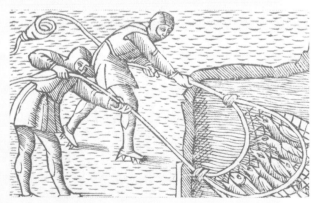

● Swallows were said to carry small sticks with them on their migratory flights so that they could stop and rest on liferafts while flying over the sea.

The Kestrel

As the only small British bird of prey to have mastered the art of hovering flight, the dark speck you see hanging in mid-air beside the road has to be a kestrel

While hunting along thousands of miles of motorway hardshoulder all over the country, hovering kestrels put on a captivating display of flying that entrances millions of motorists each year – and provide a pleasant distraction from endless tailbacks.

NEW OPPORTUNITIES

Kestrels are one of the most common, familiar and adaptable birds of prey in Britain. Not only do they exploit rodent-rich grass verges but they have found that wastelands, docks, parks and railway cuttings make happy hunting grounds too. And there are the grassy expanses on farmland, moorland, marshes or clifftops and in woodland to hunt over as well.

▶ NEAT FALCON
Only when a male kestrel takes a breather from the energetic business of hovering is there a chance to see his lovely blue-grey and ruddy-brown plumage.

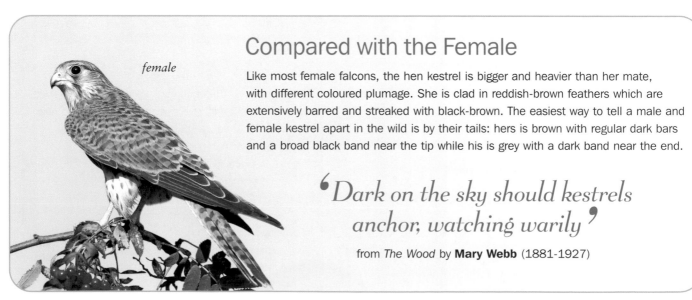

female

Compared with the Female

Like most female falcons, the hen kestrel is bigger and heavier than her mate, with different coloured plumage. She is clad in reddish-brown feathers which are extensively barred and streaked with black-brown. The easiest way to tell a male and female kestrel apart in the wild is by their tails: hers is brown with regular dark bars and a broad black band near the tip while his is grey with a dark band near the end.

'*Dark on the sky should kestrels anchor, watching warily*'

from *The Wood* by **Mary Webb** (1881-1927)

Family Life

A PAIR OF KESTRELS works as a team
to rear their single brood of the year:
the male concentrates on hunting
while the female largely stays at the
nest, caring for the eggs and chicks.

The kestrel's breeding season
generally lasts for four months, from
April to July. The timing varies,
depending on the weather, to ensure
the chicks are in the nest when there
arc plenty of rodents and fledgling
birds around to feed them on.

NEST BORROWERS

Kestrels do not build a nest: they
either take over the old stick nest of
a magpie, crow or squirrel or set up
home in a tree-hole or cavity in a
quarry wall or cliff ledge and scrape
out a shallow depression for a nest.
Old farm buildings, recesses in
church spires and lofty ruins, ledges
on buildings or under bridges are
other favourite nest sites.

MATERNAL CARE

In April or May, the female lays four
or five off-white eggs which are so
heavily blotched and spattered with
red and dark brown that they look
brick-red. She usually lays in the

morning, at two-day intervals, and
normally starts sitting after her third
egg arrives. The chicks start cheeping
from the eggs before they hatch
between 27 and 29 days later.

The tiny hatchlings are totally
helpless. At first, the hen bird stays
with them to keep them warm and
tear large prey into fine strips to feed
them. The young kestrels grow very
rapidly and are soon big enough to

▲ **TAKING HIS TURN**
*Occasionally the male kestrel takes over
the incubation while his mate has a short
feeding break. These eggs may be spread
around him to keep cool on a hot day.*

gulp down whole insects and tear
strips off larger prey for themselves.
Then the female joins her partner
in hunting for food to satisfy their
growing family.

female

Whirlwind Courtship

During the kestrel's thrilling aerial courtship displays, the birds soar and circle high
in the sky over the nest site, shrieking loudly. The male may dive-bomb the perched
female, pulling out of his dive only at the last minute, causing her to duck. He also
brings her food to seal their pair bond and build up her strength for egg-laying.

A pair of kestrels is very territorial around their nest. Even when hunting, the
female rarely wanders far and returns at once to defend her chicks at the first
sign of trouble. The youngsters respond to their parents' alarm calls
by crouching down and staying still until the danger has passed.

Even though their parents may stick together from one breeding
season to the next, the youngsters are on their own once the family
breaks up in late summer. These inexperienced juveniles are vulnerable
to starvation, predation and bad weather and many die in their first year.

male

The Hovering Hunter

THE KESTREL IS a masterful aerial hunter, floating almost stationary in mid-air as it patiently scans the ground below for its prey. It hunts over rough grassland or wasteland in daylight and selects any prey that is abundant and easy to catch. When plentiful, short-tailed voles always form the most important item in the kestrel's diet. It also takes mice, shrews, baby rabbits, birds and the odd mole, lizard, snake and frog.

Urban kestrels tend to rely more on small birds such as starlings, house sparrows and the occasional pigeon. City rubbish bins attract mice and rats which also make easy pickings for a keen-eyed kestrel.

During the winter, earthworms become more important, when they are tunnelling close to the surface or have been turned over by ploughs. The normally graceful kestrel can look quite ungainly when foraging for insects on the ground and lunging at beetles with its beak.

AERIAL HUNTING

Kestrels vary their style of hunting to suit the available prey, the weather conditions and their energy needs. In flight-hunting the kestrel flies over its territory in a regular pattern, known as quartering, hovering periodically to scan the ground for movement. Hunting heights range from 33 to 130 feet (10 to 40 metres). The keen-eyed kestrel can spot a beetle at 165 feet (50 metres) and small birds from 330 yards (300 metres).

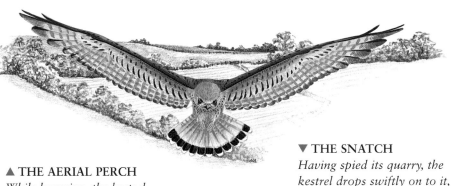

▲ THE AERIAL PERCH
While hovering, the kestrel faces into the wind, fans and lowers its tail and flutters its wings to remain stationary in mid-air. Its head is completely still, scanning the ground below for prey.

▼ THE SNATCH
Having spied its quarry, the kestrel drops swiftly on to it, pulling out of the dive at the last moment to snatch its prey in its talons.

▶ THE KILL
Grasping its prey in its feet, the kestrel flies to a killing stump to finish it off with a bite to the back of the neck. The upper bill is well notched for tearing the prey apart.

▼ GRASSY SUBWAYS
In the summer, grassland teems with field voles scurrying about unseen. The pitter-patter of vole traffic wears away bare tunnels through the base of the long grass.

Extrasensory Perception

Thanks to its large, sensitive eyes, a kestrel is superbly adapted for detecting small, active prey on the ground at a phenomenal range. The eyes are placed to the front of the head to give some binocular vision which helps in judging distances accurately. Apparently the kestrel is also able to detect ultra-violet (UV) light. This comes in handy because voles, its main prey, run along well-worn tracks in the grass, marking their trails with urine to indicate their territory, feeding routes and readiness to mate. By reflecting UV light, the urine helps the hovering kestrel map these paths and pick out its quarry.

▲ PLUCKING FOOD

Though the kestrel generally concentrates on catching small rodents, it cannot resist easy pickings and targets vulnerable, inept fledglings during the summer when it has chicks of its own in the nest.

As hovering is the most efficient way of spying food, kestrels hover more in the summer when they have chicks. Holding a hover uses up a lot of energy but is affordable when food is plentiful. Hovering is easier in a light breeze, when air flows steadily over the wings, creating lift, than on a still day or in a strong wind.

HUNTING FROM A PERCH

In winter, to save energy, the kestrel often hunts from a perch on posts and trees, telephone poles and wires, pylons and cables, even street lights. As soon as it detects its prey, it drops in a steep glide to surprise its victim.

After a good feed, a kestrel rests quietly, digesting its catch. Then it expels pellets of undigested remains that collect under roosts and nests.

Watchful Eye

Here an adult female is keeping guard while one of her fledglings eats the catch she has brought. For the first year, both male and female kestrels look like their mother so it is hard to tell them apart. The young kestrel is the one shielding the kill with its wings, a behaviour called mantling, which is used by falcons to prevent their prey being stolen. Youngsters usually make their first kill – often a beetle on the ground   about 10 days after leaving the nest.

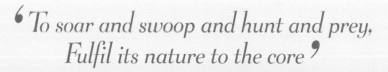

'To soar and swoop and hunt and prey,
Fulfil its nature to the core'

by **Herbert E Palmer**

juvenile

adult female

The Floating Falcon

THE ORIGINS OF the name kestrel are somewhat obscure. It may well have come from the French *crécelle*, meaning to rattle, and allude to the kestrel's shrill call. The Old French name for the kestrel was *la cresselle*. Adopted into early English, *cresselle* became *casrel*, a mere *t* away from *castrel*, another spelling of kestrel used for many years. In Devon and Cornwall the kestrel used to be known as the Cress Hawk.

The scientific name of the kestrel is *Falco tinnunculus*: *falco* stems from *falcis*, the Latin for 'of a sickle', referring to the curved shape of the beak or talons; *tinnunculus* means little bell ringer, a more generous reference to the kestrel's piercing call than the French derivation.

◄ **KEEPING CHECK**
A hovering kestrel is a study in poise, control and concentration – every part of its body is straining to spot some prey and focused on executing a swift and successful kill.

The Red Kite (*Milvus milvus*)

In certain parts of the country, notably along the M40 corridor over The Chilterns and in Oxfordshire, when you look up, the large bird of prey you see soaring rather than hovering in the sky above you is likely to be a red kite.

Such sightings represent a recent and dramatic turn around in the red kite's fortunes. In the early 20th century, the few surviving red kites in Britain sought refuge in the remote lightly wooded valleys of mid Wales. By 1932 there was just one breeding pair left. With a lot of help from their friends, numbers were up to 69 pairs in 1989. In the last 17 years, a programme of releasing foreign red kite chicks at various sites to establish breeding colonies in England and Scotland has hastened their natural recovery. Eventually the red kites will spread out from the centres of reintroduction to form a continuous population across the country. The good news is that tagged red kites have already been recorded in every county in the UK.

▲ **SIGNATURE SILHOUETTE**
Look for a deeply forked tail, long bent wings and strongly 'fingered' wingtips. The pale patches towards the jet-black wingtips clinch the identification of a red kite.

OLD NAMES

The oldest English name for the kestrel was Stanniel. In *Twelfth Night*, when Malvolio finds the letter which Maria deliberately drops in his path, William Shakespeare (1564-1616) has Sir Toby Belch remark:

And with what wing the stanniel checks at it!

In falconry, check referred to the way in which a kestrel hovered over prey that had caught its eye.

Stanniel meant *stone yeller*, from the Anglo-Saxon *stan* for stone and *gellan* for yeller, after the kestrel's loud, ear-splitting calls. Stanchel, Standhawk and Standgale were all common variants.

For seeming to float on the breeze, the kestrel was awarded many wind-related names. The best known is Windhover – but Windsucker, Windfanner, Windcuffer and Windbibber pick up on the beating wings equally graphically.

RODENT CONTROLLER

Country folk used to regard all birds of prey as a menace. Although a kestrel occasionally takes small birds, it never deserved its former scientific name of *Tinnunculus alaudaris*, which referred to it as a feeder on larks. But thousands of kestrels were poisoned, shot or trapped for this supposed sin. Now it is considered to be one of the most useful birds to have around as it patrols the countryside, keeping rodent numbers down.

POORMAN'S FALCON

As one of the smaller falcons, the kestrel was dismissed as inferior and despicable in influential falconry circles in the Middle Ages and became used as a term of abuse.

According to *The Boke of St Albans*, written in 1486 by Dame Juliana Berners, the Prioress of Sopwell Nunnery, the kestrel was the falcon used for hunting by people of lowly rank, such as peasants and knaves (male servants in the Middle Ages). Indeed, the name kestrel may originally be derived from *coystril*, an old word meaning knave.

The kestrel may have been scorned but it was far from useless. It could be tamed easily and trained

▲ **WORKING BIRD**
In a scene from the Bayeux Tapestry, a knave with a bird of prey in his hand embarks as part of the English army at Bosham on the south coast of England in about 1063. From its colouring, the bird could be a female kestrel, complete with jesses (leather leg ties used in falconry).

to catch skylarks, snipe and young partridge for the pot. In France during the reign of King Louis XlII (1610-1643), agile kestrels were even taught to catch bats.

Lore and Legend

• From ancient times, falcons have usually been much revered as symbols of freedom, victory and ascension. This was the theme that Gerard Manley Hopkins (1844-1889) developed in his poem about a kestrel, *The Windhover*.

Dapple-dawn-drawn falcon, in his riding
Of the rolling level underneath him
steady air and striding.

• Writing in his famous epic poem, *The Faerie Queen*, Edmund Spenser (c.1552-1599) used the kestrel to represent lack of honour and morality:

No thought of honour did assay
His baser breast, but in his kestrel kynde
A pleasant veine of glory he did find.

• One of the Fables of Pilpay, an ancient book of proverbs from India, told how a falcon chided a hen for being ungrateful: after all the food and shelter she received she still would not let anyone catch her, whereas he, who had

to work for what little he got, was prepared to cooperate. The hen agreed that's how it appeared but pointed out

that she really did not have much to be thankful for: while few hawks ended up roasting in front of the fire, plenty of fat hens did. The moral of the story was that circumstances alter attitudes.

• Kestrels are remarkably unperturbed by the hustle and bustle of city life. In 1871 a pair of kestrels nested on top of Nelson's Column in the middle of Trafalgar Square in central London. In 1952, another pair chose to rear their family on a ledge behind a cherub's leg on the Savoy Hotel, high above The Strand, off Trafalgar Square. Today they are often found nesting on office blocks, on the balconies of high-rise flats and under railway bridges.

The Pheasant

Today, the pheasant is a familiar sight and sound in fields and lanes, so much part of the country scene that it's hard to believe it was once an exotic alien from Asia

It is thought that pheasants were originally brought to Britain nearly two thousand years ago by the Romans, who bred them in captivity because they were so beautiful and made good eating. Before long, the pheasant had made itself at home and become a naturalised and popular gamebird.

ALL OVER THE PLACE

Today, pheasants are widespread and common almost everywhere, except on high rocky peaks. They are frequently spotted on farmland which is dotted with hedges, copses and thickets that serve as cover for feeding and nesting. Occasionally, pheasants may wander into gardens or be seen on the seashore.

MULTICOLOURED STOCK

Over the years, various races of pheasant have been introduced and interbred to produce the variety of coloured forms seen in the wild today: the Old English cock pheasant,

with his plain dark neck, seems to be a descendant of the original stock from central Asia; in the 1700s, ring-necked males with white collars were imported from China. There are also all-over darker types with more black and purple in their plumage and lighter buff ones too.

▲ **MAJESTIC POTENTATE**
Of all British birds, the cock pheasant has the most opulent colouring and regal demeanour: he swaggers around for all the world as if he owns his adopted country.

cock pheasant

What a To-do!

Although conspicuous in the open, cock pheasants in cover are more easily identified by their alarm call, a raucous *kocock, kocock*. In the breeding season, the cock pheasant also crows a cockerel-like *kokorok*. When used in displays, this is accompanied by a loud but brief bout of wing-flapping, called wing-drumming.

The cock pheasant is a flagrant poser and roué: his exquisite plumage, bright wattle and belligerent behaviour are intended to seduce as many females as possible to join his harem, thereby maximising the number of offspring he sires. During courtship, he shows off his most flamboyant features, strutting in front of a hen pheasant, his head down, feathers puffed, wattles inflated and ear tufts erect.

Pheasant Fare

SMALL GROUPS OF pheasants spend much of the day roaming across pastures, among tall crops, along hedgerows and in copses, wherever there is food to eat and good cover to protect them from predators while they are foraging.

EATING OUT

In spring, pheasants nibble at the tender young shoots of grass and cereal crops. During the summer, they start scratching around to find more seeds to eat. Berries, beech mast and acorns play an important part in their diet over the winter. A pheasant will also feed on slugs, snails, earthworms, insects and spiders, and has even been known to catch lizards and small rodents.

FLIGHT PLAN

When threatened, a pheasant either crouches in cover or sprints to safety. If surprised, a cowering pheasant takes off with a startling clatter of wings and a volley of irritated *orrk-orrk* coughing calls. It rises steeply into the air on its short rounded wings, its tail slightly fanned.

Once airborne, a pheasant climbs quickly and steeply to clear the nearest hedge or obstacle. The flight rarely lasts long; the pheasant soon switches to glide mode and usually returns to earth within half a mile of take off. With such a short flying range, pheasants rarely move more than six miles from their birthplace.

▲ FEMALE MODESTY
Disguised by her mottled sandy and dark brown plumage, a hen pheasant moves almost unseen through a flowery meadow.

> ' *Ah! what avail his glossie, varying dyes,*
> *His purple crest, and scarlet-circled eyes,*
> *The vivid green his shining plumes unfold;*
> *His painted wings, and breast*
> *that flames with gold?* '
>
> from *Windsor Forest* by **Alexander Pope** (1688-1744)

Part of the Rural Economy

Every year, a staggering 20 to 30 million young pheasants are released into the countryside in time for the start of the pheasant-shooting season on 1 October. The natural pheasant population doesn't get much support from the management of the pheasant industry any more. Gamekeepers used to cosset their pheasants, feeding and creating shelter for them and massacring thousands of nest robbers to protect them every year. Now that so many pheasants are bred indoors under intensive artificial conditions, and let loose only when nearly full-grown, there's no need for keepers to maintain breeding and nesting grounds. Instead, they develop winter cover, from which pheasants can be bullied into flying in front of the guns. Wild pheasants get shot too but the self-sustaining population is boosted by any released birds that escape unscathed.

good pheasant country, with hedges, spinneys and open fields

female

◀ FIGHTING COCKS
In territorial confrontations, two cock pheasants advance on each other until they are beak to beak. Then they leap into the air and lash out with their feet and spurs like duelling swordsmen.

Lord and Master

FOR THE PHEASANT in the wild, the breeding season can start as early as January, when the cock birds start crowing noisily to attract females and establish their territories.

The competition among cock pheasants to woo and defend a harem is so intense that territorial disputes often arise. Posturing cock birds have a sideways dance, where they spread their wings and tail, then shiver in front of each other, to make themselves seem as large as possible and intimidate their rivals. If one or other doesn't back down, fierce foot-to-foot combat can ensue.

PROTECTION RACKET

The pheasant is the only British bird with harem-defence polygamy as its breeding system. A cock pheasant's territory is composed of two distinct habitats: some open space where he can perform his courtship displays and areas with ground cover to shelter the nesting hens. He woos a group of hen birds, then spends his time on look-out duty, defending his territorial boundaries to keep conjugal access to his harem all to himself. In the pheasant's world, territoriality is an exclusively male

affair: it's all about creating a dominance hierarchy, where the bigger cock birds prevail over the smaller ones, not about picking the best nest sites.

MATRIARCHAL FAMILY

The cock pheasant doesn't lift a feather to help raise his chicks. Each hen picks out her own nest site, normally in dense vegetation, such as tall grass or at the bottom of a hedge within his territory. She scratches out a shallow depression in the leaf litter or bare earth and lines it roughly with dried grass and leaves. Each day she lays an egg in the nest, then settles to incubate her clutch.

CHICK FEED

For the first few days out of the egg, pheasant chicks eat little, relying on

male

▲ BEATING A RETREAT
When flushed from cover, a cock pheasant bursts into the air in a flurry of whirring wings, 'clearing its throat' noisily. It's enough to make even seasoned country walkers jump out of their skins.

' *See! from the brake the whirring pheasant springs, And mounts exulting on triumphant wings* '

from *Windsor Forest* by **Alexander Pope** (1688-1744)

Motherly Touch

Each hen pheasant lays one pale greeny-brown egg a day until her clutch of anything from 8 to 15 eggs is complete. Only then does she start incubating them. Like other ground-nesters, pheasant eggs have a large yolk to nourish the embryos for 23 to 28 days of incubation. Cheeping from the eggs synchronises the time of hatching: the well-developed chicks break out of the eggs within hours of each other and can run around straight away, camouflaged by their marbled buff, chestnut and black down.

Independent as they are, pheasant chicks still rely on their mother to shelter them from hot sunshine and chilling rain. When danger looms, the hen pheasant gives a warning call and the young either freeze on the spot or rush for cover under her wings.

▶ **SUBDUED AND PRACTICAL**
The hen pheasant's subtle brown markings are rather beautiful and really come into their own when she is incubating her eggs. By sitting still, she merges invisibly into the undergrowth.

a yolk store that became absorbed into their bellies before hatching. Once that is used up, the chicks begin feeding, chaperoned and guided by their mother for around 80 days. Scratching the earth with her strong feet, she uncovers edible morsels that she drops in front of her chicks to encourage them to peck in the earth.

Initially, the chicks feed mainly on animal food, especially spiders. During the second week of life, the proportion of plant food starts to increase, beginning with leaves and buds but eventually including seeds.

AFTER THE BREEDING SEASON

Female pheasants stay in small flocks of anything from five to 20 birds all the year round. During the winter, the males relax their fierce territorial behaviour and join the hen pheasants and youngsters in roaming the fields and hedgerows in search of food.

At night, pheasants are more tree-based than most gamebirds. They often roost off the ground, perching among the branches of a tree.

Half Grown

In the early days, pheasant chicks on the ground are easy pickings for predators. As early as 12 days old, the half-grown chicks can fly weakly on rudimentary wings to escape their enemies. At this stage, many are killed in encounters with traffic on the country roads.

At first, juvenile pheasants look like short-tailed females and can be mistaken for gangly partridges, quails or corncrakes, especially in the air. The young males start getting their bronze feathers in an autumn moult.

juvenile

The Grey Partridge

The grey partridge was once a common bird on open country over much of the British Isles but in the last quarter of the 20th century its numbers fell by a scary 80 per cent

As a native British gamebird, the grey partridge has long been hunted for food and sport. It was once so common that in the 1920s it was said to be *'too familiar to need description'*. Sadly, that is no longer the case: numbers have fallen so drastically that it is now on the RSPB's Red List of Birds of Conservation Concern.

LOSS OF HABITAT

For most of the year, partridges live in small groups known as coveys. From habit, they would spend the winter feeding and sleeping in stubble fields and hedgerows. Unfortunately, both are in short supply these days because of changes in arable farming.

▶ **COMPLICATED CAMOUFLAGE**
At a distance, a cock partridge may look like a dumpy, dull grey-brown bird. But close to, he is covered with an intricate pattern of chestnut, brown and black.

female

juvenile

Escape Strategies

Most of the time, the grey partridge relies on its tweedy-brown markings to help it melt into the background in muddy stubble fields. The hen partridge looks similar to the cock bird but is less flamboyantly coloured and marked. Her head is streakier and a paler orange than his and her breast is usually paler and plainer. Some young females display a horseshoe marking like their mates, but this becomes much smaller and less obvious in older hens. A juvenile partridge is smaller and browner than its parents and lacks the adults' orange head and chestnut stripes on its flanks.

When approached by predators or people with guns, the partridges' initial inclination is to crouch down and freeze, becoming brown blobs that look like clods of earth. Their second choice is to run away, scurrying off through the stems of wheat or barley or across the stubble to the haven of a nearby hedge. If forced to fly, the group takes off together with a noisy whirring of wings. The birds skim swiftly and strongly over the ground for a short distance, alternating a flurry of rapid flaps with bent-wing glides, clucking an indignant *it-it-it* as they go.

Out in the Fields

PARTRIDGES FEED MOST actively first thing in the morning and in the late afternoon: your best chance of seeing them is to walk around a cereal field at dawn or dusk.

Of all British birds, the partridge is among the most earthbound, eating, nesting and roosting on the ground. Traditionally, the adults have always found enough grain, seeds, fruit, leaves and shoots to eat by roving across cereal and stubble fields, or in the hedges and on the grassy verges around those fields.

But since the 1960s, many arable farmers have been messing up the grey partridge's habitat and lifestyle. There is a clash of cultures and the problems are manifold, affecting the partridge's food and nesting sites.

PLIGHT OF THE PARTRIDGE

Cereal crops are now heavily sprayed with chemicals: herbicides kill the weeds which used to feed the insects that partridge chicks eat for the first 10 days of their lives; insecticides wipe out the insects directly.

Ploughing up stubble fields has deprived partridges of their staple winter diet: the weed seeds and grains once found there. Autumn sowing of cereals means the crop stands so tall in spring that the chicks cannot reach the sawfly larvae they used to eat.

Hedges have been uprooted and fields ploughed to the edges, reducing cover for both nests and chicks and exposing them to heavier predation.

▲ BROADCASTING OWNERSHIP

At dusk on a spring evening, a cock partridge stops feeding and stretches up to broadcast his presence. His hoarse keev-it, keev-it *call, which sounds like a rusty key being turned in a lock, carries a long way across the fields, warning other males in the vicinity that this is his patch of stubble.*

Killing Fields

The numbers of grey partridges in the wild may be boosted temporarily each year by the release of birds raised in captivity by gamekeepers. Eggs are hatched in incubators and the chicks reared in pens. The adults are released into the fields in time for the start of the shooting season, which for partridges is on 1 September. The problem is that such releases mask the true decline of the grey partridge and its habitat while adding few birds to the wild breeding stock, as most of the captive-bred partridges are shot.

' *The thundering guns are heard on every side,*
The wounded coveys, reeling, scatter wide '

from *Brigs of Ayr* by **Robert Burns** (1759-1796)

The Partridge Family

HAVING SPENT THE winter together, grey partridges start to pair up in January and February. Aggressive territorial and flirtatious courtship displays are similar: both involve some loud crowing from the males and lively chases. Successful pairings are reinforced with a bonding session: the male and female partridge stand breast to breast, heads stretched up, rubbing necks and beaks together.

PREPARING TO NEST

While the cock bird stands guard, the hen partridge scrapes out a shallow hollow on the ground and lines it with dry grasses and leaves. This nest is usually well concealed in thick grass and weeds under a hedgerow, along a field margin or among a cereal crop. A hen can take over two weeks to finish laying her huge clutch of eggs and to start incubating. As hatching draws near, the cock bird stays close to the nest.

EARLY DAYS

Most chicks hatch in June. As soon as they are dry, the tiny fluffy buff-brown spotted chicks start running around, looking rather like big brown bumblebees on legs. Very young partridges eat a protein-rich diet of insects, picking up masses of sawfly larvae and wireworms, small caterpillars, beetles, ants, bugs and aphids in and around the fields and under hedges. After about 10 days, the chicks begin to feed on young shoots and seeds like their parents.

▲ AERIAL PROFILE
In flight, the wings are slightly bowed and the stumpy tail is spread.

▶ ATTENTIVE PARENTS
Both the male and female partridge escort their chicks on early feeding expeditions: the cock bird leads, followed by his little cheepers, as the chicks are called. The hen brings up the rear to make sure that any stragglers don't get left behind.

female   male

Plucky Partridge

When danger threatens their chicks, either parent partridge is capable of putting on a frenzied, bravura performance of pretending to have an injured wing to distract the would-be predator. The apparently wounded and weakened bird lures the enemy away, buying the family time to make good its escape.

' A wounded partridge dropped agen my feet
She fluttered round and calling as she lay
The chickens chelped and fluttered all away '

from *The Partridge's Nest* by **John Clare** (1793-1864)

HAZARDOUS CONDITIONS

Neither young partridges, nor the insects they eat, thrive in cold, wet weather in the late spring and early summer. Tramping over sticky fields, the chicks' feet get caked with mud, which can hamper their movement so badly that they starve or become incapable of running away from predators, such as foxes and crows.

Unlike most birds, which grow to their full size before they can fly, a young partridge flies at 15 days but does not reach its adult weight until it is 100 days old. Until then, the brown juvenile can be mistaken for a quail or a young pheasant.

FOR THE WINTER

The family sticks together as a covey throughout the autumn and most of the winter, eating and sleeping together. In bad weather, several families or unrelated adults usually join up to form one larger party. There is often a senior cock partridge in each covey to chivvy and watch over the hens and younger birds. Family groups only go their separate ways the following spring when pairing takes place before breeding.

▲ EASILY OVERLOOKED

Sitting low and still on her nest, a hen partridge is nearly lost among the leaves and grasses at the bottom of a hedge.

Monster Clutch

Partridges lay the largest number of eggs in a single clutch of any land bird in the United Kingdom. During late April and early May, the hen partridge lays one pale olive-brown egg in her nest each day until her clutch of 10 to 25 eggs is complete. While incubating her eggs for 23 to 25 days, the hen is extremely hard to budge from her task. She sits in four hour stints, interrupted by short breaks. On vacating the nest, she always covers her eggs with leaves to preserve some warmth and to hide them from prying predatory eyes.

Partridge in a Pear Tree

PROBABLY THE BEST known partridge of all is the one perched in a pear tree, which an extravagant lover presented to his true love in the children's rhyme *The Twelve Days of Christmas*:

> *On the first day of Christmas*
> *my true love sent to me*
> *a partridge in a pear tree.*

Originally the rhyme was a sort of memory game for children in the 18th century. Each child recited a verse until someone missed their turn and had to pay a forfeit. The idea that the verse was a way of helping Catholic children remember their catechism at a time when it was illegal to be a Catholic in England has been discredited as a hoax.

The poor grey partridge is a much maligned bird: famously portrayed

> ' *The partridge too, that scarce can trust,*
> *Will in its clumps lie down, and dust* '

from *Spear Thistle* by **John Clare** (1793-1864)

▲ EASY TARGET
During the shooting season, a male partridge has to keep his wits about him as he wanders across a snow-covered field. In a white world, he sticks out like a sore thumb.

Health Spa

The sand flies as a partridge enjoys a good dust bath. Squirming about in a hollow of dry earth, using their wings to flick dust over their backs, is a favourite pastime of partridges. This routine plays a vital part in keeping them free from parasites such as fleas and the dreaded partridge feather louse. These lice nibble away at the feathers and suck blood from their growing bases: a heavy infestation can cause serious damage and lead to feather loss. A regular shower of dust particles makes the feathers too dry for the pests' liking.

Lore and Legend

• The present spelling of partridge dates from the 16th century. It was arrived at by a convoluted route from the original Greek, *perdix*. It seems that the partridge named itself because apparently this is how the Greeks interpreted the bird's creaky call.

• According to an Ancient Greek legend, Perdix was the creative nephew of a mythical Athenian craftsman called Daedalus. The story goes that Uncle Daedalus was so miffed when his nephew invented the saw that he pushed him off the Acropolis. Luckily, Athene, goddess of arts and crafts, caught Perdix and turned him into a plump partridge with a call like a saw being sharpened.

• Before becoming the partridge, it was known as the *partrich* and *pertriche*. This came from the Old French of the Norman invaders, *pertriz*. In French today the partridge is still called *le perdrix*.

• In Scotland, the partridge was better known as the *pertrick*, *pairtrick* or *partrick*. These were further contracted to *patrick* and often confused with the Irish patron saint's name.

• The sleeping arrangement of a covey of partridges, when the birds gather

round in a circle, all facing outwards, is called a *jug*.

• An alternative name for the grey partridge is the English partridge to differentiate it from its continental cousin, the French or red-legged partridge, which was introduced into southern England in 1770.

• Another old country saying was *good farming and partridges go hand in hand*, which is rather borne out by the demise of the partridge when a less holistic approach is adopted.

• To mark the start of the partridge-shooting season, 1 September was known as St Partridge's Day. Partridges could relax again at the end of January, just in time to start winding themselves up to breed.

▼ GATHER ROUND
A covey of partridges huddles down to feed in a muddy field of kale. By pooling their watchfulness, the members of this close-knit group afford each other protection from predators.

as sitting in a tree when it never perches. And all the thanks it gets for eating pests is to be hunted.

ESTEEMED GAME

During the 16th century, partridge-hawking – using goshawks to catch partridges for the table – was a popular pastime among the gentry. The playwright Ben Jonson (1572-1637) wrote *To Penshurst* in praise of a large country estate in Kent:

The painted Partrich lies in every field
And for thy messe (meal) is
willing to be kill'd.

CRUEL SPORT

Later, when guns replaced hawks, partridges were shot in vast numbers. Thomas Hardy (1840-1928) wrote on behalf of all *Puzzled Game Birds*:

They are not those who
used to feed us
When we were young –
they cannot be!

red-legged partridge

THE RED-LEGGED PARTRIDGE

(Alectoris rufa) Two different partridges are found in Britain: the native grey partridge and the red-legged partridge which was introduced from France in the 18th century. Although similarly dumpy and short-tailed, the red-legged partridge is flashier. It is distinguished by its red beak, white eyestripe, black-bordered white face, speckled breast, heavily-barred flanks, plain brown upperparts and red legs.

The Barn Owl

Sightings of barn owls are all too rare, because they generally prefer to sleep by day and only come out to hunt under cover of darkness

With its flat heart-shaped face, dark button eyes and distinctive pale colouring, the barn owl is regarded by many as the prettiest and most appealing bird living in Britain today.

Hungry barn owls hunt along roadside verges and hedge banks at night. If you are lucky, you may just catch a tantalising glimpse of a phantom-like bird in your headlights as a barn owl takes off from its perch or flies across a country lane in front of your car.

REGULAR HABITS

Otherwise, your best chance of spotting a barn owl is in the half-light at dusk or dawn, as it starts hunting or is flying back to its roost. If you do spot one, make a note of

▶ **ALL-ROUND VIEW**
Looking backwards presents no problems to a barn owl as it has an extremely flexible neck. It has to turn its whole head to see what is going on because its eyes are too big to swivel in their sockets.

Feather Care

Every strand of each barn owl feather has long, fine extensions which give the feathers a fluffy fringe. Such soft feathers are fragile and easily ruffled or damaged. It takes regular preening to keep them well arranged and in good condition. A highly mobile neck comes in handy for tidying up unruly wing feathers. (A barn owl can turn its head through 135° to right and left.)

where you are, as barn owls are creatures of habit and hunt over the same ground each night. Then you can return another day, soon after sunset or at sunrise, for a chance of seeing the barn owl fly past again.

EERIE SCREECHER

Sightings of the nocturnal barn owl may be few and far between but its drawn-out screech is often heard shattering the peace of a quiet night. The shrieking *kee-yak*, called with a quaver in the voice, is spooky enough to send a shiver down most spines.

Future Generation

FROM FEBRUARY ONWARDS, male barn owls step up their screeching to stake their claim to a roost in a hollow tree or derelict building. To attract a mate the male gives a display of hovering accompanied by a twittering cry. He then wins her over and fattens her up with tasty morsels of food.

STARTING A FAMILY

A pair of barn owls gets away without building a nest. Instead, the female scrapes out a slight hollow on the floor of a tree-hole or in the dust on a dark ledge or beam in a barn or deserted outbuilding.

Most eggs are laid in late April or early May. A female barn owl starts incubating as soon as she has laid her first egg. Then she continues laying at two to three day intervals until her clutch of four to seven eggs is complete. While she is sitting on her eggs, the female drags in fur from regurgitated pellets in the roost around her to form a soft insulating pad of felted hair under the eggs. As long as she stays at the nest, the female relies on her mate to hunt for food for her and their family.

STAGGERED HATCHING

After between 30 and 32 days the first chick chips its way out of the shell. A few days earlier, it may be heard calling in the egg and the female responds. The rest of the eggs hatch at two to three day intervals in the order in which they were laid, over a period of eight to 14 days.

Because the hatching is staggered, there are soon chicks of various sizes and different stages of feathering sharing the same tree-hole or beam. If the food supply dries up, the youngest and smallest may be sacrificed so that the rest can survive.

All being well, young barn owls grow quickly, reaching their top weight, which is heavier than their

parents, 36 to 40 days after hatching. Over 10 to 11 weeks, the gawky owlets' down is gradually replaced with feathers. The flight feathers appear late on but by the time they are 55 to 75 days old the chicks are fledged in adult-coloured plumage and ready to fly for the first time.

▲ FEEDING TIME
When one of their parents returns to the nest with a dead mouse, fluffy barn owlets hiss hoarsely to encourage their mother or father to hand over the catch. As the chicks grow, their hissing deepens to a snoring sound.

Protective Instincts

On hatching, barn owl chicks are scantily covered in white down and their eyes are shut. Their mother stays at the nest for two or three weeks after her first chick hatches to feed, warm and guard her family. When her nest is threatened, the female crouches down in front of her chicks and spreads out her wings to shield them. Then her head starts swaying while she hisses loudly and snaps her bill to intimidate and deter the intruder.

Silent Hunter

IN THE MAIN, barn owls hunt at night over rough grassland: in damp meadows, beside streams, rivers, drainage dykes and ditches, along the edge of fields and woodland, on hedgebanks, roadside verges and in graveyards. They are looking for short-tailed voles, mice, common shrews and the odd mole, frog and fledgling birds.

FLIGHT HUNTING

When on the prowl, a barn owl cruises slowly back and forth across an area of grassland, a technique known as quartering. Flying at about 3 metres (10 feet) seems to be the optimal height from which its ears and eyes can scan the ground for prey. Once it detects something moving in the grass, the owl flies lower and hovers briefly to get an accurate fix on its target, before plunging down to capture it.

MOVING IN FOR THE KILL

As it drops on its prey, a barn owl keeps its head aimed at the target until it is just above the grass. At the very last minute its long legs and feet swing forward. The toes are spread to their maximum as the feet reach down into the grass to grab the scurrying victim.

▲ FINAL DETAILS

As a barn owl homes in on its prey, it can even work out how fast and in which direction its target is moving and align its approach and feet accordingly.

◄ HUSHED APPROACH

The softened edges of the flight feathers help to deaden the sound of air rushing through the wings as it flies, allowing the barn owl to take its victims by surprise.

► BUOYANT FLIGHT

In the air, the barn owl bobs along with a slow, leisurely beat of its long broad bent wings, which give it plenty of lift. When it is carrying prey, these large wings take the extra loading in their stride.

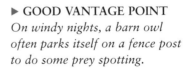

► GOOD VANTAGE POINT

On windy nights, a barn owl often parks itself on a fence post to do some prey spotting.

Sound Tracking System

The barn owl is a formidable nocturnal hunter because it has large light-sensitive eyes and phenomenal hearing. In fact, it can detect prey by sound alone in inky blackness, even when the quarry is buried in the matted stems of long grass or under a blanket of snow. The short bristly feathers that cover the front of the head and the beak form a flat, heart-shaped facial disc, which is outlined by a ruff of stiff mobile feathers. Together they create two shallow 'dishes' that catch and funnel the faintest whispers to two large ear holes hidden under the feathers just below the eyes. The ear on the left is directed slightly downwards and is a little higher than the one on the right, which points upwards. By tilting its head, adjusting the ruff feathers and shifting position a couple of times, a barn owl uses the different information it receives in each ear to pinpoint the source of the sound.

◄ **HUNTING IN DAYLIGHT**
During the summer, when the length of darkness is too brief for a barn owl to catch enough food to satisfy its brood, it may have to be out hunting before nightfall and after sunrise.

▲ **INESCAPABLE CLUTCHES**
To get a firm grip on its prey, the barn owl has a massive talon at the tip of each toe. For a more secure grasp, the outer toe on each foot is turned back and the skin lining the toes is roughened.

The barn owl grasps its wriggling prey in one foot and squeezes until the needle-sharp talons stab it to death. At the same time, it rises into the air again and heads back to the roost or nest. On the way, it transfers the corpse to its beak to make landing easier.

TROUBLE FINDING FOOD

Persistent heavy rain is bad news for barn owls, especially during the summer when they have a family to feed. A barn owl's soft, lightly-oiled plumage gets waterlogged easily, which makes flying awkward. It usually doesn't hunt in a downpour, preferring to wait for a break in the weather to snatch some prey.

The barn owl's prey may also be less active in bad weather. Small rodents are certainly harder for the barn owl to find in the wet, as the sounds of their activity are muffled in the soggy grass.

Prolonged dry spells are not good for hunting either. Grass growth falls off in summer droughts and can lead to a slump in the number of voles. Vole populations fluctuate wildly on a three or four year cycle anyway. Numbers build and build until the bubble bursts and the population crashes and voles become scarce for a year or so. The barn owl's egg laying dates follow the vole cycle, with earlier laying in peak vole years.

NOTHING IN RESERVE

Starvation is now probably the most common cause of death among barn owls. To stay buoyant, the barn owl carries little body fat. If it cannot find food, because prey is scarce or it is too wet to hunt, a barn owl may use up its fat stores in as little as eight days and be too weak to hunt properly after that.

Good Meal

A barn owl carries a vole back to its chicks in the roost. While the owlets are very young, the female bird tears up the catch and feeds them small pieces; when they are bigger, both adults leave the prey whole for the chicks to shred and go straight back to hunting. At other times of the year, a barn owl swallows its catch whole, digests it and then brings up neat pellets of unwanted fur and bones.

National Treasures

IN 12TH-CENTURY England, a preacher called Odo of Cheriton in Kent came up with an explanation for why owls hunt at night. Apparently, an owl once stole a rose, a prize given for great beauty. The other birds ganged up on it and have allowed owls to come out only at night ever since.

DRAMATIC OWLS

As a bird that flies by night, the barn owl was often associated with death and its hair-raising screeching was widely regarded as a portent of disaster. A dead barn owl used to be nailed to a barn door to ward off evil spirits. Frequently, Shakespeare used the imagery of an owl to elicit fear and set up a doom-laden scene for his audience, as in Act ii, Scene 2 of *Comedy of Errors*:

This is the fairy land. O spite of spites!
We talk with goblins, owls and sprites.
If we obey them not, this will ensue:
They'll suck our breath, or pinch
us black and blue.

ALL CHANGE

Even so, life used to be good for the beautiful barn owl in rural Britain. On the whole, farmers approved of

▲ WHITE OWL
It is easy to see how the barn owl got its ghostly reputation – and why it used to be known as the White Owl – when its pale feathers are caught in a shaft of light as it lines up a landing on a headstone.

barn owls – and still do – as they help to keep mice and rats under control. Indeed, they built their barns with a special owl window to allow them to come and go freely.

But farms are no longer the barn-owl friendly places they used to be. Grassland has been ploughed up for arable crops. The horses and stables, the haystacks and their rodent camp followers have gone. Haysheds are used as lambing sheds when the barn owl needs peace and quiet to nest. Old barns have been converted into dwellings for people. Today, special barn-owl nesting-boxes are offering barn owls an alternative venue in which to roost and rear a family.

LEGAL COTTONWOOL

Legislation stops people disturbing a brooding barn owl on her nest and makes it illegal to take eggs and chicks from the nest. A licence is required to remove young barn owls from

Grave Digger

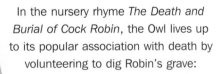

In the nursery rhyme *The Death and Burial of Cock Robin*, the Owl lives up to its popular association with death by volunteering to dig Robin's grave:

'Who'll dig his grave?'
'I,' said the Owl,
'With my spade and trowel,
I'll dig his grave.'

An old illustration of the rhyme clearly depicts a barn owl struggling with a spade to excavate a hole in which to bury Cock Robin.

Dangers in the Dark

● The barn owl has few natural enemies. Occasionally rats, stoats and weasels may attack chicks in the nest. Yet in the past 60 years, barn owl numbers have fallen by an alarming 70 per cent in Britain.

● Every year, many barn owls drown in cattle troughs, water butts, rivers, ponds and lakes. Once their feathers are waterlogged, their fate is sealed.

● Up to 60 per cent of barn owl deaths each year occur as a result of collisions with traffic on the roads, motorways and railway lines. Some of their best hunting grounds are along embankments and verges where their low hunting flight means many, especially young birds in the autumn, get clipped by vehicles and their aerials or sucked into their slipstream.

● Flying into overhead power cables and barbed wire fences in the dark can be a problem for barn owls hunting in the dark.

● In the 1950s and 1960s, barn owls suffered from eating the rats and mice that ate seeds dressed in pesticides, such as DDT. The use of rodenticides around farms can still accidentally poison barn owls when they eat the dead or dying rats and mice. Choosing pesticides less poisonous to birds and quick removal of the corpses help to save the barn owl.

their nest to ring and keep track of them throughout their lives.

Barn owls kept in captivity have to be captive bred. It's against the law to release a captive-reared barn owl into the wild without a licence in case it is unable to fend for itself or so lacking in barn-owl etiquette that it might upset the local population.

'*Now the owl on wheaten wing,*
And white hood scowling o'er his eyes,
Jerking with a sudden spring,
Through three-cornered barn-hole flies'

from *Evening* by **John Clare** (1793-1864)

The Little Owl (*Athene noctua*)

Introduced into England from Europe in the 19th century as a voracious insect exterminator, the little owl is now the most common owl found on farmland, orchards, hedgerows, wasteground and quarries. Thanks to the little owl's habit of sitting out in the open in broad daylight, it is the most frequently seen owl too. It is also easily overlooked because its greyish-brown colouring, beautiful mottled markings and squat shape are well camouflaged against the trunk of the tree. But if you spy a dumpy brown blob perched on a fence post, low branch, overhead cable or telephone wire, which bobs about as you approach, then flies off, you have probably disturbed a little owl's daylight vigil. It is actually one of the easiest birds in the country to identify: almost everyone recognises an owl, and if it is a small owl – no bigger than a chunky song thrush – it must be a little owl. Its most striking features are its two luminescent yellow eyes glaring out from under white brows.

▼ **LITTLE AND LARGE**
Less than half the size of a tawny owl, the most common woodland owl in Britain, the little owl is sometimes mistaken for a tawny fledgling. On rare occasions, tawny owls are known to prey on little owls, when they find them roosting.

tawny owl

little owl

The Fieldfare

Just as the first swallow of the year is said to mark the arrival of summer, the first fieldfare of the autumn has always been taken as a sign that winter is fast approaching

The fieldfare is a common winter visitor to the British Isles. Large numbers arrive in October and most will have departed again by the following May, although a few stragglers may hang around until June. Every year, a handful of pairs stays behind to breed in the English Peak District and Scotland.

ROVING FLOCKS

Fieldfares are highly gregarious birds, travelling around in noisy, rather disorganised flocks, which are generally seen at a distance, flying over open farmland on their way to roost in hedges and woods.

In the air, the fieldfare has an obviously relaxed, slightly undulating

▶ **CHUNKY THRUSH**
The fieldfare is distinguished by its striking grey head and rump, black tail, chestnut back and spotted breast.

Berry Hungry

Fieldfares prefer foraging on rough fields and pastures as they don't like being enclosed. Most gardens are too small for them; they are only likely to drop in if there are loads of ripe berries going begging or the weather is extremely cold in the countryside, leaving the ground too hard for digging up worms or insects. Then fieldfares descend on urban parks and gardens, stripping bright red berries from trees, bushes and hedges – hawthorn berries are their favourites – or pecking at windfall fruit.

flight action: it gives several strong wing beats, then either glides for a while on open wings or flicks them back and coasts for a bit.

SHY OR BOLD

In Britain, over-wintering fieldfares are alert, wary and flighty birds, which stay mostly in the countryside. However, during the summer, when they are nesting in Norway and Russia, they are far bolder and frequently live in built-up areas. Fieldfares are a regular tourist attraction around Trondhjem Cathedral and the residents of St Petersburg often see them nesting in parks and gardens.

Scandinavian Nesters

EVERY SPRING, ALMOST all fieldfares leave Britain and fly north to breed in Scandinavia and Russia where they become a familiar feature of the summer landscape.

Fieldfares build their nests in trees, mainly in birch, alder and pine woods. Groups of between three and 50 pairs nest in close proximity, forming rowdy, restless colonies which are easy to find. Communal nesting affords added protection against predators and intruders. When alarmed while there are chicks in the nest, adult fieldfares will dive-bomb predators, such as owls and crows, shrieking hysterically and spattering the enemy with droppings and vomit to make them go away.

EARLY SITTING

A fieldfare's nest is bulky but well built, wedged in the fork of a tree. It is a typical thrush construction: a cup of twigs, moss and woven grasses, strengthened with mud and lined with finer grass. Most of the building work is done by the female. When the reinforced cradle is complete she lays between four and seven glossy pale blue eggs with light reddish-brown splotches.

Unusually for a small bird, the hen fieldfare does not wait until her clutch is complete before starting to incubate her eggs but begins sitting after laying her second or third egg. The chicks hatch 11 to 14 days later, on different days. A pair of fieldfares breeding in the south of their range may rear two families a year but most only manage to fit in one clutch each summer.

▲ **TEAM EFFORT**
While the female fieldfare is incubating her eggs, her partner brings her food and stands guard nearby to warn her of approaching danger. Generally she stays put to avoid drawing attention to the nest and to protect her eggs.

fledgling fieldfare

Growing-up

On hatching, young fieldfares are covered in long buff down and have broad yellow gapes outlined in pale yellow flanges. Fed on an abundance of worms by both parents, the chicks grow rapidly. Sometimes they leave the nest after only 12 days, before they can fly very well, so they stay on the ground and wait for their parents to feed them. By the time they are 16 or 17 days old the youngsters are fully fledged and flying properly but they still stay with their parents. Some 30 to 35 days after hatching, the juveniles join small flocks before emigrating to warmer regions for the winter.

After fledging, young fieldfares are freckled all over and look less clearly marked than the adults. In their first autumn moult they renew their body plumage but not their flight feathers. They emerge looking more like adult birds, although the head and rump are still browner, the underparts more spotted and the tail shorter.

▲ EMERGENCY RATIONS
When there is snow on the ground, putting out bruised fruit may lure fieldfares into your garden. While there, they will also take seeds and kitchen scraps from the ground.

Viking Raiders

IT IS A SURE sign that winter is here when fieldfares start plundering the hedgerows for their berries. For the fieldfare, the plethora of red berries ripening in hedgerows and gardens is one of the main attractions of spending the winter in the British Isles. During their stay, fieldfares eat berries as they ripen, so ivy, for example, lasts well into the winter.

Arriving on the northeast coast of England after an overnight flight from Scandinavia, the fieldfares' priority is to find food. Their first choice is stripping the scarlet hips and haws from the hedgerows. The birds chatter noisily and quarrel among themselves all the time while feasting greedily on the bunches of red berries.

GRUBBING ABOUT

When fieldfares are not pillaging hedgerow berries, they are feeding on the ground in ploughed fields and rough pastures. There they hunt for worms, slugs, snails, beetles and leatherjackets, spiders and centipedes in the soil and among the roots of the grasses.

Before settling to feed, a flock of fieldfares wheels gracefully over a field for a while. On landing, the birds spread themselves out and work their way across it on foot like an advancing army, leaving no stone or blade of grass unturned. They run or hop over the ground, stopping frequently, standing upright with wings drooped, to check that they are in no imminent danger, before continuing their quest for food.

WINTER SAFARIS

As winter drags on, mixed flocks of fieldfares, redwings, starlings, mistle thrushes and blackbirds roam far and wide, taking food wherever they can find it. The distribution of the fieldfare varies from one winter to the next. It is nomadic throughout its winter sojourn in Britain, moving

' *Flocking fieldfares, speckled like the thrush,*
Picking the red haw from the sweeing bush
That come and go on winter's chilling wing '

from *The Shepherd's Calendar: March* by **John Clare** (1793-1864)

Orderly Flocks

Generally, fieldfares travel about in flocks of between 30 and 200 birds, often in the company of redwings. When feeding in ploughed fields or grassland, a flock appears well-organised, as all the birds space out, to maintain their personal space, and face into the wind, ready for a quick getaway. If any bird breaks rank, fieldfares can be quite belligerent: noisy squabbles break out, drawing attention to the flock. When disturbed, the whole flock rises vertically, as one, with loud cries of alarm, and flies off to perch in trees nearby.

In Hard Times

Lean spells in harsh winters call for desperate measures. Here, a mixed flock of fieldfares, redwings and blackbirds is reduced to raiding boxes of rotting apples to avoid starvation. If all else fails, fieldfares have been known to attack turnips and mangolds put out to feed cattle and sheep or eat snails on the seashore.

wherever food is to be found. A flock may appear suddenly and vanish again just as suddenly as soon as it has exhausted the local food supplies.

In long or cold winters, when food stocks fail or become locked away under snow and ice, flocks of fieldfares usually migrate farther south and west in what are described as hard-weather movements. By the

▲ PILLAGING HORDES

In the winter, a berry-laden pyracantha is manna from heaven for a flock of hungry fieldfares. In fact, any berries on trees and shrubs, such as cotoneaster, rowan and holly, are fieldfare magnets.

end of April, early May, huge flocks of fieldfares start gathering in the northeast before flying north to their Scandinavian breeding grounds.

The Redwing (Turdus iliacus)

Another Nordic nomad, the redwing joins the fieldfare in this country for the winter. In fact, they often travel around together. The redwing's pale buff eyestripe, russety-red flanks and the orange flush under its wings distinguish it from all the other 'spotty' brown thrushes.

The redwing's diet is much the same as most other thrushes: insects and earthworms supplemented by berries and fruit in the winter. Bright red haws are its favourites, although it guzzles yew, holly and rowan berries as well. Given half a chance, redwings would eat earthworms at any time of the year: they are often drawn to flooded pastures, meadows and playing fields where the ground is soft and it is easier to excavate the worms.

In icy spells or when wild berries are scarce, redwings may seek sanctuary in gardens, looking for windfall apples. They only stay long enough to denude shrubs of any red berries and take grated cheese and soaked dried fruit from the lawn.

▲ FLYING IN TOGETHER

Flocks of redwings fly fast and straight, in loose formation, often changing course only at the last minute to avoid obstacles. At times, the hurried flicking action of the wings seems more lark-like than thrushy. From some angles in silhouette, an airborne redwing's pointed wings look rather starling-like. While in the air, members of the flock issue coarse whistling tseeeip-tseeeip *contact calls which can be heard from the ground.*

CHAPTER 2 · WOODLAND & COPPICE

The Nuthatch

If you see a bird coming headfirst down a tree trunk it is definitely a nuthatch, as it is the only one capable of executing such a gravity-defying feat of gymnastics

Dancing up or down a tree, jinking to left, then right on the trunk or going upside down under a branch, it is all the same to the highly nimble nuthatch. This energetic little bird is constantly flying from tree to tree in search of food. Before taking off from one tree, it often gives a sharp *tsit* contact call to let its partner know that it is moving on. Then it flies strongly, along a slightly dipping flight path, to another nearby. There it weaves erratically over the bark, hunting high and low for insects to eat.

WOODLAND BIRDS

Nuthatches are in their natural element in mature coniferous and broadleaf forests, woods and copses, especially those with large oak and beech trees. Wooded parks and nearby gardens with trees offer them sanctuary in urban areas.

long toes and sharp claws are essential aids for climbing

Astonishing Grip

To perform such fly-on-the-ceiling climbing stunts, the nuthatch relies entirely on its huge, powerful feet to provide good anchorage on a tree trunk or branch. It has the conventional songbird arrangement of toes, with three pointing forwards and one back (rather than the woodpeckers' two forward, two back). Each toe is armed with a long, needle-sharp claw that pierces the bark to give a nuthatch unshakeable grip on vertical surfaces and when it turns upside down.

▲ **HEADLONG DESCENT**
With its back foot anchored on the trunk and its front one tucked under its chest, this nuthatch is demonstrating its technique for going headfirst down a tree.

In Britain, the nuthatch breeds mainly in Wales, the Midlands and southern England. Over the past hundred years, nuthatches have been gradually extending their range from established populations in England and Wales, heading northwards and westwards. A few pairs are now established in Scotland. And the good news is that there are still plenty of woods in northern England and Scotland for it to colonise.

Hatching-out

MARCH IS THE best time of year to look out for nuthatches in a wood. The male's plumage is at its brightest in spring and he is at his noisiest then too, flying around calling *twee, twee* loudly to establish and hold his territory against competitors.

In his courtship display to a female prior to breeding in April and May, the male ruffles his flanks to expose his richest chestnut feathers and fans his tail to show off its white spots. At the same time, he floats down to meet the female, with nodding head and open wings so that she can see the black patches on his silvery underwing feathers.

MUDDY BARRICADES

Nuthatches nest in tree-holes and old woodpecker nests. The final choice of nesting site is down to the female, who is up against strong competition from starlings.

To keep out rivals and predators, she takes the extraordinary precaution of plastering the entrance hole with mud until only she and her mate can just squeeze through the tailor-made opening. She collects sticky mud

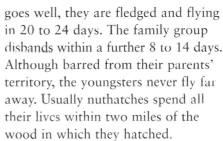

▶ **GOOD JOB**
The female nuthatch's plastering around the entrance hole to her nest is so neat that it is often hard to tell where the bark ends and the mud begins. If the mud cracks as it dries, she soon repairs the damage.

from the margins of puddles, then works it into pellets which she smooths around the nesting hole with her beak. She may also line the cavity with mud to draughtproof it. Such masonry work and nest-building take her two to three weeks to complete.

FAMILY BUSINESS

A pair of nuthatches rears only one brood a year. When the eggs hatch, both parents work hard to keep their grey, downy nestlings filled with caterpillars, flies and aphids. If all

goes well, they are fledged and flying in 20 to 24 days. The family group disbands within a further 8 to 14 days. Although barred from their parents' territory, the youngsters never fly far away. Usually nuthatches spend all their lives within two miles of the wood in which they hatched.

Flakes of Comfort

The nuthatch's nest is a heap of thin bark flakes, often from a nearby pine, larch or yew tree, piled on to a base of wood chips. (As many as 6695 scales of pine bark have been counted in one nest.) On this mound the female lays six to nine white eggs, lightly sprinkled with reddish blotches, which she incubates for 14 to 18 days. She rarely leaves the nest, so the male ferries food to her. When she goes out to stretch her wings, she covers her eggs with bark chippings so that predators assume the nest is empty.

'*You intent on your task and I on the law
Of your wonderful head and gymnastic claw*'

from *The Nuthatch* by **Edith M Thomas** (1854-1925)

Spirit of the Woods

FOR MUCH OF the year, a nuthatch feeds on the insects and their grubs that it finds by scouring the bark on tree trunks and branches. Nuthatches lack the woodpecker's long probing tongue so they cannot investigate insect boreholes and drag out any grubs residing there.

Instead they use their powerful, dagger-like beak, more as a hammer than a chisel, to dislodge loose flakes of bark in search of anything edible underneath. Such excavations are often accompanied by urgent loud rapping sounds – a sure sign that there is a nuthatch in the trees somewhere nearby.

The straight spike of a beak is also the perfect weapon for prising insects and their grubs from crevices in the bark and for splitting nutshells to get at the sweet edible kernel inside.

ADROIT HUNTER

Because they are so agile, nuthatches are able to catch running woodlice, spiders and insects, such as beetles, which they crush against the bark

▲ CRACKING THE CASE
Having firmly plugged a hazelnut into a slit in a bough of rotting oak, the nuthatch positions itself over or above it. Then it bends back its body and repeatedly punches the spike of its beak into the shell until it splits open, revealing the kernel.

Cracking Nuts

The nuthatch really begins to live up to its name in autumn when, as insects become harder to find, it starts eating nuts and seeds. Acorns, chestnuts, beech mast and hazelnuts are all on the menu. The large, hard seeds hidden inside the yew tree's soft red berries, which are deadly poisonous to mammals, are another favourite.

To eat a hazelnut, the nuthatch needs to open the hard shell to get at the sweet, crisp, edible kernel inside. This is how it tackles a nut.

● First the nuthatch finds a cleft in the bark of a tree or on an old trunk softened by decay into which it can wedge the nut to hold it steady.

● Then the little bird sets about breaking the shell. It leans back and brings its whole body weight hammering down behind its beak on to the shell. Bang! Bang! Bang! It goes on bashing at the nut until it smashes the hard case and can start chipping away at the kernel. All the tap-tap-tapping is another clue to alert you to the presence of nuthatches among the trees.

acorns

with their powerful beaks. A flying nuthatch can hover briefly in mid-air like a kestrel, so it can also catch a few flies on the wing. Occasionally, it stops, perching on a branch to frisk the foliage for greenfly.

IN THE COLDER SEASONS

In autumn and winter, nuthatches start feeding on the ground, hopping about searching for seeds or nuts in the leaf litter on the woodland floor. During cold weather, they can spend almost all their time looking for food. A pair of nuthatches may join

up temporarily with loose mixed flocks of blue, great and long-tailed tits as they flit through their territory, feeding as they go. If food supplies run really low, nuthatches may have to feed on tree sap.

SQUIRRELLING AWAY NUTS

Nuthatches are renowned hoarders of nuts, acorns and seeds, as an insurance policy against periods of severe food shortage. They wedge nuts and seeds into rotten wood and bark, but instead of cracking them straight away, they cover their booty

'*Into the woods I went to hear the birdis song,*
Which on the branches, both in plain and vale,
So loudly y-sang, that all the wood y-rang,
Like it should shiver in pieces smale'

from *Four Birds* by **John Lydgate** (c1370-1451)

with moss, lichen or wood chippings. They may also bury stores under leaves on the ground or hide them in cavities in stone walls. The food in these larders is called upon when the temperature drops. A detailed mental map of the territory is needed to find the caches again. This may be one good reason why nuthatches never roam far from home base.

CHATTERBOXES

Not only does the nuthatch's tapping give it away but its voice livens up woodland no end. It is a very vocal little bird with a broad vocabulary of loud, clear calls, which help partners keep track of one another among the tree trunks and branches while they are busy feeding. When startled, a nuthatch issues an abrupt gurgling *twit* note. If it gets very excited, the *twit-twit-twits* come rattling out at least seven times every second.

SINGING SEASON

Nuthatches sing particularly noisily in spring before the breeding season. The male repeats a trio of drawn out, boyish whistles, *pwee-ah, pwee-ah, pwee-ah*, from the upper branches to declare his presence to rivals,

partners and would-be mates. The adults only fall silent when the chicks hatch. Then it seems as though all the nuthatches have deserted the area – but they haven't. They are just preoccupied with chick-rearing.

▲ GOOD HUNTING
Rough bark and dead wood offer rich pickings for a nuthatch looking for insects and their grubs. There are plenty of nooks and crannies where its next meal could be hiding.

Cold Fare

During spells of very cold winter weather, nuthatches are often driven to leave the shelter and privacy of the woods and seek food in nearby gardens. On bird-tables, they impatiently barge and bully their way past the regular, more timid clientele to have first choice of the sunflower seeds, nuts, fat and bread on offer.

The nuthatch's natural agility and strong feet stand it in good stead when it comes to hanging on to bird-feeders as well. With a firm grip on the wire or nylon mesh, it can arch its back, throw back its head and hack into the shelled peanuts inside with its strong beak.

The Treecreeper

*With its mottled brown back, thin beak and long tail,
a treecreeper looks for all the world like a feathery little
mouse as it busily shuffles its way up a tree trunk*

Treecreepers may look sweet and mousy but they are voracious hunters. No bark-dwelling insect or spider is safe when these little tree-climbers are on the loose in broadleaved and mixed woodland, tall hedges, well-wooded parkland or the gardens nearby.

DOWN IN THE WOODS

A treecreeper's plumage blends in well against the rough bark of a tree. Were it not for the odd flash of its white underparts, it would be all but invisible. The best time to look out for treecreepers is in spring, before there are any leaves on the trees. They are at their liveliest and noisiest then, busy setting up breeding territories and courting females.

▶ EVER UPWARDS
Aided by its large, strong feet and stiff, supportive tail, the treecreeper spends its life climbing up the vertical trunks of trees in search of insects and spiders.

male singing

Rallying Calls

Treecreepers sing at most times of the year, but become particularly vocal between mid February and mid May, in the build-up to the breeding season. Only the male sings, frequently opening his beak wide to repeat the same high-pitched, tinkling song – *tsee-tsee-tsi-tsi-si-si-si-si-sisisisisisi-tsee*. Each time, the lyric gathers volume and speed on a descending scale, ending on a trilling flourish like a miniature bugle call. Rival males exchange calls in lively song-duels to establish their territories among the trees. To woo his mate, a male treecreeper eagerly pursues her in and out of trees and up and around trunks. These lively chases are punctuated by hovering displays, wing quivering and courtship feeding.

Woodland Hideaways

THE TREECREEPER'S NEST is one of the best camouflaged of all woodland birds. Instead of excavating or adopting a nesting hole, treecreepers tuck their nest away behind a flap of bark on a decaying tree or into a cleft in the trunk shielded by ivy. Sometimes they wedge it in crevices among loose brick or stonework, behind wooden cladding on buildings or in a log pile. All that is likely to give it away are a few strands of nesting material and the adults' visits.

WORKING TOGETHER

As part of his courtship display, the male treecreeper presents his mate with food and nesting material at their nest site to reinforce their pair bond and initiate nest-building.

Both birds get on with assembling their cup-shaped nest from strips of bark, wood chips, dry grass, moss and lichen. When the foundations are prepared, the female takes over to line it with soft warm feathers, hair, wool, lichen and spiders' silk. It takes a pair of treecreepers roughly two weeks of hard work to complete their building.

NESTING HABITS

A female treecreeper usually lays five or six white eggs with a ring of reddish-brown freckles around the broad end. She is also responsible for incubating them for 18 to 19 days. As hatchlings, the chicks are covered in blackish-grey down. With both parents feeding them, they are ready to fly the nest in 14 to 15 days.

Many treecreepers manage to rear two families each year. Often the male is building a new nest and the female is laying a second clutch of eggs while they are still feeding their first brood of fledglings. Usually the youngsters receive after-nest care from one parent or the other for up to 14 days after fledging.

KEEN CLIMBERS

Be warned and stand back if you happen to be around when a family of young treecreepers leaves the nest for the first time. They have been known to land on the only upright thing around, regardless of whether it is a tree trunk or a person, and start climbing up right away.

▲ BIT OF A SQUEEZE

Invisibility is the treecreepers' motto. Not only do they get lost against the bark but they also pick hidden crannies in which to build their nests. Usually these are so narrow that even the fledglings find it a tight squeeze getting out.

Out of the Nest

Juvenile treecreepers are paler brown than the adults, with a yellower tinge to their white areas. They often have a faint bib of brown spots on their throat and more white spots on their back. Their beaks are shorter and less curved too.

Having left the nest, the youngsters follow their parents about from tree to tree, with the whole family trooping up the trunk in single file. If threatened, they freeze, beaks up, relying on their ability to blend into the background to keep them safe. The youngsters make their first attempt to feed themselves about seven days after fledging. For their first few nights of freedom, they return to the nest to roost.

juvenile

No Hiding Place

SMALL, ACTIVE BIRDS such as the treecreeper need to eat thousands of tiny insects and spiders each day to keep themselves going. A treecreeper is always busy, searching each tree thoroughly and methodically as it moves up the trunk, so that it does not miss any small insects, such as ants, earwigs, beetles, their eggs and larvae, or spiders, mites, centipedes and woodlice living on the bark.

According to one theory, the treecreeper's gleaming white breast reflects a little extra light into nooks and crannies where its prey is hiding, making it easier to find.

SEARCH PATTERN

The treecreeper clambers up from the base of the trunk, searching for insects in the bark as it goes. Having reached the top, and investigated the larger branches, it flies down to the base of a neighbouring tree and starts its search all over again.

A treecreeper's wings are well-rounded but it is not a strong flier; in the air it is fluttery and looks almost moth-like. While it is feeding, flights from tree to tree are brief and wavy, hardly long enough for any passer-by to catch sight of the whitish wingbar on each wing.

▲ UPWARDLY MOBILE
A treecreeper climbs in short, jerky hops with its feet wide apart, aided by its stiff pointed tail feathers which are pressed against the trunk to support it.

> ' *The protectively coloured weevil, the crouching spider clinging to its web, the coccoon enshrouded pupa do not elude its keen eye* '
>
> from *Birds of the Wayside and Woodland* by **T A Coward** (1936)

Creating a Cosy Roosting Place

young treecreepers roosting

● Although they may seek shelter in dense ivy or inside outbuildings, treecreepers generally roost in tree crevices – behind loose bark, in hollow trees or in cavities they dig out for themselves in rotten stumps. Each regular visitor to a tree hollows out several holes around the trunk so that, regardless of the direction of the wind or rain, they always have a dry, draughtproof bunker for the night. Several treecreepers, especially young ones, may share a suitable tree each night and move around the trunk if the weather changes.

● As tiny birds, treecreepers are vulnerable to the cold. In icy weather, as many as 13 or 14 birds may huddle up together. A roosting treecreeper fluffs out the feathers on its lower back to keep itself warm and improve its camouflage against the bark.

● It was first noted in Ireland in about 1924 that treecreepers were roosting in large cracks in the soft, thick, very fibrous bark of the majestic *Wellingtonia*, an ornamental giant redwood pine tree imported from America. Now, all over Britain, treecreepers are using their beaks and sharp claws to scratch out well-insulated mattresses in the spongy bark of Wellingtonias. Then they squeeze in headfirst and flatten themselves against the trunk (see left).

◄ **HOME IS THE HUNTER**
After another successful hunting trip, a treecreeper returns to its nesting cleft in the bark carrying a feast of insects in its beak.

▲ **LIKE A COCKTAIL STICK**
The treecreeper is the only British songbird to have a crescent-shaped beak. Long, fine and down-curving, with a needle-sharp tip, it is the perfect tool for tweaking prey out of narrow crevices in the bark.

Flying and hunting are accompanied by needle-sharp contact notes of *tseee* and a slightly softer *tsit*. Most of the time, these calls are repeated rapidly and frequently and can give away the presence of a treecreeper in the area. However, their calls often go undetected because, being so high-pitched, they are beyond the range of human hearing.

SHARING THE SPOILS

Finding enough food is never easy, especially as the treecreeper is far from the only bird hunting for insects in the woods. To reduce competition, different birds feed on various parts of the trees in a number of ways. While the treecreeper frisks every crack in the bark, the great spotted woodpecker eats wood-boring insects under the bark and the nuthatch takes seeds as well as insects from bark and dead wood. The coal tit, blue tit, goldcrest and willow warbler are all small and light enough to find insects among the leaves and twigs on the flimsiest outer branches.

Even when insects and spiders are hard to find, treecreepers in this country rarely eat seeds. On short visits to gardens in the winter, they usually stick to exploring the bark on tree trunks. Occasionally, they may be spotted scouring rocky walls, the sides of buildings, fences and turf for something to eat or hovering very briefly to catch flies in mid-air.

Toughest Season

Winter is a cruel time for treecreepers. When a prolonged spell of freezing fog or rain forms a slippery icy coating on tree trunks, they cannot get a firm enough grip on the bark, or push their beaks into the iced-up cracks, to hunt normally and effectively.

Even under such extreme duress, treecreepers hardly ever visit bird-tables, although they have been known to land on peanut-feeders and take crushed nuts, porridge oats or suet after they have been pressed into crevices in coarse-barked trees.

The Green Woodpecker

You'll know when there is a green woodpecker in the area: even if you miss its brilliant markings you may still see it bouncing along through the air and hear its laughing call

Green woodpeckers favour open woodland, copses and parks where there are a few dead and dying deciduous trees. They can excavate a nest-hole in the softened timber with their beak or use their long tongue to seek out wood-boring insects.

HAPPILY GROUNDED

Although it lives and nests among trees, the green woodpecker often leaves the shelter of a wood and lands on grassy fields or lawns to eat ants. For a bird that feeds out in the open, the green woodpecker's bright plumage and noisy calls are amazingly conspicuous. It compensates for this by being very wary and ready to take flight at the first sign of danger.

▶ **AT FULL STRETCH**
Flying away from his nest-hole (just visible behind his left wing) a male green woodpecker resumes a non-stop food shuttle to keep his family well fed.

female

Spot the Difference

Although it can be hard to see clearly in the wild, one visible feature distinguishes male from female green woodpeckers: on each side of his beak the male (above) has a red moustache-like stripe with a black border; the female (left) has similar markings but hers are all black. In other respects the male and female look the same: they share the same bright yellow rump, grass green back and wings, scarlet crown and black patches around their pale eyes.

Woodland Carpenters

AT THE END OF March, normally solitary green woodpeckers start to show an interest in other green woodpeckers in their area. When the resident male and a passing green woodpecker confront each other, they sway from side to side, with beaks outstretched.

A full turn of the head reveals the definitive moustachial stripes. If they are red, the male chases off his rival; if black, he starts courting the female with noisy pursuit flights and mock nest-hole drilling.

PICKING THE HOLE

A pair of green woodpeckers prefers to adopt an existing tree-hole as their nesting site. Outside of the breeding season, green woodpeckers roost in deserted tree-holes and often choose to use the female's winter roosting hole as their nest.

If the green woodpeckers have to excavate a new hole, they usually settle on a site high up in a dead or dying tree where the timber is rotten and soft. The woodpecker's skull is specially adapted to withstand all the rapid-fire hammering involved in drilling a hole in a tree. To prevent brain damage, the space between the beak and skull is packed with shock-absorbing cartilage.

ARCHITECTURE OF A HOLE

When drilling a nesting hole, a green woodpecker hacks in horizontally for 5 to 7.5cm (2 to 3in), creating an oval entrance hole. Then it digs down for about 30cm (12in), opening up a 12.5cm (5in) chamber at the base. The bottom of the nest-hole is lined with a thin layer of wood chippings.

A pair of green woodpeckers may take two to three weeks to hollow out a new nesting chamber. And after all that hard work, some may still be ousted from their nest-hole by a pair of bullying starlings.

NESTING ETIQUETTE

The female lays five to seven white eggs on a bed of wood chippings in the nesting chamber. Both parents take it in turns to incubate them for 18 to 19 days, then share the care of their nestlings. To keep the nest clean, they swallow the chicks' droppings, rather than carry them away.

▲ HANGING ON BY HIS TOENAILS
The green woodpecker's two forward, two back toe configuration gives this male secure anchorage on the trunk of his nesting tree. His stiff tail feathers play an invaluable supporting role.

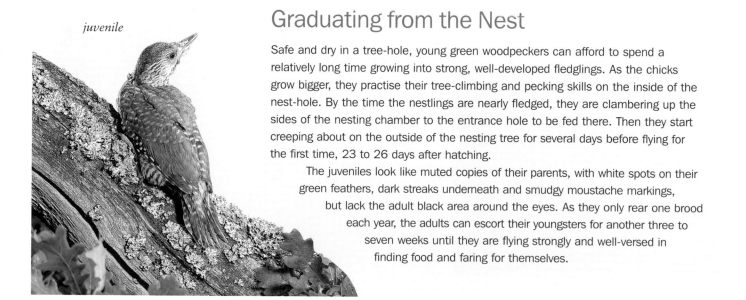

juvenile

Graduating from the Nest

Safe and dry in a tree-hole, young green woodpeckers can afford to spend a relatively long time growing into strong, well-developed fledglings. As the chicks grow bigger, they practise their tree-climbing and pecking skills on the inside of the nest-hole. By the time the nestlings are nearly fledged, they are clambering up the sides of the nesting chamber to the entrance hole to be fed there. Then they start creeping about on the outside of the nesting tree for several days before flying for the first time, 23 to 26 days after hatching.

The juveniles look like muted copies of their parents, with white spots on their green feathers, dark streaks underneath and smudgy moustache markings, but lack the adult black area around the eyes. As they only rear one brood each year, the adults can escort their youngsters for another three to seven weeks until they are flying strongly and well-versed in finding food and faring for themselves.

Flame of the Wood

GREEN WOODPECKERS FEED mainly on the ground and almost entirely on ants; even when looking for food in trees, they are mostly following ant trails up the trunk and searching for ants under loose bark.

Although a green woodpecker's beak looks fearsome, it is not as strong as other woodpecker's. It is used for digging into the earth and anthills more than it is for prising off bark or drilling holes in trees.

RECORD-BREAKING TONGUE

The green woodpecker has a long and phenomenally mobile tongue. It is the longest of any British woodpecker, extending about four times the length of the beak and reaching 10cm (4in) beyond its tip. While it is being flicked out, the tongue gets thickly coated with sticky saliva produced by glands

female

▶ **JESTER'S OUTFIT**
The full array of a green woodpecker's red, green and yellow plumage and the white spots on the black flight feathers are best seen as it takes off.

' *Under the crag, where the tree-tops lean Flashed your feathers in green and gold, Stroke by stroke, with a dip between* '

from *The Yaffle* by **A C Benson** (1862-1925)

Feathery Anteater

The green woodpecker can wriggle its long, agile tongue through the maze of tunnels and breeding chambers in an anthill, seeking out ants, their eggs and pupae. On sunny afternoons worker ants carry pupae to the upper chambers in the nest where it is warmer. Crafty woodpeckers sweep away the leaves on top and lick up the ants. On a diet of ants, green woodpeckers produce cigarette ash-like droppings, containing the indigestible remains of hundreds of ants.

Between April and October, woodpeckers often ambush ants marching along their trails across the woodland floor. In winter, when ants go farther underground, woodpeckers will even clear snow from the top of an anthill to attack them.

Angry ants defend their nest ferociously by squirting concentrated formic acid all over the place. If any lands on the green woodpecker's feathers, it can help to purge them of mites, lice and other parasites.

in the lower bill. Sometimes, a green woodpecker leaves a shiny trail of saliva on the bark of the tree or over an anthill where it has been feeding.

The most sensitive, mobile part of the tongue is its tip, a flattened pad which scoops up every ant it touches. The tongue is frequently drawn back into the beak so that the woodpecker can swallow its prey. To be fully withdrawn, it has to be wound over and around the back of the skull.

DOWN TO EARTH

On the ground, a green woodpecker hops about rather clumsily, dragging its stiff tail through the dirt. It cocks its head, stares intently at the grass and stabs the turf fiercely in search of small insect grubs. Although not common garden visitors, green woodpeckers are sometimes seen drilling furiously into large lawns in search of insects, leaving beak-holes. In harsh winters, they may also take suet, bird cake and mealworms from a bird-table. While prodding the ground, a green woodpecker raises its head frequently to look around and check for danger before going back to its digging.

UP IN THE TREES

When looking for food in trees, the green woodpecker flies in and lands with a final upward swoop, low down on the trunk. From there it works its way upwards, spiralling around the trunk in jerky hops.

As it goes, a green woodpecker chips away at any loose bark and exposes tunnels made by wood-boring insects. These it can probe with its long tongue and reel in insect grubs living inside. When it has exhausted the possibilities on one tree, the green woodpecker sweeps

▼ GETTING STUCK IN
Head down, a green woodpecker is intent on finding ants buried in the woodland floor.

Winter Rations

During the winter, when ants and their grubs are well beyond its reach, a green woodpecker may be forced to use its dagger-like beak to eat any nuts, acorns, berries and fruit, such as these windfall apples, that it can find. After his autumn moult, this male green woodpecker's back looks a browner, more olive shade of green than it would have done during the spring and summer.

down to the base of a neighbouring tree and starts all over again.

CLUES TO IDENTITY

As you walk across a field, the first inkling you are likely to get that there is a green woodpecker nearby is when you hear its loud cackling flight call. If you look up quickly enough, you may catch sight of a green bird with a yellow rump and red crown flying away, tracing a distinctive switchback path to the trees in a nearby wood.

In the air, a green woodpecker is swift, although quick bursts of flapping interspersed with regular closed-wing glides result in choppy, deeply undulating progress. Among the trees, its green plumage soon vanishes against the foliage and green-stained bark on the trunks.

The Laughing Yaffle

IN LATIN, THE green woodpecker's scientific name, *Picus viridis*, simply means woodpecker green. More interesting are the numerous nicknames based on its conspicuous plumage, cackling cry and pecking.

LAUGHING BIRD

To many, the green woodpecker used to be the Yaffle. To the ear, *yaffle* mimics the barking quality of the green woodpecker's call – as Thomas Gisbourne (1758-1846) observed in *Walks in a Forest:*

> *Green-yellow bursts from*
> *the copse the laughing yaffle.*

The green woodpecker's neighing call has given rise to an extraordinary number of local names. Many sounded like a guffaw of laughter: Heigh-wawe, Hickwall, Hecco and Highhoe, to pick out just a few.

In Gaelic, the red-capped green woodpecker was aptly known as the

▶ **EVER ALERT**
As nimble as a squirrel, a watchful green woodpecker dodges behind a tree trunk at the first sign of danger, then peeps around to check whether it is safe to carry on probing the bark for insects.

Wet Weather Warning

• In many cultures, the bright green woodpecker is linked with wet weather and, by association, agriculture. Its green plumage symbolised rain, new growth and fertility. Using its beak to plough up ants' nests and dig into bark also suggested farming.

• A woodpecker cult developed in ancient times. Among Neolithic tribes and the Welsh Druids, the green woodpecker in particular was seen as a rain-maker.

• Wet and rain names persisted throughout Europe: the green woodpecker was variously called the Rain Bird, Rain Fowl or Rain Pie (pie after its variegated plumage).

• The green woodpecker was also the Wet-Wet Bird or Wet Tail, which became contracted to Whetile or Whittle and changed to Greenile.

• In Germany one of the green woodpecker's names is *geissvogel*, the torrent bird; its Danish name, *regnkrake*, is a compound of rain and croak.

• *Lorsque le pivert crie il annonce la pluie* (When the woodpecker cries it announces the rain) is a French proverb.

Bee-eater

- In winter, when ants' nests are frozen, green woodpeckers turn to digging out bee and wasp nests in hollow trees or banks and breaking into bee hives to eat the grubs within.

- In Germany, the green woodpecker was so closely associated with bees that one of its names was *Bienenwolf* or Bee-eater.

- Green woodpeckers do not appear to be bothered by bee stings. This gave rise to a German belief that anybody carrying a woodpecker's beak would be protected from being stung by bees.

- The Post Office used to have trouble with woodpeckers boring holes in telephone poles. Although not strange feeding behaviour for woodpeckers, in this case it was fruitless as the poles were sound, having been chemically treated to prevent insect and fungal infestation. It seems that the woodpeckers were drawn to the poles by the humming of the telegraph wires, which made them think that there were bees' nests hidden inside. Once the vibrations of the wires were suppressed, the buzzing was silenced and the woodpeckers stopped vandalising the poles.

flame of the wood. The eye-catching gaudiness of the green woodpecker's plumage has always been an exciting if somewhat incongruous sight in the British countryside. As he noted in his poem *Walks in a Forest*, Thomas Gisbourne evidently enjoyed seeing – and hearing – such a vibrant bird.

Joy glistens on her verdant plumes,
And bright scarlet sparkles
on her crest.

ANCIENT RIDDLE

As long ago as the 8th century, apparently, people enjoyed brain-teasers. In Exeter Cathedral there is an Anglo-Saxon book of riddles in which number 24 is about the green woodpecker. The puzzle ends with a jumble of the six letters in *higora*, one of the Old English names for the green woodpecker, from the Anglo-Saxon word for a laugher, *higera* (with a soft g).

I am a wonder. I vary my voice,
Sometimes bark like a dog,
Sometimes bleat like a goat . . .
. . . G suggests me,
Also A and R, with O,
H and I. Now I am named,
As these six letters clearly say.

'*Laugh, woodpecker, down in the wood;*
What do you find that moves your mirth?
Should I laugh if I understood
All that you know of the merry earth?'

from *The Yaffle* by **Arthur Christopher Benson** (1862-1925)

KEY TO ANY DOOR

According to Pliny (23-79), the Roman natural historian, a small fern called moonwort could open any lock. But it took a woodpecker to find the magical plant. First you had to locate a woodpecker's nest and block the entrance. With access to its chicks barred, the woodpecker would fetch some moonwort. When it rubbed the root over the blocked entrance, the plug would fall out.

TRANSMOGRIFICATION

In ancient mythology, a few badly behaved gods were punished by being changed into woodpeckers. Celeus, for example, was turned into a green woodpecker after trying to steal honey from the baby Zeus.

male golden oriole

female golden oriole

THE GOLDEN ORIOLE (*Oriolus oriolus*)
The green woodpecker is in the top 10 of most commonly misidentified birds in Britain. Some people get overexcited when they see a green-and-yellow bird flying out of woodland, believing that they have seen a golden oriole – now a very rare summer visitor to eastern England. Seen fleetingly in flight, the female's green back and yellow rump may look a bit like a green woodpecker, but she is thrush-shaped.

The Nightingale

Long before Elvis Presley earned the title of king of rock 'n' roll, the nightingale was acclaimed as a singing superstar, even though it has always preferred to shun the limelight

E ach April, nightingales come back to England to breed, having spent the winter in tropical Africa, south of the Sahara. Many cross the English Channel at its narrowest point and arrive in Kent, from where they radiate out into Sussex, Essex and East Anglia.

MODEST GENIUS

The nightingale is renowned for the brilliance of its voice and for singing in the dark. But its brown plumage and secretive, nocturnal lifestyle make it hard to see as it sings from tangled undergrowth. Nightingales hug the shelter of shadowy thickets of coppiced hazel in copses and on railway embankments and heaths, in spiky hawthorn, dog rose and bramble in hedgerows and in dense clumps of nettles and bracken.

With its brown colouring, the nightingale looks like an overgrown robin without a red breast. A striking feature of the plumage is its broad rounded tail, which is a rich, almost brick-dust-red colour. The tail is most noticeable when it is spread in flight or during courtship displays.

The nightingale also shares many of the robin's mannerisms. The perky posture, long legs, sudden hops and pauses, when it stands erect with its feet planted well apart while feeding on the ground, are typical. So are the frequent bobbing, tilting of the head and flirting of the tail.

▲ STAYING UNDERCOVER

A nightingale finds all the food, shelter and nesting sites it requires in the mesh of stems, leaves, thorns and stumps in woodland and coppice undergrowth.

FINDING FOOD

Nightingales feed mainly on the ground, hopping about on their long brown legs and stopping occasionally to cock their heads, just like robins. They use their strong pointed beak to turn over leaf litter and pick out insects and spiders to eat. From time to time, they plunge it into the soil to pluck out juicy worms. Its large dark eyes, outlined by pale eye-rings, help it to see better at night and when it is moving through poorly lit thickets.

Musical Virtuoso

HEARING A COCK nightingale deliver his song with all his might on a still moonlit evening in spring is bound to stop you in your tracks and take your breath away.

The most obvious and astounding quality of the nightingale's song is its enormous power. A volley of clear notes simply explodes from the thicket in which the little bird is singing. Despite the force of his delivery, there is no sense that the singer is straining to sing his notes with such bravado. Keats's description of *full-throated ease* captures the confidence of genius perfectly.

EXPECTANT PAUSES

Another extraordinary part of the nightingale's song is the pauses. It is a fitful but ecstatic melody: the male sings in short snatches of five or six second long phrases, punctuated by brief periods of quiet. In the darkness, these silences add an element of breathless suspense to the song.

Not all nightingales are cathedral choristers but each one uses the full range of his versatile voice. A single nightingale can have 300 different love songs in his repertoire. Phrases are repeated but varied in pitch, rhythm, intensity or timbre; he can switch from sounding as if he is plucking metallic strings to churring gruffly, even croaking. His voice seems wistful one moment, merry the next. Throughout, he adds trills and crescendos and holds long notes at will. To hear such a virtuoso live on stage is thrilling – once heard, the nightingale's song is never forgotten.

▶ HEART AND SOUL
The nightingale's throat throbs and his whole body and tail quake with excitement as he performs his brilliant song with astonishing vehemence. Yet the opening and closing of his beak seem unsynchronised with the phrasing of his melody.

' 'Chee-chew chew-chew,' and higher still:
'Cheer-cheer, cheer-cheer,' more loud and shrill:
'Cheer-up cheer-up cheer-up,' and dropt
Low: 'tweet tweet jug jug jug,' and stopt
Wew-wew, wew-wew, chur-chur chur-chur '

Part of **John Clare's** transcription of the nightingale's song
in *The Progress of Rhyme*

Courtship Concerts

Arriving back in Britain about 10 days before the females, male nightingales start singing at once to stake out their territories and warn off other males. They only come into full voice when the females start flying through their area.

Having enticed a female down to join him, a male nightingale performs a courtship display that is rarely seen because he is hidden low down in dense cover. It involves much posturing, with his wings slightly outspread, drooping and quivering, and his tail fanned. Sometimes a male makes himself visible by climbing up to the top of the thicket or choosing a perch on the outside of a bush from which to sing.

A male nightingale mounts guard over the ground he claims as his own. Sometimes, neighbouring nightingales get embroiled in an exciting choral duel, when one bird sings, then waits in silence for the other to respond.

Hermit's Nest

MALE NIGHTINGALES ARE loyal to familiar nesting sites, returning each year to areas where they have bred successfully before. Newcomers are thought to be attracted to a site by hearing older birds singing. Usually a breeding area has to sustain several pairs, as nightingales tend to nest in loose colonies. This could be because the combined power of many songs is better at attracting females. Often it is difficult to work out why one thicket is deemed to provide acceptable cover while another seemingly identical patch nearby remains uncolonised.

FAMILY HOME

Meanwhile, as her mate sings his heart out to defend their territory, the shy female

▼ FULFILLING HIS BRIEF
Until his chicks hatch, the male nightingale's job is to concentrate on his singing, which will win him a nesting territory and his mate, and defend their nest.

▲ DIRECT FLIGHT
In the air, nightingales fly quickly, straight from one patch of cover to another.

▼ OLIVE EGGS
A dense spattering of translucent brown freckles over a blue-green shell makes a nightingale's eggs look olive-brown. On the base of the deep nest-cup, their dull colour is perfect camouflage in shadowy locations.

'*The nest is made a hermit's mossy cell,*
Snug lies her curious eggs in number five,
Of deadened green or rather olive brown;
And the old prickly thorn bush
guards them well'

from *The Nightingale's Nest* by **John Clare** (1793-1864)

Nest in Privacy

The female nightingale is in charge of building a nest, low down in bushy tangles, either on the ground or at the base of a dark thicket, even in a bed of nettles. It starts as a scruffy heap of dried grass, fine roots, moss and dead leaves, which she fashions into a deep cup lined with hair or wool. When finished it is a well-disguised extension of the undergrowth. Then she lays her eggs and settles down to incubate them. With her ruddy chestnut tail and pale throat, a hen nightingale sitting on her eggs is as well-camouflaged as the nest itself.

nightingale builds her secret nest in the inaccessible depths of a thorny thicket. Then she lays four to six eggs and incubates them for about 13 days, until the chicks emerge. The newly hatched nestlings are covered in dark grey down and have an orange lining to their mouths, with pale yellow flanges around their beaks.

NO MORE TIME FOR SINGING

Now the male gives up singing to help care for his chicks. Nightingale voices are rarely heard after 21 June, Midsummer Day. At first he tries to do both while he is still hopeful of attracting another female. He is often heard trying to sing his sweet song through a beakful of insects and spiders he has collected to feed his family in the nest.

Nightingales only have time to bring up one brood each year, before they have to start preparing to leave these shores again. Towards the end of July, berries such as wild

strawberries and elderberries are ripening. These are a valuable source of sugar which helps the nightingales put on fat reserves for their long journey back to Africa, which starts in August or September.

▲ **PART OF THE LEAF LITTER**
If it were not for the five golden food funnels of the chicks begging to be fed in this nightingale's nest it would be very hard to distinguish the loose leafy cradle from the leaf litter.

Cases of Mistaken Identity

fledgling nightingale

fledgling robin

female redstart

● With a bit of wishful thinking, it is possible to mistake a mottled brown young robin for a mottled brown young nightingale. When in doubt, check out the tail. The nightingale has a much brighter, richer chestnut tail than the robin.

● The nightingale's ruddy tail can also lead to confusion with another brown-feathered summer visitor to open woodland, the female redstart. Like the nightingale, her most conspicuous feature is her bright chestnut tail but, unlike the nightingale's, hers always has a band of darker brown feathers down the centre.

Love's Chorister

THROUGHOUT HISTORY, the singing of the nightingale has been fêted by poets and musicians, who were entranced by the combination of desire and sweetness they heard in its voice. In his book, *Through the Woods*, H E Bates vividly described hearing a nightingale's fabulous song *flaring out in a moment into a crescendo of fire and honey.*

To the 18th-century poets, the nightingale was Philomel, the tragic heroine of a Greek myth about the origins of the nightingale. Today, the scientific name of the song thrush is *Philomela*, a tribute to its lovely song.

In the myth, Philomel was tricked into marrying her brother-in-law, Tereus, thinking her sister Procne was dead, which she wasn't. After a scurrilous tale of revenge and death, the gods intervened to avert more bloodshed, by changing Tereus into a hawk, Procne into a swallow and Philomel into a nightingale.

▶ **FACT AND FICTION**
Thorny wild roses and brambles create impenetrable defenses around the nightingale's nest. But in legend, the nightingale is said to prick himself with a thorn to calm down his passion.

Listening for Nightingales

You have only about six weeks each year – from the last week in April until mid June, when their eggs start hatching – to hear male nightingales singing. The male sings from cover in coppiced hazel and open woodland. During the day, his exquisite voice cuts through the general hubbub of birdsong because it is so beautiful; but after dark, singing alone, he sounds perfectly spine-tinglingly fabulous. To appreciate the song at its best, try creeping as close as you can to one bird in the dark, so you are enveloped in his wondrous music. The males usually fall silent before sunrise and sunset and take no part in the spectacular dawn and dusk choruses.

Beware of wishful thinking though: at times, it is possible to mistake a robin singing under a street light for a nightingale. Even the nightingale that famously sang in Berkeley Square was probably an insomniac blackbird or robin.

Lore and Legend

● According to legend, a nightingale and a blindworm (an old name for the slow-worm, a legless lizard that looks like a snake) had only one eye each. When the nightingale was invited to the wren's wedding it was ashamed to attend with only one eye, so it stole the blindworm's eye. The blindworm promised to steal its eye back if it ever found the nightingale sleeping. It is supposed to be the fear of being caught napping that keeps the nightingale singing day and night.

● In one medieval myth, the nightingale was so terrified of being bitten by a snake that it pressed its breast against a thorn all night to keep itself awake. For ages, its song was taken to be a cry of pain:

Now the nightingale, the pretty nightingale,
The sweetest singer in the forest's choir,
Lo, yonder she sitteth, her breast against a briar
from *The Song* by **Thomas Dekker** (1570-1641)

● An Eastern version of the thorn myth said that the nightingale, Bulbul, was in love with the rose and had to stab himself with a thorn to keep his passion under control.

● An old proverb declared that to hear a nightingale sing before a cuckoo in spring promised luck in love:

Thy liquid notes that close the eye of day,
First heard before the shallow cuckoo's bill,
Portend success in love
from *To the Nightingale* by **John Milton** (1608-1674)

● In Renaissance Europe, *listening to the nightingale* was euphemism for sexual frolicking.

● The purity, range and agility of the legendary Stockholm-born soprano Jenny Lind's (1820-1887) voice won her the nickname of the Swedish Nightingale.

MIXED EMOTIONS

Like many duped lovers, the literary critic Joseph Warton (1722-1800) empathised with Philomel's suffering in his *Ode to the Nightingale*.

Oh fail not then, sweet Philomel,
Thy sadly warbled woes to tell,
In sympathetic numbers join
Thy pangs of luckless love with mine!

On the other hand, the poet William Wordsworth (1770-1850) heard almost unbearable romance and passion in the nightingale's voice:

O nightingale! Thou surely art
A creature of a fiery heart:
These notes of thine –
they pierce and pierce.

The most famous poetic nightingale has to be the bird so much envied by a sickly John Keats (1795-1821).

That thou, light-wingëd
Dryad of the trees,
In some melodious plot
Of beechen green and
shadows numberless,
Singest of summer
in full-throated ease.

MUSICAL PLAGIARISM

An illustrious roll call of composers – Vivaldi, Handel, Tchaikovsky, Haydn and Saint-Saëns among others – has attempted to copy the nightingale's musical excellence. Probably the most realistic reproduction of its song is in *Catalogue d'Oiseaux* by the French organist and composer, Olivier Messiaen (1908-1992). With his keen ear, he could analyse and transcribe birdsong, within the limitations of musical notation, into fiendishly complicated but beautiful music.

Broadcasting Debut

In 1924, the nightingale was the star of the first live outside radio broadcast. Superstardom beckoned when the well-known British cellist, Beatrice Harrison was practising Rimsky-Korsakov's *Chant Hindou* in her garden and a nightingale started to sing along with her cello.

Beatrice thought it would be lovely if more people could hear her songster singing. With some trepidation, Lord Reith, then Director General of the BBC, agreed to a live broadcast of Beatrice and her nightingale making music together.

On the night of Saturday 19 May, dressed in her concert finery, Beatrice sat in her garden in Surrey playing her cello in front of a microphone to coax the nightingale to accompany her. Like a true star, the coy nightingale kept its audience waiting until well into the evening before he started singing with the cello. All over the country, a million people stayed up late to listen, absolutely spellbound.

The Willow Warbler

It may come as a surprise to learn that around five million willow warblers spend the summer in the British Isles each year. You hardly ever see them, so where are they?

Willow warblers are our most numerous summer visitors and the eighth commonest breeding bird in the country. They are among the earliest arrivals to get back each spring. In late March or early April these little pale yellow and olive brown birds suddenly start appearing in woods and copses across Britain. But it is always difficult to watch willow warblers, because they forage in the tree-tops and their plain yellow-olive plumage merges with the foliage.

ANYWHERE WITH TREES

Hungry and weary after their flight from Africa, willow warblers dive straight into hedges and trees looking for insects and spiders to eat. Their favourite haunts are open woodland, preferably birch, oak and ash groves, hedges and scrub across the country.

A willow warbler is a restless little bird, always darting from tree to tree, then dashing from one leaf to the next twig in the upper branches in an urgent search for insects. It used to be called a willow wren because it is so tiny and frenetic.

PICCOLO PLAYER

The willow warbler has a small sweet tinkling voice which sounds like a plaintive trill played on a high-pitched flute. Throughout May and early June, there are willow warblers incessantly singing their hearts out in woodland, copses and hedges all over the country.

Normally the cock bird sings from a lowish perch. His vivacious song starts quietly, then rises in volume and pitch before falling away in a thinner cascading trill and fading out with a soft flourish. A pair of willow warblers uses a mournful whistling *hoo-eet* contact call that becomes a more anxious *pui-pui* whenever danger threatens.

▲ SPRING IS IN THE AIR
A cock willow warbler is singing his sweet melody for all he's worth from a birch tree. He is inviting any female warblers in the area to pair up with him and warning other males to keep clear.

'*The willow wrens begin their ethereal whisperings*'

from *The Joy of Music* by **Mary Webb** (1881-1927)

Busy Little Birds

THE MAIN WAVE of willow warblers arrives back in Britain in April, just as trees and hedges are bursting into leaf and in time to take advantage of a population explosion of insects that feed on the tender young leaves.

CATCHING FLIES

The willow warbler's thin, pointed beak marks it out as an insect-eater. It spends most of its time fluttering through twiggy hedges and leafy tree-tops, looking for caterpillars, aphids, flies, small moths, ants, weevils and beetles, spiders and mites which it daintily picks off the leaves and bark. Sometimes it snaps up flies on the wing or hovers in mid-air to take insects from the undersides of leaves.

POPULATION TRENDS

Willow warblers generally feed and roost on their own, except during the breeding season. If you see several at once it is usually a coincidence and indicates there are lots in the area.

In recent years, the willow warbler's abundance has shown diverse trends in various parts of the country. Their numbers fell drastically in the 1980s over southern England but stayed steady in Scotland. In the 1990s, numbers levelled off and may have picked up slightly since then. Smaller clutch sizes and higher chick mortality account for some of the fall but fatalities during migration and droughts in sub-Saharan West Africa are probably more significant.

▲ HEDGEROW FEAST
An overgrown hawthorn hedge is prime hunting territory for a willow warbler. It can flit largely unnoticed through the spiky leafy branches, snapping up beaks full of insects and spiders.

Preparing to Migrate

In autumn, willow warblers that have nested in Britain generally head off to spend the winter in the forests of Côte d'Ivoire and Ghana in West Africa. Their route takes them down the west coast of France, through Spain and North Africa.

Before departing, a willow warbler needs to build up its energy reserves and overhaul its flying equipment. In late summer, it gains weight by gorging itself on elderberries and honeysuckle berries that are rich in sugars. In the autumn, willow warblers may pop into gardens where there are plants that attract insects, such as greenfly on roses or brambles. Although it will stop off *en route* to feed, it needs to lay down a good store of fat to fuel its journey across the Sahara Desert.

Long-distance migrants such as willow warblers need their wing feathers to be in top condition for their arduous journey. Unusually, willow warblers moult twice a year: a quick change of feathers in the summer after breeding takes about five weeks; a more leisurely moult lasts about 10 weeks in Africa. Return migration begins in late February and is faster and more direct than the autumn passage south.

willow warbler in winter plumage

Summer Family

EVERY SPRING, WILLOW warblers fly a long way to reach this country and to spend the summer rearing a family. The males get back from Africa from late March, before the females. Most return to the vicinity of their birth each year.

When he reaches his destination, the cock bird starts singing all day long to set up his territory and attract any passing females. Several willow warblers trying to out-sing each other to protest their rival claims to the same territory or female sounds really beautiful.

Courtship starts in earnest as soon as the females arrive about one week later. The tiny birds chase each other about, darting in and out of trees and shrubs. When they alight, the cock bird fluffs out his feathers, spreads his quivering wings and flies diagonally towards the female.

male in spring

▲ FLYING PHENOMENON
Almost unbelievably, the willow warbler's wings carry it thousands of miles from Africa to Europe each spring. Here they raise a family before making the return journey in the autumn.

▲ MUSICAL WARBLER
A cock willow warbler is an irrepressible singer: he even warbles away in a rather disjointed manner while he is insect hunting.

COSY CRADLE

Willow warblers begin nesting soon after pairing up at the beginning of May. The hen weaves coarse grass, dead leaves, bracken, green moss and hair into a domed structure with a tiny entrance on the side, rather like a wren's. Then she packs it with masses of feathers. Her nest is well

concealed in a shady spot on the ground: among tangles of rough grass along a bank or in the debris at the bottom of a hedge.

GROWING UP

For four days or so after the chicks hatch, the male finds all the food for his young family while the female

chiffchaff

In the Pink

Six to eight tiny pinky-white eggs, dusted with faint red spots, are incubated for 13 to 14 days, mainly by the hen bird. Meanwhile her partner sings his heart out and brings her titbits to eat several times a day. If disturbed, she flies out, making lots of noise and pretending to be injured to distract the intruder. Strangely, willow warblers often abandon their nests for no apparent reason, before the eggs are laid or after sitting on them for several days.

THE CHIFFCHAFF

(Phylloscopus collybita) Even an experienced birdwatcher finds it challenging to tell a willow warbler and its close relative, the chiffchaff, apart. Those who are defeated often record having seen a willowchiff. Their colouring and markings are virtually identical: seen side by side, a willow warbler is generally brighter and usually has a clearer blond stripe over its eye, paler legs and slightly longer wings. Their songs are more distinctive: the willow warbler sings a clear fading trill while the chiffchaff repeats its name over and over again.

▲ TAXING BROOD

Just before fledging, a large family of willow warblers makes huge demands on their parents. At this stage, the adults are visiting the nest up to four times a minute, bringing in hundreds of insects to fuel the nestlings' rapid growth.

stays on the nest to keep her family warm. During the 13 or 14 days the young willow warblers spend in the nest, their parents may have to catch up to 10,000 insects, mainly small moth caterpillars, and tiny spiders for them to eat.

Mortality rises when the fledglings leave the nest. By sitting out in the open, young willow warblers attract the attention of jays, magpies and squirrels that snatch them. Their parents try to warn them of danger with a persistent *hooeet* alarm call. Most willow warblers raise only one brood each year, so it is important that as many as possible survive.

Jazzy Youngsters

After just 14 days in the nest, the tiny grey hatchlings are looking a brighter yellow than their parents. Once the fledglings leave the nest, they start exploring the woodland beyond the boundaries of their parents' territory. The adult birds escort and feed their fledglings for a couple of weeks.

By mid June, as soon as the youngsters are independent, singing ceases as adult willow warblers go through a quick moult. Afterwards, cock willow warblers resume singing until late summer when they start leaving the country. The song changes from a merry greeting in spring to a mournful ditty in September. Echoes linger on in southern England as the final stragglers prepare to depart.

' The little yellow willow wrens were dropping their little songs – a cool, measured trickle of refined etherealised notes '

from *England's Birds*
by **W K Richmond** (1936)

juvenile willow warbler

The Bullfinch

Even people who curse the lovely cock bullfinch for stripping buds from their fruit trees and ornamental shrubs are impressed by his exotic colouring and bold markings

Opportunities to admire the gaily-coloured cock bullfinch are few and far between. It has always been shy but now it is becoming scarcer in this country too.

QUIETLY UNOBTRUSIVE

Usually all you see of a bullfinch is a glimpse of its white rump as it bounds along a hedge or darts into cover. It rarely flies far from the shelter of dense foliage in hedgerows, copses and thickets.

A bullfinch's piping calls, short wistful *deu* notes which sound like muted pan pipes, are often so faint that they are overlooked too. Bullfinches call a lot in flight, with a clear, carrying whistle which, once recognised, makes them easier to spot.

▶ **SUPER SMOOTHY**
With his ultra-sleek, hot-pink breast, jet-black skull-cap and beak, grey back and white rump, the male bullfinch is a strikingly handsome bird.

female

Lifelong Partners

A cock and hen bullfinch stay together throughout the year and almost certainly pair for life. The hen bullfinch has a jet-black skull-cap like her mate, but her brownish-pink underparts and olive-grey back are more sombre than his pink breast and grey back. They both have a square patch of dazzling white rump above their black tail feathers and a single white flash on each wing, which are particularly prominent in flight.

Bullfinches flit about in pairs or small extended family parties over the winter, rather than forming large groups or joining mixed flocks like other finches. Only on a cold winter's night may bullfinches join other woodland birds in mixed roosts to keep warm. A bullfinch is not as tough as its big head or thick neck suggest and its beak is too feeble to crack large seeds.

Nippy Budpicker

ADULT BULLFINCHES ARE vegetarians, although nestlings are reared on large quantities of insects and spiders. They rarely feed on the ground, collecting most of their food from seed- and fruit-bearing plants, bushes and trees.

Throughout the summer and autumn and into winter, as long as stocks last, bullfinches eat a huge variety of seeds – anything from tiny grass seeds to the seeds of birch, privet, bramble, nettle, meadowsweet, dock and rattling bunches of ash keys (winged seeds from ash trees).

BIT OF A MENACE

From December onwards, when the supply of wild seeds and fruits starts to dwindle, bullfinches turn to eating the small buds developing on trees and shrubs. These contain the future leaves and flowers but are not very nutritious. A bullfinch has to husk hundreds to sustain itself, strewing the ground below with litter. This earned them an unfair reputation for being vandals, inflicting malicious damage.

In spring, bullfinches antagonise some fruit growers by stripping leaf and flower buds from fruit trees in orchards and ornamental shrubs and trees in gardens. Their large buds swell before the smaller wild ones on hawthorn, blackthorn, elm, willow and oak.

ODD ONE OUT

The glowing colour of the cock bullfinch's cheeks, throat and breast puts other British finches in the shade. It is variously described as brick or strawberry red, salmon pink or matching the colour of red horse chestnut blossom. In bright sunlight it can look almost blood red.

In other ways, too, the bullfinch is an unusual finch. It always appears more ponderous than the perky chaffinch or agile goldfinch. And, unlike the greenfinch and chaffinch,

it rarely visits the ground, where it can only hop about awkwardly. Neither is it an accomplished nest-builder like the hen chaffinch, nor a great singer in the fine musical tradition of those irrepressible songsters, the cock chaffinch and the tinkling goldfinch.

▲ **SPOILING THE BLOSSOM**
The bullfinch's stubby beak is the ideal tool for nipping off and dismantling buds from flowering blackthorn. It systematically strips immature flowers and leaves from the branches, starting at the tips and working inward.

Visiting the Garden

In winter the bullfinches' rovings in search of food sometimes bring them into gardens, where they are fond of rape and sunflower seeds. They also take shelled peanuts from mesh bags but cannot crack unshelled peanuts. Their stubby sharp-edged beaks make short work of crushing and peeling seeds and fruits or shelling small snails. (Bullfinches are the only finches to tackle snails.)

Garden plants also provide bullfinches with a variety of nourishing seeds and berries. Early in the year they concentrate on cracking the pods of ornamental shrubs such as *Weigela*. In spring they tuck into buds on fruit trees and bushes; come the summer, soft fruits are the main attraction. In autumn they start feasting on the seeds in *Delphinium*, *Antirrhinum* and *Campanula* pods and sunflower hearts.

male

Family Planning

BULLFINCHES WAIT UNTIL there is thick leafy cover to provide maximum privacy for their nests before starting to breed. Between late April and September, most pairs attempt to rear at least two broods of four to six chicks. When there are plenty of seeds about, some energetic couples manage to fit in a third brood.

WINNING HER OVER

To catch a female's eye and ear, the male bullfinch perches on the tallest tree-top. Then he throws back his head, fluffs out his red breast and belts out his loudest call, wagging his cocked tail to the beat and bobbing his head up and down.

When a female lands on a branch nearby, he flies to join her. Leaning forwards, they gently touch beak to beak. Then he flies back to his perch at once and she moves on; he follows and more bill caressing ensues until she accepts his advances.

NESTING GETS UNDERWAY

The male selects a site in the heart of a thorny hedge, prickly bush or evergreen, such as holly or yew.

male

female

male

female

◄ ENGAGEMENT TWIG
As part of his courtship display, the cock bullfinch offers his mate a twig to initiate nest-building.

Red Alert!

Bullfinches are becoming a rare sight in woodland, hedgerows and orchards. According to a recent census, numbers have fallen by nearly two-thirds in the past 30 years. They are now on the Red List of British birds at serious risk of disappearing altogether.

Although the reasons for the dwindling population are unclear, loss of the bullfinch's traditional food plants, shelter and nest sites due to the uprooting of hedges and the widespread use of herbicides in intensive farming are likely culprits. The much-sprayed, well-pruned and trained fruit trees in modern orchards are also far less hospitable to bullfinches than the mature trees of old.

▶ CLOSE COUPLE

As partners, a male and female bullfinch go everywhere together at all times: drinking from pools, feeding in trees, flitting along hedges or flying across open ground in typically bouncy fashion.

There his mate constructs a platform of loosely interwoven twigs and moss, with a shallow cup of rootlets and hair in the centre.

Then she lays four to six pale green-blue eggs with dark purple-brown spots and streaks and starts incubating after the last egg is laid. The hen does all the incubating as her dull plumage is less conspicuous on the nest. While she is sitting, she rarely leaves the nest, so only the male risks giving away its location when he delivers food occasionally.

All the eggs hatch together, usually in about 13 days. The chicks are covered in long grey down and have pink linings with puce spots and yellow flanges to their mouths.

SECURITY PRECAUTIONS

Bullfinches do all they can to avoid drawing attention to the location of their nest. Parents keep their feeding visits to the nest to a minimum and sneak into the bush, tree or hedge together so that predators get fewer chances to follow them.

Early on, both parents feed the chicks by regurgitating a partially digested mash of insects, spiders, snails and fluffy seeds. As the chicks grow, their parents include more seeds in their diet until, by the time the fledglings leave the nest after 14 to 16 days, they have been weaned on to eating seeds alone.

◀ FOR SAFETY'S SAKE

The adult bullfinches forage as a pair and tend their young together. Both parents develop large cheek pouches that they cram with so much food that they need to return to the nest only every half an hour or so to feed the chicks.

> ' *The honours of his ebon poll*
> *Were brighter than the sleekest mole;*
> *His bosom of the hue*
> *With which Aurora decks the skies* '

from *On the Death of Mrs Throckmorton's Bullfinch*
by **William Cowper** (1731-1800)

Chip off the Old Block

Although this drab brown young bullfinch has yet to be painted in its full family colours, it already has many of the bullfinch's trademark features – a thick beak, stocky neck, white rump and black wings and tail – but, as yet, no glossy black cap. However, by September or October, this youngster will have moulted into its adult plumage. For the first week or so after leaving the nest, juvenile bullfinches issue a persistent squealing double note, demanding food from their parents. The family travels around together for several months.

juvenile bullfinch

Cock-a-Hoop

IN THE 15TH CENTURY, the bullfinch was commonly known as the Alp, from the Latin word *albus*, meaning white, after its prominent white rump. The current common name of bullfinch appears to have come into use in the 16th or 17th century. It alludes either to the thickness of the bird's bullneck or to its general chunkiness when compared with other finches.

LOCAL NAMES

A host of vivid nicknames testify to how familiar and controversial the colourful cock bullfinch used to be, particularly in fruit-growing regions. Understandably, his brilliant pink underparts attracted most attention. In Somerset, he would have been recognised as the Blood Hoop or Red Hoop. Names with hoop in them, such as Ting Hoop and Cock Hoop, were picking up on his call too. In other parts of the country, his bold black helmet inspired the nicknames of Coal Hood, Monk and Pole.

The Hawfinch (Coccothraustes coccothraustes)

With its massive conical beak and bold, bright plumage, the hawfinch is a joy to behold and should stand out from the crowd. Instead, its quietness and wariness makes it exasperatingly elusive. In spring and summer, hawfinches spend most of their time among the densest foliage and shadiest spots in the highest branches of tall, mature trees in deciduous and mixed woodland, parks, gardens and orchards, coming down occasionally to drink at pools and streams.

In autumn and winter, hawfinches spend more time on the woodland floor, feeding in small flocks. The distribution of hawfinches across Britain mirrors the location of hornbeam trees, one of its main food sources for the winter, which grow naturally south and east of a line drawn from Worcestershire to Norfolk. In autumn, the hawfinch also plunders the hedgerows for purple sloes. It strips away the sour flesh to reach the stone in the centre which it cracks in its vice-like beak to get at the edible kernel inside – once described as the equivalent of *a man cracking a coconut in his teeth*.

▲ BOLD FLIER
A hawfinch always looks much more comfortable in the air, as it traces an undulating path between branches and over trees, than it does on the ground. When it comes down to the woodland floor to feed or drink, it hops or waddles on its shortish legs.

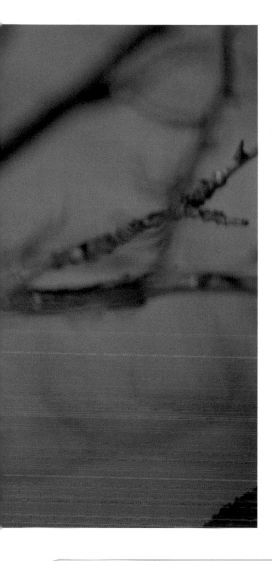

In Welsh, the bullfinch is the *coch y berllan*, which translates rather graphically into English as the Red One of the Orchard. The bullfinch's scientific name, *Pyrrhula pyrrhula*, describes it as the red, red-coloured bird, from *purrhos*, the Greek for flame-coloured.

PEST CONTROL

In the orchard, the bullfinch's destructive habit of stripping buds from fruit trees and shrubs made it the Budpicker, Budbird or Budfinch. The bullfinch is the only British bird to have been designated as a pest. As long ago as the 15th century, it had a bounty on its head. In the 1950s and 1960s, bullfinch numbers rose so much that fruit growers in southern England were granted licences to cull them. Using live-decoy baited traps, thousands were destroyed each year.

◀ **SPLASH OF COLOUR**
Seeing a majestic cock bullfinch sitting among the bare branches of a tree has always been one of the great joys of spring, but is now becoming a rare sight.

Yet it was not until the 1970s that numbers began to drop dramatically. Interestingly, the rise and fall of the bullfinch parallels the decline and recovery of the sparrowhawk, a bird of prey that is its main predator

MUCH-LOVED PETS

For centuries, cock bullfinches were popular cage birds. Apparently, they made affectionate, even jealous pets. In his eulogy *On the Death of Mrs Throckmorton's Bulfinch* the poet William Cowper (1731-1800) related how greatly Bully was mourned.

In captivity, wild bullfinches were quick to learn tunes such as *God Save the King* or *Queen*. In the 18th century, bullfinch was slang for a simpleton, possibly because the bird was so willing to learn new tunes. William Cowper praised Bully's musical versatility:

> *And though by nature mute,*
> *Or only with a whistle blest,*
> *Well-taught, he all the*
> *sounds expressed*
> *Of flageolet or flute.*

Menace in the Orchard

During the first part of the winter, bullfinches eat the seeds of trees and wild weed plants. Only when the supply of wild seeds dwindles do bullfinches start raiding orchards and attacking the buds on fruit trees.

They are particularly keen on ash samaras, or keys, the bunches of winged seeds dangling on ash trees. Depredation in orchards and gardens is much lighter in the years when there is a good crop of ash seeds than in alternate ones when the ash trees take a break from seeding.

● Growing seed-headed plants and berry-bearing shrubs in gardens can help bullfinches get through the winter.

● Bullfinches can systematically strip a tree at a staggering pace. Rates of 10 to 30 buds per bird per minute are common. One bird can eat half the buds on a pear tree in a single day.

● Bullfinches show a curious unexplained preference for the buds of certain varieties of apples, cherries, pears and plums, while turning their beaks up at others. James Grieve apples, Morello cherries, greengages and Conference or Williams pears are sought after but Bramley apple and Comice pear buds are ignored.

● It was thought that bullfinches shredded bud after bud from fruit trees

just for the sake of it, as they left behind so many trimmings under the fruit trees. But bullfinches have to strip away bud casings to find the tiny nutritious growing hearts of the buds.

The Sparrowhawk

A sparrowhawk is a supreme aerial hunter: stealthy while locating and targeting its prey, totally committed to the chase and swift in the capture

Often, a kerfuffle at the bird-table and a few downy feathers floating in the air are the only signs that a sparrowhawk has just launched a lightning raid on your garden, grabbed a chaffinch or tit and flown off with it in its talons.

AMONG THE TREES

Normally sparrowhawks hunt small birds over all kinds of country, along hedgerows and riverbanks or through woods, only occasionally trespassing into gardens. They need accessible open woodland that offers good cover for nesting: preferably in conifers, although they do build in deciduous trees as well.

▶ **FEATHERY PREY**
Even during the winter, an elegant male sparrowhawk is the scourge of small songbirds in hedgerows and woodland all over the country.

The Powerful One

female

As with many hawks, the male is much smaller than the female but in sparrowhawks the differential is extreme: she may be twice as heavy as he is. The sexes show marked differences in colouring too. While the adult male has rusty-orange underparts and a bluish-grey back, the female has fine grey barring on her pale underside and is brownish-grey above with a pale streak over her eye.

*'As thou dost watch the small young birds,
With such deadly care'*

from *The Hawk* by **W H Davies** (1871-1940)

Pine Parents

A PAIR OF SPARROWHAWKS divides up the effort involved in raising a family: the female usually stays at the nest to take care of the eggs and chicks, while the male does most of the hunting for his mate and family.

Sparrowhawks leave nesting until later in the season so that they have chicks in the nest in June when there are plenty of inexperienced young songbirds about. Their lack of flying skills makes them easier for the hard-pushed male sparrowhawk to catch.

FANTASTIC AEROBATICS

The male and female sparrowhawk pair up early in spring and soon pick out a nesting territory, usually in coniferous woodland. To assert their claim to the area and strengthen their pair bond, the birds soar and wheel overhead, gaining height, then swooping down and climbing again.

This roller-coaster ride always ends with a spectacular dive from a great height. Being larger, the female is usually more visible during these magnificent display flights. Once nesting begins, sparrowhawks become more low profile.

SETTLING DOWN

First they build their nest in the fork between the trunk and a branch, around 10 metres (33 feet) above the ground. Sometimes it is based on an old magpies' or crows' nest. Both birds collect building material but the female does most of the construction work involved in assembling a flat bulky platform of loosely overlaid twigs, with a shallow cup in the centre.

She lines the cup with flakes of dry bark and lays three to six bluish-white eggs, blotched with dark reddish-brown spots, on top. Later, while incubating the eggs for about 35 days, the hen adds a downy lining, plucked from her breast.

MOTHERING MATTERS

When her chicks hatch, the female sparrowhawk is a very conscientious mother. She keeps the nest clean by removing the remains of catches; she stretches her wings to shade her nestlings from strong sunshine and to shelter them from rain; at night they huddle under her to keep warm.

▲ IN THE EARLY DAYS

Sparrowhawk chicks are clad in white down at first but dark feathers soon start to come through. Droppings on the lower branches and trunk, and loose down that floats into branches nearby, often give the nest away.

Feeding the Family

While the female is sitting on the eggs, the male brings fresh kills for her to eat. He whistles to let her know that he has left a catch on a nearby plucking post. After the eggs hatch, he continues to deliver roughly plucked bodies of small birds that she strips down quickly and feeds to the frail nestlings. Young sparrowhawks grow fast and can soon deal with carcasses themselves. Then they start hopping along branches around the nest and flapping their wings.

In 24 to 30 days the young hawks are fledged and look like browner, streakier versions of their mother, with the same piercing yellow eyes and lethal hooked beak. For a while they pester their parents for food with mewing calls.

juvenile

Stealthy Hunters

ARMED WITH KEEN eyesight, swift reactions, a sharp beak, lethal talons and speedy flight, the sparrowhawk is an awesome hunter. Usually small songbirds are its target prey. Woodland and hedgerow birds recognise the danger: while a gang of songsters may mob a resting tawny owl, the first bird to spot a sparrowhawk approaching sounds a general alarm that the others recognise as a warning to take evasive action. Sometimes the tits and finches dive for cover but often they take to the air: a small bird is usually able to evade a sparrowhawk in open flight.

ELEMENT OF SURPRISE

Unlike the kestrel, the sparrowhawk never hovers while hunting. To avoid a long, exhausting chase, which it may well not win, it has perfected the art of ambush. One favourite hunting ploy is to perch patiently in a tree, waiting for a flock of small birds to fly close by, before darting out to snatch its victim.

The sparrowhawk has large feet and long toes tipped with needle-

▲ MENACING SILHOUETTE
From an early age, songbirds recognise the shape of a hawk in flight as a sign of danger. The combination of small head, short neck, broad wings and long tail give it away.

◄ SPEED IS OF THE ESSENCE
When a sparrowhawk swoops down and seizes a small bird as it is flying along, the attack is over in a flash. Very aptly, in falconry a sparrowhawk's claws were called pounces.

' Suddenly down he dropped:
She heard the hiss of his wing,
Fled with a scream of terror '

from *The Hawk* by **A C Benson** (1862-1925)

Hedge-hopping

After soaring to a lofty height to get the general view, a sparrowhawk usually dives down to patrol at low level. It flies rapidly along one side of a hedge, darting over the top from time to time to catch an unwary little bird perched on the other side. It also hunts at speed along the edge of woods or riverbanks and follows wider woodland tracks. Some days this life-and-death drama may even be played out in your own garden. Sparrowhawks generally attack finches and tits, while females take thrushes, blackbirds and starlings as well. A plucky, well-built female may also kill woodpigeons and partridge. This helps to avoid competition between the sexes for the same prey.

▲ PINNED TO THE POST

A sparrowhawk usually carries the little bird it has just caught back to a regular killing cum plucking post or bough to eat it. Sometimes with heavier prey it may have to land almost immediately on the ground to deal with its victim.

sharp talons. Each middle toe is exceptionally long to help a charging sparrowhawk grab and hold on to a small bird tightly. Its spindly long legs hold the prey well away from its body to save it getting pecked or scratched by its struggling victim.

AERIAL SURVEILLANCE

The sparrowhawk also prowls on the wing, often soaring majestically over its territory to survey the scene for prey. Its glaring yellow eyes can detect the slightest movement from several hundred metres above.

Alternatively, a sparrowhawk patrols along streams, hedgerows and woodland fringes with swift, low-level passes. Thanks to its short,

broad wings and long tail, the sparrowhawk is very precise and manoeuvrable in the air. It weaves its way around trees and along hedges at speed in hot pursuit of its prey. With explosive acceleration, it can hop over the hedge to the other side and catch songbirds unawares.

Occasionally a sparrowhawk also catches rodents, such as mice and voles, and moles, frogs, large insects and slugs to eat.

Eaten Alive

When eating its prey, a sparrowhawk stands on its victim with both feet to hold it down, droops its wings to throw a tent over it and spreads its tail to help keep its balance. Then it starts vigorously plucking feathers and tearing off strips of breastmeat. Small birds such as finches and tits get squeezed to death in the talons, but larger victims such as starlings are still screaming for their lives while they are being ripped to pieces.

a male sparrowhawk mantling his prey with his wings

The Priest's Hawk

THERE ARE NO prizes for guessing that the sparrowhawk got its common name because of the large number of sparrows it used to catch. There is an amusing story of how an elderly Duke of Wellington, the victor at the Battle of Waterloo, was called in by Queen Victoria to get rid of large flocks of sparrows that were causing a nuisance in the glass houses of the Crystal Palace at the Great Exhibition of 1851. The Iron Duke's answer was a cryptic 'Sparrowhawks'.

With fewer sparrows around, it might soon be more appropriate to change the sparrowhawk's name to tithawk. *Accipiter* is derived from the Latin verb *accipio*, to seize, and refers to all the short, blunt-winged hawks. Today the sparrowhawk is known as *Accipiter nisus*. *Nisus* could be taken from a Latin word for striving or refer to Nisus, a mythical king of Megara in Ancient

Holy Hawks

- The hawk has always been one of the great solar birds. In *The Compleat Angler* Izaak Walton (1593-1683) wrote

  Hawks soar up on high, and when they are lost in the sight of men, then they attend and converse with the Gods.

- Sun gods are often depicted with a hawk's head. The hawk was sacred to the Egyptians as the form assumed by the Sun god Ra. In Ancient Greece, Homer described the hawk as *the swift messenger of Apollo*, a god of light.

- According to ancient belief, a hawk never ate the heart of its victims. There was an Icelandic saying: *a hawk never recognises his sister until he devours her, and when he comes to the heart he departs in remorse.*

- It was seen as an omen of eventual success when a hawk chased its prey to the right and failure when it went to the left.

- An ancient Greek fable is an early version of the bird-in-a-bush proverb. When a hungry hawk caught a nightingale, the songbird pleaded for mercy, pointing out that it was hardly worth eating because it was so small. But the hawk replied that the little bird he had would satisfy his hunger better than a bigger bird he had yet to catch.

▲ WAY UP HIGH
When soaring high in the sky on a spying mission, a male sparrowhawk looks as though he is floating along. His fanned tail and parted flight feathers at the tips of his wings help maximise lift.

Greece who, according to Ovid in his epic *Metamorphoses*, was changed into a sea eagle.

HAWKING FOR FOOD

Hunting with trained hawks for food and sport was known as falconry or hawking. Falconry was a favourite pursuit of kings and gentry in Europe during the Middle Ages, until the development of the shotgun. It is still popular in some parts of the world, especially in the Middle East. Swift and agile, hen sparrowhawks were used for hunting small game birds such as partridges and quail. The smaller male sparrowhawk was known as a musket.

Echoes of Falconry

Many words and phrases in the English language were once used by falconers.

- *At one fell swoop*, a sudden event which is over and done with quickly, alludes to the hawk's headlong dive or stoop on its quarry. In Macbeth, Act iv, scene 3, Shakespeare has Macduff ask *At one fell swoop?* on hearing that his wife and children have been killed. Fell came from an Old French word *fel*, meaning cruel, which conveys a sense of cruelty in such decisive action.

- Today, to be *fed up* means to be in low spirits but it used to describe a lethargy in hunting hawks caused by them being too well fed.

- Hawks were carried to the hunting field on a frame called a *cadge* (see below right) by an elderly falconer called a *cadger*. He was unpaid and had to ask for tips, which led to the expression *to cadge a favour*.

- When the hawks were being carried, they wore hoods to convince them that it was night time. From this comes the word *hoodwink*, to deceive.

- Many of the hawks used for falconry in Britain were captured in Holland. An old Dutch word, *busen,* meaning to drink to excess, was adopted by falconers: when a hawk drank it was *bowsing*; a bird that drank for a long time was called a *bowser*, which in due course became *boozer*, a heavy drinker or a place to drink.

- Originally, *mews* referred to special buildings where hawks were kept safely while they were moulting. The word mew is derived from the old French word *mue*, to change or moult.

FALL FROM GRACE

In 300 years, the sparrowhawk went from being a falconer's pride and joy to being heavily persecuted by gamekeepers for killing game-bird chicks reared for shoots during the first half of the 20th century.

No sooner were sparrowhawks showing signs of recovering from being hunted themselves than they hit another crisis in the late 1950s and 1960s. High adult mortality, thin-shelled eggs, which broke easily, and failure to hatch, were blamed on an excessive and widespread use of organo-chlorine insecticides such as DDT and Dieldrin. Numbers were sent crashing again.

Although population levels seemed to be rising again after the slump in the 1960s, it looks as though numbers peaked in the late 1990s and have since been declining.

▶ CLEANING UP
Killing small birds and mammals can be a bloody, messy business. As a hunter that relies on its speed and agility in flight to catch its prey, a sparrowhawk often needs a good wash to keep its feathers and talons clean.

' *Swooping upon your unsuspecting prey A dusky blot upon the face of day* '

from *Hawk* by **Clinton Scollard** (1860-1932), American poet and author

CHAPTER 3 · HEATHLAND & MOORLAND

The Nightjar

The nightjar takes its common name from its habit of hunting for insects after dark and its rattling song, which eerily breaks the silence on summer evenings

On warm evenings, from mid May until the end of July, the male nightjar's weird churring song is generally the first and only indication you get that there is a nightjar nearby. Actual sightings are extremely rare.

LOWLAND HEATHS

The nightjar is found in areas of bracken, heather and gorse on open commons and heathland, hillsides and moorland, in woodland and on sand-dunes from southern and eastern England to western Scotland. It is concentrated on lowland heath in the West Country, Surrey and East Anglia and in West Wales.

▶ **VANISHING ACT**
A nightjar whiles away the daylight hours resting on a low stump, protected by its mottled plumage, which serves as its cloak of invisibility.

Haunting Voice

Crouching at the end of a bare branch, a male nightjar usually starts singing about 30 minutes after dusk. His deep, slightly hollow, mechanical churring sounds like the soft persistent put-put-putting of a two-stroke engine. He can purr without a break for up to five minutes but generally sings in shorter bursts. His murmuring carries a long way, up to a mile on calm evenings. It rises and falls as he turns his head from side to side with a ventriloquial effect which makes him hard to locate.

'Lone on the fir-branch, his rattle-note unvaried, Brooding o'er the gloom, spins the brown eve-jar'

from *Love in the Valley* by **George Meredith** (1828-1909)

Twilight Hunter

THE NIGHTJAR'S METHOD of feeding is unique among British birds: it flies about in the dark, chasing down airborne insects. It hunts over heaths and dunes, above pastures where there is livestock grazing and across large woodland clearings, engulfing insects in its shovel-like mouth.

CAVERNOUS GAPE

The nightjar's beak may be stubby but it is very broad at the base. When opened, its mouth stretches from ear to ear. In addition, the lower bill is jointed halfway along its length on either side so that the tips of the two bills can be parted to widen the gape still farther. The beak is also fringed with long bristles that funnel flying insects into the bird's open mouth and deflect them away from its eyes.

AGILE FLIER

With its long, slender, soft-feathered wings and light body a nightjar can fly slowly and silently enough to catch individual insects. The wing beats are leisurely and full as it flies low, zigzagging and twisting about in the air to grab its prey. It can even hover briefly with relative ease.

CREPUSCULAR ACTIVITY

Nightjars are active mainly in the twilight at dusk and just before dawn. In the semi-dark, their huge eyes can pick out large, relatively slow-flying moths and beetles. One of the most common dung beetles, the dor beetle, which is up to 25mm (1in) long, swarms over cattle pastures on summer evenings. Blundering about in the dark, these cumbersome beetles are unable to evade the manoeuvrable nightjar.

As nightjars fly through the night sky, they are always colliding with moths. Scales from the moths' wings lodge in their feathers. A nightjar uses a comb-like claw on each foot to keep its plumage spick-and-span.

▼ OPEN WIDE
A mother nightjar feeds her young chicks in a nest on the ground. She is tenderly delivering some mashed insects that she caught on a recent hunting expedition to their already wide gapes.

Tracking Nightjars

Sightings of the nightjar in daylight are rare and usually accidental. It spends the day dozing, often lying along a fallen log, out in the open on a patch of bare or sparsely vegetated ground. As long as a nightjar stays still, and keeps its shiny eyes closed to slits, which protects them from sunlight as well, it merges into the background, thanks to the intricate mosaic of grey, brown and buff in its plumage.

If you stalk a nightjar's call at night, you may be lucky enough to catch a shadowy glimpse of the male responsible flying away. (But don't forget that nightjars are specially protected and intentionally disturbing them is an offence.) You may also hear the sharp *coo-ic* call he uses on take off and in flight to stay in touch with his mate in the dark.

Another very rare summer visitor, the wryneck has similar cryptic markings to the nightjar. But any confusion is remote, as this small woodpecker-like bird lives among trees.

male nightjar catching insects on the wing

wryneck

Timing a Family

male

NIGHTJARS ARE SOME of the last summer visitors to get back from Africa to breed. Generally, a pair returns to the same area each year, with the male arriving first to set up a breeding territory. Nightjars rarely get down to nesting before the end of May or early June, mainly because moth numbers don't start increasing significantly until then.

SEDUCTIVE PERFORMANCE

A male nightjar's nuptial display is highly flirtatious. He lazily follows a female around. From time to time, he glides or hovers in front of her, holding his wings high, and turns to show off the white flashes near his wingtips and on the corners of his tail. Suddenly, he may break the silence with a volley of wing claps, up to 25 at a time, which sounds like a whip cracking. Any rival males are also driven from his territory with the same scary wing clapping.

▶ WHITE WING SPOTS
Although male and female nightjars share the same colouring and markings, only the adult male has white flashes near the tips of his wings and on the corners of his tail.

GROUND-BASED

Nightjars nest out in the open on the ground, in a shallow, unlined scrape among the dry twigs, bracken and debris on heathery heathland and in pine plantations after clearance. The farther off the beaten track they settle, the more secure the nest will be.

If approached, the sitting bird is amazingly steadfast, only leaving the nest at the last moment before being trampled on. She may take off with one wing trailing, apparently injured, to draw attention away from her eggs or chicks. Any disruption is bad news for the nightjar. The incubating

▼ TIME OFF
The female does most of the incubating. The male flies in at dusk and dawn to relieve her briefly so she can fly off and feed. He calls coo-ic *to identify himself; she usually replies with a* kee-ic *call.*

female

Fearful Displays

Like any ground-nesting bird, the nightjar's nest and chicks are all-but defenceless against predation and disturbance, however accidental. On hatching, the chicks are covered in thick grey and brown down. They remain in the nest but they are not totally helpless: their eyes are open and they can move about a bit. Against all the odds, nightjars do stand up for themselves from an early age. When alarmed at the nest, a chick can perform a strange, retching threat display: opening its beak wide, it exposes a vast expanse of pink-lined mouth, throws its head back and forth, and issues a snake-like hissing. It's an intimidating performance that should scare away all but the boldest assailants.

'*As through the rustling ling with heavy tread*
He goes, nor heeds he tramples near its nest
That underneath the furze or squatting thorn
Lies hidden on the ground'

from *The Fern Owl's Nest* by **John Clare** (1793-1864)

to defend itself, a young nightjar opens its vast mouth and hisses

▲ HIDDEN IN DEAD BRACKEN

It is only when a female nightjar moves to stretch her wings and shuffle about on her nest that there is any chance of spotting her. After she has settled down to incubate her eggs again, she will vanish into the background.

bird may not return to the nest for at least 20 minutes, leaving the eggs to cool down. Her absence also gives a long queue of predators, including stoats, foxes, badgers, hedgehogs, adders, crows and magpies, a chance to raid the nest.

SECOND TIME AROUND

The male and female share the care and feeding of their chicks for at least 12 days until the female lays a second clutch of eggs. She is left to incubate them without help from her partner, while he takes responsibility for their first family.

Generally the chicks can fly short distances by the time they are 16 to 17 days old, but rely on their parents to feed them for another three or four weeks. Regardless of gender, the fledglings look like the female bird, without any white patches on their wings or tails. When the first brood is able to fend for itself, the male can rejoin his mate to help her feed their second family. By August, adults and juveniles have to be ready to leave on their long pilgrimage to southern Africa for the winter.

By Moonlight

Within a day or two of mating, the female nightjar lays her first grey-white egg marbled with grey and dark brown spots. A second egg laid two days later completes the clutch. Around 17 or 19 days later the first chick emerges from its shell. Eggs are generally laid so that they hatch during a full moon. Because it hunts by sight, a nightjar stands a better chance of catching insects to feed its hungry chicks on moonlit nights.

Night Jarring

A CENTURY AGO, the nightjar was a common summer visitor and its hollow murmuring song would have frequently been heard reverberating over heaths and across woodland glades on still, warm evenings. But numbers have been declining, and its range shrinking, ever since, not just in Britain but all over Europe too.

GOING DOWN

Those old bugbears, agricultural changes resulting in a lack of food and loss of suitable breeding sites were in the frame again. Urban expansion and widespread ploughing up of heathland for cultivation in the 1940s swallowed up huge tracts of potential breeding territory.

Lowland heath is a delicate, high-maintenance habitat. Left unchecked, it eventually becomes overgrown by trees. Wild fires and grazing used to keep the vegetation under control but fires are no longer allowed to burn themselves out and grazing is poor, so almost half of all heathland has been lost since the 1950s.

Numbers of nightjars reached an all-time low in 1981 when only 2100 males were heard churring. There was a real threat that this evocative sound would disappear for ever.

COMING UP

The challenge has been to create sustainable habitats for the nightjar. It has benefited from more conifer plantations, doing best in the early years, while the ground cover is low and sparse. Regular clear-felling to harvest young pines maintains the open habitat nightjars crave. The management of heather and pine plantations in Suffolk encouraged more nightjars to nest between 1982 and 1989. Numbers had recovered to about 3400 pairs by 1992. With any luck, a census due shortly will find more nightjars are purring now.

> ‘ *The buzzing dor-hawk, round and round is wheeling,*
> *That solitary bird is all that can be heard* ’
>
> from *Benjamin the Wagonner* by **William Wordsworth** (1770-1850)

Lore and Legend

- Owing to its nocturnal activities, silent flight and mottled plumage, the nightjar came to be thought of as an honorary owl. Thanks to its habit of hiding itself in brackeny heathland, it became the Fern Owl; on account of its churring song it was known as the Churn Owl.

- Other nicknames picked up on the nightjar's superficial resemblance to a hawk. One of its most familiar regional names was Dor Hawk after its penchant for eating dor beetles (below left). Taking insects on the wing earned it the names of Moth Hawk or Gnat Hawk.

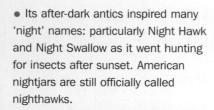

- Its after-dark antics inspired many 'night' names: particularly Night Hawk and Night Swallow as it went hunting for insects after sunset. American nightjars are still officially called nighthawks.

- In some places the nightjar became the Eve-jar.

- Some local names, such as Wheel Bird and Jenny Spinner, referred to the similarity between the male's churring and the droning of a spinning wheel. In Ireland the nightjar was known as the Flax Spinning Wheel.

- To others, the male's churring call sounded like scissors or a blade being sharpened on a grinding wheel and the nightjar became better known as the Scissors Grinder or Razor Grinder.

- Like owls and bats, which are also active after dark, the nightjar used to be associated with death, under the alias of Lych Fowl or Corpse Bird. In the Yorkshire Dales, people gloomily believed that nightjars carried the souls of dead unbaptised infants, who were doomed to wander for ever in the sky.

- In the north of England, nightjars were better known as Gabble Ratchets, which was another name for the Gabriel Hounds, a pack of spirit dogs that were supposed to run across the night skies making weird noises.

- In Somerset, people believed that a nightjar was a witch and could be eliminated only by shooting it with a gun loaded with a silver sixpence.

◀ **NIGHT FLIER**

As a nightjar takes off from the ground, its wings and tail feathers are fully spread to achieve maximum lift. Its huge bright eyes are designed to capture as much as possible of the little light available in the darkness and help it find its insect prey.

'*Fern-Owl, Churn-Owl, or Goat-Sucker, Night-Jar, Dor-Hawk, or whate'er Be thy name among a dozen*'

from *The Dor-Hawk* by **Mary Howitt** (1799-1888)

The Milk Thief

- In the 17th century the nightjar was better known as the Goatsucker. This strange name dates back to Ancient Greece where no lesser an authority than Aristotle accused it of sucking milk from goats' udders with its huge mouth.

- The myth is enshrined in its scientific name *Caprimulgus europaeus* meaning European goat milker, after the Greek for goat, *capri*, and *mulgus* meaning milker.

- In Gaelic the nightjar is *Gabhar Adhar* (gower ah-ar) – 'the goat of the air'.

- By stealing milk, the nightjar was believed to infect cows with a disease called *puck* and so it became the Puck Bird or Puckeridge. In folklore, Puck, alias Robin Goodfellow, was an impish spirit of the night who also stole milk. In Shakespeare's *A Midsummer Night's Dream* it dawns on a Fairy who Puck is:

You are that shrewd and knavish sprite Call'd Robin Goodfellow: are not you he That frights the maidens of the villagery; Skims milk, and labours in the quern?

The Dartford Warbler

The dainty Dartford warbler is a charismatic emblem of the campaign to save lowland heathland for the unique community of rare plants and animals that live there

The fate of the Dartford warbler is inextricably linked to the future of gorse- and heather-clad lowland heaths. The gorse bushes create an important microhabitat for Dartford warblers. An internal maze of branches and young growth provides them with shelter and nesting sites and harbours the insects and spiders they eat.

HEATHLAND SPECIALIST

Most Dartford warblers still live on the remaining sandy lowland heathland in southern England – on Studland Heath in Dorset, the New Forest in Hampshire, and around Frensham Ponds and the Devil's Punchbowl near Hindhead in Surrey.

▶ **GORSELAND SPRITE**
The male Dartford warbler is a perky little bird, with his extraordinarily long, mobile tail and striking orange-red eyes, set in a red eye-ring.

Paler Shadows

juvenile

The female Dartford warbler is a much duller, more muted, version of the male: where he has a grey head, slate-grey back and claret-brown underparts, she is more browny-grey all over, although her upperparts and wings are slightly darker than her underparts. The female's eyes and eye-rings are yellow-brown rather than scarlet like the male's. A juvenile Dartford warbler is even plainer, paler and browner than its mother.

A few pairs are also found among the gorse on the clifftops along the south coast in Kent and Sussex.

PIONEERING SPIRIT

Recently, a reviving population has been colonising new haunts. Dartford warblers have turned up on sites as far apart as Lizard Point in Cornwall and East Anglia. After vanishing from Suffolk in 1939, Dartford warblers appeared again in 1987 and are now breeding on the Sandlings Heaths. Since 1995, they have been nesting in Ashdown Forest in Kent. One pair bred in Buckinghamshire for the first time in 2003.

Threats to Survival

UNTIL RECENTLY, THE odds were heavily stacked against the Dartford warbler surviving in Britain. Part of the problem was that it is restricted to living on dry lowland heathland: an ancient man-made environment that was vanishing rapidly until conservation groups stepped in to protect this precious habitat.

CHALLENGING CLIMATE

Nothing can alter the fact that Dartford warblers are living at the northern limit of their range in the south of England or that they stay here for the winter. Not so long ago, the Dartford warbler was the only warbler to risk spending the winter in England – now more and more blackcaps and chiffchaffs are staying all year round too.

As dedicated insect eaters, the Dartford warblers gamble on being able to find enough food to keep them going. Spiders sheltering in gorse bushes are one of the keys to their winter survival.

In winter, many Dartford warblers form into small flocks. Most stay on their breeding grounds, though there are signs of a southwesterly drift from southeast England to the southwest where winters are milder.

Cold weather sends populations crashing: down to 11 breeding pairs in 1963 after an exceptionally long bitter winter. Thanks to a recent run of milder winters, numbers have been steadily increasing. In 1966, 22 pairs were found rising to 900 in 1990 and to 1600 by 1994. By rearing two or

▲ PROMISING FUTURE
A male Dartford warbler collects masses of caterpillars, plus flies, beetles, moths and spiders from the local heather and gorse to feed his nestlings – new recruits to the Dartford warbler's comeback.

three families each year, Dartford warblers can recoup losses sustained in hard winters quite quickly.

thriving gorse and heather bushes are the Dartford warbler's life-support system

Heathland Husbandry

Left to its own devices, heathland reverts to woodland: first bracken, then trees (usually Scots pine, sycamore and silver birch) move in and take over from the heather and gorse. Most heathland now lies within nature reserves where it is diligently managed: regularly cut and carefully burned to safeguard a continuous progression of gorse and heather of different ages. The controlled burning knocks back invading saplings while the smoke encourages heather seeds to germinate.

❛ I love to see the old heath's withered brake
Mingle its crimpled leaves with furze and ling ❜

from *Emmonsales Heath* by **John Clare** (1793-1864)

Heath and Home

female

male

DARTFORD WARBLERS start breeding in late April and can carry on nesting well into June. They are notably loyal to their breeding sites: many adults stay on the same territory all year round. Wanderers usually return to their old territories every spring.

▲ WOBBLING ALONG

In the air, as it switchbacks from one bush to the next trailing its long tail like a banner, a Dartford warbler looks similar to dark brown long-tailed tit.

GOOD OPPORTUNITY

In England, the cock Dartford warbler stands out as the most colourful member of a family of pale little birds, but it still takes patience and perseverance to spot him. Probably your best chance comes in March or April, when he is singing in the open on bracken or gorse. As he gets excited, a male Dartford warbler raises his grey crown into a high peak and puffs out his speckled white throat feathers.

'It is a sight of fairy-like bird life which cannot soon be forgotten'

on the Dartford warbler in *Birds and Man* by **W H Hudson** (1841-1922)

▲ COCK TAIL

The male's extraordinarily long tail makes up to half of his whole body length of 12.5cm (5in). He wags and pumps it all the time, especially in flight, and lifts it high over his back on landing.

On the Nest

The female lays a clutch of three to five white eggs with brown speckles. She does most of the incubating, which lasts for roughly 12 days. From time to time, the male relieves her at the nest and takes his turn at sitting. The hatchlings are bare, with yolk-yellow gapes and pale yellow flanges to their beaks.

Because the nest is so close to the ground it is vulnerable to disturbance: predators and dogs running off the lead over the heath are the main hazards. Wildfires are another risk, especially in long hot summers when the heathland vegetation becomes tinderbox dry. In the drought of 1976, when Dartford warblers were perilously rare, the wildlife on Hartland Moor at Studland Heath in Dorset was almost totally consumed by fire. More recently, a colony of 10 pairs of Dartford warblers was lost in the blaze that swept across 300 acres of Trendlebere Down on Dartmoor National Park in the spring of 1997.

Apprentice Dwarblers

A pair of Dartford warblers generally lays two clutches of eggs each year, occasionally three: the first in April and the second in June, sometimes as late as July. When the fledglings leave the nest after about 14 days, their tails are still very short but these grow to full length within 10 days. Their parents continue to feed them until they are fully mobile.

In October, the young Dartford warblers leave their parents' breeding territory in search of vacant heathland. Dartford warblers have a good record as parents: on average, more than two chicks fledge from each brood they raise.

fledgling

▲ HEAR YE! HEAR YE!

In spring, a normally shy male Dartford warbler perches on top of a gorse bush and sings heartily to let others within earshot know he is looking for a mate.

NESTING ARRANGEMENTS

As part of his courtship display, the male Dartford warbler builds several rather flimsy trial cock's nests with the aim of impressing his prospective mate. After pairing, it is the female which builds the real nest just above the ground in dense gorse, heather, bracken or brambles. She weaves dry leaves and grass stems, moss, rootlets and soft young gorse and heather shoots into a cup, binding them together with spider and insect silk. Then she lines the cup with horse hair and plant down.

SECRET WORLD

Most of the time, particularly on breezy days, Dartford warblers stay under cover, creeping stealthily through the dense gorse and heather, finding food or looking after their chicks in their well-hidden nest. They are not particularly vocal little birds but their drawn out, buzzing *chrr* calls can give them away.

BREAKING COVER

Once in a while, a flustered Dartford warbler may flutter out of a bush, and issue a shrill explosive *tut tut tuc* scolding cry if you go too close to its nest in the gorse. When the Dartford warbler does break cover, no sooner has a little dark blob trailing a wavy streamer emerged from the gorse and taken to the air than it slips into another bush nearby and disappears again. To stay airborne, the Dartford warbler has to beat its short rounded wings very rapidly. The frantic flapping generates a low whirring sound as the little bird wavers from bush to bush.

The Dartford warbler's tail is very long – up to half of its length – and the little bird wags and pumps it all the time. When it lands on a spike of gorse, it twitches its tail so that it stands erect over its back, which makes a Dartford warbler look quite like an extremely long-tailed wren.

' On the rude heath yclad in furze and ling
And oddling thorns that thick
and prickly grow '

from *The Shepherd's Fire* by **John Clare** (1793-1864)

The Watford Dabbler

LOWLAND HEATH IS a very special British habitat. For centuries, these areas of dry sandy heath played an important role in the rural economy, providing grazing and fuel. Such activities shaped the open landscape and the unique array of animals and plants that lived there. At the end of the 19th century, there were Dartford warblers breeding in all counties south of the River Thames and west into Dorset and Cornwall.

During the 20th century, large areas of heathland were abandoned, neglected and lost. Agricultural and urban development encroached on swathes of gorse and heather; reafforestation and mining for sand or gravel accounted for further losses.

Building right up to the edge of a heathland is almost as damaging as building on the land itself because the heath becomes too accessible. It gets trampled on and burned in uncontrolled ways and the local wildlife – including amphibians, reptiles and ground-nesting birds like the Dartford warbler – is killed by local dogs and cats.

But at last the tide running against the Dartford warbler seems to have turned: ancient heathland is now

> ' *Furze ling and brake all mingling free*
> *And grass forever green*
> *All seem the same old things to be*
> *As they have ever been* '

from *Emmonsales Heath* by **John Clare** (1793-1864)

By Other Names

- The Dartford warbler was named after the town of Dartford in Kent. Reputedly, in April 1773, Dr John Latham described a wine-coloured warbler with red eyes after seeing a pair that had been shot on Bexley Heath near Dartford. This gives it an extra claim to fame as one of only two birds to be named after a British town – the Sandwich tern takes its name from the Earl of Sandwich after the town of Sandwich in Kent.

- Scientifically, the Dartford warbler is known as *Sylvia undata*: *Sylvia* from *sylva*, the Latin word for wood; *undata* means undulating, from *unda*, a wave, and refers to the little bird's rather up-and-down flight.

- Birdwatchers have affectionately nicknamed the Dartford warbler the Watford Dabbler.

carefully protected and managed in nature reserves. New heathland is being created by planting gorse and transplanting heather turves, shoots and top soil on to old farm fields.

CAUSE FOR OPTIMISM

Another hopeful sign for the future is that a few Dartford warblers in Dorset have started occupying less than optimum habitats: heathery undergrowth in young conifer plantations and gorse growing with squat blackthorns. The downside of this expansion is that, among this less protective vegetation, the pioneers are probably even more vulnerable to the privations of a severe winter than they are on their traditional heathland sites.

▲ HOPEFUL SIGN

Due to all the hard work and lobbying of a number of environmental agencies, the chances of catching a glimpse of a male Dartford warbler among the summer gorse are increasing.

UNPREDICTABLE ENEMIES

On the heaths, the future for the Dartford warbler is looking purple and gold. At the moment, it seems as though this little bird has a fighting chance of survival. But it would only take a stray spark to start a wildfire one summer or a lengthy icy spell in winter to set the population figures back by more than 40 years. Such uncontrollable events could still have potentially devastating consequences.

Something to Sing About

● When a male Dartford warbler goes a-wooing, he performs a dancing song-flight to impress the females. With tail fanned and drooping, he launches himself from one gorse bush and flutters over to another. On his way, he sings a scratchy melody.

● At last Dartford warblers really do have something to sing about: for the first time in recorded history, the area of lowland heath actually increased in the 1990s.

● It's not just the Dartford warbler that benefits from the restoration of English heathland: the gorse and heather are home to other rare, beautiful animals and plants, including the smooth snake and sand lizard; the natterjack toad, our rarest amphibian; the lovely silver-studded blue butterfly; and the stunning insect-eating sundew plants.

The Stonechat

Bold by nature and in appearance, the cock stonechat is colourful enough not be outshone by the radiant yellow gorse bushes on which he habitually perches in spring

Stonechats frequent the wilder areas of the country, especially the coastal heathland covering cliffs and dunes in western England, Wales, Scotland and Ireland. Patches of open, short grassland, where they can feed, among gorse bushes, heather, brambles and bracken in which to nest and shelter, are ideal.

CHARMING CHAT

The cock stonechat is an endearing little bird. It is hard not to admire his dark head, smart white collar and chestnut waistcoat; it is impossible to ignore the verbal assaults of several agitated cock stonechats, each bravely defending his territory, mate and nest.

▶ **HEATHLAND HARLEQUIN**
Posing out in the open on a spray of golden gorse to sing his heart out or warn off intruders, a boldly painted cock stonechat looks extremely photogenic.

female in late summer after moult

Faded Beauty

While the male stonechat is showing off his dandy colours from the highest song-post in the area, his mate keeps a much lower profile, aided by her stonewashed version of the same markings. After a post-breeding moult, both male and female stonechats look duller and browner. Over the winter, the buff tips on the male's dark feathers gradually wear away to expose his strong black head again by the following spring, in time for the breeding season.

'Mountain gorses, ever golden
Cankered not the whole year long!'

from *Lessons from the Gorse* by **Elizabeth Barrett Browning** (1806-1861)

Hardy Survivors

THE STONECHAT HAS the fine pointed beak typical of many insect-eaters. From its perch on a gorse bush or bracken spire, a stonechat scans the ground and lower vegetation for potential prey. Its large eyes help it to spot the slightest false move of any caterpillars, moths, beetles, ants, spiders and flies.

Then it swoops down and pounces on its prey. Sometimes it has to hop or run a short distance across the turf to pluck its fleeing victim from the grass or lower branches of a bush. On the way, it may suddenly stop to pick up a worm, slug or snail from the ground. It then flies back, either to its original perch or a new one, to eat its catch. A stonechat is perfectly capable of flying out from its perch occasionally and hovering briefly to snatch an insect flying past.

PERILS OF WINTER

It is always difficult for small insect-eaters such as the stonechat to find enough to eat during the winter. Many stay on their heathland haunts all year round. Like other heathland songbirds, the stonechats' chances of surviving a harsh winter are closely linked to the architecture of the gorse and heather bushes they live in.

As the weather cools in autumn, some stonechats drift towards the coast where the climate is milder than inland. They make for the sand dunes and clifftop gorse bushes, saltmarshes and reedbeds where they can find food and shelter over the

▲ FEASTING ON THE HEATH
This female stonechat has caught a juicy caterpillar, just one of many thousands she will catch during the summer to feed herself and her family.

winter. A stonechat perched on a tuft of marram grass or hunting for sandhoppers along the strand line on a wintry beach is a common sight.

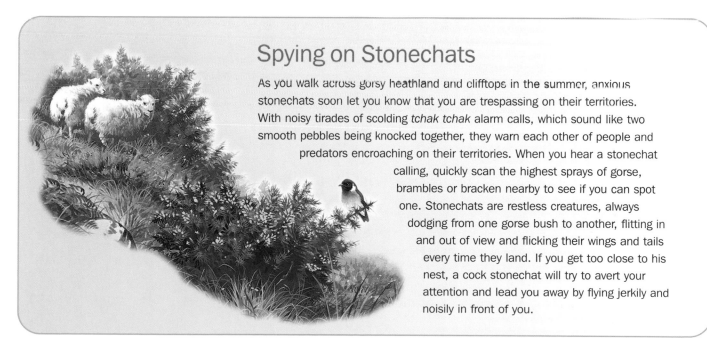

Spying on Stonechats

As you walk across gorsy heathland and clifftops in the summer, anxious stonechats soon let you know that you are trespassing on their territories. With noisy tirades of scolding *tchak tchak* alarm calls, which sound like two smooth pebbles being knocked together, they warn each other of people and predators encroaching on their territories. When you hear a stonechat calling, quickly scan the highest sprays of gorse, brambles or bracken nearby to see if you can spot one. Stonechats are restless creatures, always dodging from one gorse bush to another, flitting in and out of view and flicking their wings and tails every time they land. If you get too close to his nest, a cock stonechat will try to avert your attention and lead you away by flying jerkily and noisily in front of you.

The Furze Family

EVERY SUMMER, STONECHATS labour long and hard among the gorse to rear their heirs and plenty of spares. They start nesting as early as March. Many hold on to the same territories among the heather, bracken and gorse on heathland and dunes throughout the year and for several seasons running. During spring and summer, each male stonechat woos and supports his mate by singing a cheery jingle from a gorsy perch, the top of a stone wall or wire fence.

SORTING OUT PARTNERS

Although some stonechats stay paired for life, there are signs of a lively reshuffle among partners in the spring. On Jersey in 1955, the antics of eight pairs of stonechats were closely scrutinised. All the birds had spent the winter with a partner. Then at the end of March, everything suddenly changed: two males and one female selected new mates from recent arrivals; two pairs from adjacent territories swapped mates;

◄ **FAVOURITE LANDSCAPE**
On a virtually treeless heath, gorse bushes are key to the stonechat's survival, providing elevated vantage points and song-posts, as well as shelter and food.

Stonechatlings

juvenile

With its speckled brown plumage and blushing breast, a just-fledged stonechat looks rather robin-like. After fledgling stonechats have left the nest, both parents remain in attendance for about five days. Then, while the youngsters dog the male's every move as he continues to look after them, the female builds a second nest. Before the next clutch hatches, the previous family will move on or be driven off their parent's territory. By the end of the summer, the gorse-topped cliffs on the Lleyn Peninsula in northwest Wales are teeming with noisy young stonechats.

Between March and July a pair of stonechats are usually able to rear up to three broods. Fledging success is remarkably high: up to 80 per cent is not unusual, which means that even heavy losses sustained during a harsh winter can be recovered within a few years.

► AERIAL OUTLINE
As a male stonechat flits from one gorse bush to another, his short, rounded wings and stumpy tail are on show.

male

▲ HEATHERY HIDEAWAY
Four golden 'food hoppers' are raised in noisy unison to greet a cock stonechat when he returns to feed the chicks in the nest that his partner buried in the base of a clump of heather.

▲ ► TO BE OR NOT TO BE SEEN
While the dandyish male stonechat stands guard, his more subtly shaded mate moves secretly through the gorse, building her nest, then settling down quietly on her eggs.

female

one pair set up a new territory and one male took a second mate – most have only one mate but a few cock birds run two families simultaneously. Only one pair stayed together.

As part of his courtship display, a cock stonechat performs a brief but joyous song-flight, in which he flutters up and glides down like a butterfly, warbling squeakily. The sight and sound of stonechats in their internest chatrooms among the gorse and heather is one of the cheeriest aspects of heathland life each summer.

DAYS IN THE NEST

Hatchling stonechats are a helpless brood, covered by only a wispy coat of brownish-grey down. Both parents attend to their chicks, approaching and leaving the nest cautiously to avoid attracting a predator's attention to it. The chicks stay in the nest for 12 to 16 days before fledging.

' *Then suddenly the sun-enkindled fire*
Of gorse upon the moor-top caught his eye
And that golden glow held all his heart's desire '

from *The Gorse* by **Wilfrid Wilson Gibson** (1878-1962)

Hidden Away

The female stonechat frequently tucks her nest into a tussock of thick grass at the base of a gorse or heather bush. She weaves the nest-cup from grass, moss and sprigs of thistle or gorse and lines it with hair, wool and feathers. Then she lays between four and six pale blue eggs, speckled with reddish-brown, and incubates them for 13 to 14 days. While sitting, she leaves the nest only briefly, often called away by the male to feed.

The Meadow Pipit

*Few birds have a greater claim to be described as an LBJ –
a little brown job – than the meadow pipit, which looks like
a song thrush but is barely bigger than a robin*

Over 1.5 million meadow pipits breed in Britain each summer. A walk across any rough open space with low, fairly sparse vegetation, on hill pastures, heaths, moorland and downs, dunes and saltmarshes, usually disturbs a few meadow pipits and sets off a chorus of plaintive squeaking. They are only absent from big city centres.

FOR THE WINTER

In autumn, meadow pipits from higher, cooler ground move downhill. A few flock to the coast to spend the winter on marshes, along estuaries and on beaches. The rest stay on their breeding grounds all year long.

▶ **BEAUTY IN THE DETAIL**
*Before dismissing the meadow pipit as
a dull brown bird, it is worth taking
a closer look at its intricate markings
and the subtle shading in each feather.*

*a cock meadow pipit sings his
lyrical song as he paraglides
gently back to earth on quivering
outspread wings*

Aerial Serenade

male

Like other birds that breed in an open, largely treeless landscape, the male meadow pipit has to create his own song-post to broadcast his presence and potential as a good mate to any female in earshot. In the absence of a tall tree or fence post, he takes to the air and performs his distinctive tinkling song-flight. He rises from the ground or a low perch with fluttering wings and spread tail, and climbs steeply to about 15 to 30 metres (50 to 100 feet). On the way up, he sings a series of *pheet-pheet-pheet* notes which come out faster and faster as he climbs. The song switches to a slower, more tinkling melody as he parachutes slowly back to earth on stiff outspread wings, which shiver rather than flutter, with his narrow tail tightly closed and raised vertically over his back. On landing, he signs off with a sweet trilling finale.

Merry Mipits

MEADOW PIPITS – OR mipits as they are called – feed mainly on the ground, gleaning insects, such as caterpillars and small moths, beetles, flies, crickets and grasshoppers, and spiders, small snails and slugs from the vegetation. On moorland, crane-flies and their grubs are an important part of their diet. Over a summer, meadow pipits polish off millions of insects – and are themselves the staple diet of the merlin, a small bird of prey hunting on the hillsides.

A meadow pipit usually works its way nimbly through the coarse grass, heather, gorse and bracken. From time to time, it breaks cover to run after an insect, then dashes back to the shelter of the longer grass and bushes. As it hunts, the meadow pipit repeats a quiet *lit-tit* or *pip-it*.

IN GOOD COMPANY

During the winter, when insects are harder to find, meadow pipits are nomadic, often travelling around in flocks, sometimes with skylarks and wagtails. Groups are seen feeding in ploughed fields, turnip fields and coastal meadows, supplementing their diet with a few earthworms and seeds, or pecking insects and shrimp from seaweed on the shore. In frosty weather, they may seek refuge in urban areas and take soft food, suitable for dunnocks, from garden bird-tables.

At the end of the day, meadow pipits usually sleep on the ground, unless they are travelling with wagtails and reed buntings when they may roost in reedbeds.

SPOTTING PIPITS

Pipits belong to the same family as the wagtails and rush about in a similarly frenetic fashion. One of the meadow pipit's claims to fame is that it is the smallest bird that runs over

▲ EASY PECKINGS
Having collected an overflowing beakful of insects from the heather, a meadow pipit makes its way back to its nest to feed a choir of gaping beaks.

the ground – smaller birds always hop about. Each hind toe is equipped with an exceedingly long claw, rather like the skylark in a similar situation, which helps to hold down the long blades of grass as it runs across rough pasture.

When disturbed by walkers and their dogs, a meadow pipit flutters up from cover, and often immediately gets swept away on the breeze like a shuttlecock, only to fall back to earth farther along the hillside. In flight, it always looks as though

it is struggling to gain height. Headway is weak and hesitant in spite of deep wing beats. Progress comes in spurts like an erratic series of up, along and down steps.

As it flits about, the meadow pipit issues an insistent *tissip-tissip* call, which turns to an hysterical *peep-peep-peep* if danger threatens. In winter flocks, a meadow pipit makes shorter calls of *pip-it*, as though it is calling out its name.

▶ RAISED VIEWPOINT
A meadow pipit spends most of its time scampering about on the ground but you may sometimes see it perched on a fence post or stone wall or on heather, bilberry and gorse bushes.

Moor Peepers

BREEDING STARTS EARLY in the year for meadow pipits. The cock birds are back singing over the hills from March onwards. On a warm spring day, moors and heaths are aflutter with cock meadow pipits rising from the heather on their brief aerial courtship flights and showering their tinkling songs down on the heather.

MERRY MEMORIES

The meadow pipits' singing and calling makes a significant impact on the country soundtrack. In *The Charm of Birds*, Viscount Grey of Fallodon (1862-1933) reflected that '*the meadow pipit is a bird that, being gifted with only a small song, displays it to the best advantage.*'

He also recalled how its joyous song-flight had made '*a minute but perceptible contribution to the happiness of the day*' when he was salmon fishing on a moorland river. With evident pleasure, Viscount Grey considered that the moor must be pervaded with the scent of meadow pipits. He noticed how his dog, a pointer, would suddenly stop and stare at a bush. '*At length, a titlark (a folkname for a meadow pipit) flits unconcernedly out of the heather, the dog relaxes and wags its tail.*'

THATCHED CRADLE

Meadow pipits nest on the ground in a cup-shaped nest woven from dry, coarse grasses and lined with finer

▲ BEST TO BE BROWN
The meadow pipit's dark wing feathers, outlined in buff, and its brown-streaked plumage are good camouflage as it moves among the heather and dry grass on moors and heaths. Its white outer tail feathers are conspicuous only when it flies, especially in low-level song-flight.

▲ BASKET WEAVING
The meadow pipit winds blades of coarse, dry grass into a small bowl that it binds to the base of a grassy tussock or overhanging bush.

'*The cuckoo's double note*
Loosened like bubbles from a drowning throat
Floats through the air
In mockery of pipit, lark and stare'

from *Wiltshire Downs* by **Andrew Young** (1885-1971)

Unwelcome Company

The meadow pipit suffers from being one of the cuckoo's favourite foster-parents. Despite attempts to conceal the nest, a male meadow pipit singing overhead gives away its location. A female cuckoo susses out when a meadow pipit starts laying, then she whips in and dumps her egg in the nest. Both pipits accept their role as foster-parents amazingly meekly. The female incubates it as her own and the pair pour all their parental urges into rearing the giant foundling when it hatches.

In Wales the meadow pipit is known as *gwas-y-gog*, which means the cuckoo's servant, as it accepts the cuckoo's egg and chick so submissively. In the north of England, the meadow pipit was derided as the Gowk's Fool, where Gowk was a local name for the cuckoo, because it was so easily duped by the nest parasite.

grasses, moss and some horsehair. The female fashions a bulky nest under a clump of heather, a spray of rushes or marram grass on sand dunes or in grassy tussocks.

Then she incubates her eggs on her own while the male continues to serenade her overhead. His singing may reassure his mate but can give away the concealed nest's location.

HEROIC STAND

Meadow pipits are brave little birds. If alarmed at the nest, the female sits tight to protect her eggs, fluttering away only at the last possible minute, pretending to be injured to divert the intruder. Although a meadow pipit is little bigger than a robin, it mobs larger birds, such as crows, rooks or cuckoos that get close to its nest.

Even so, the hatching success is generally low: just over half of all eggs laid produce chicks, of which only a third survive to fledge. At that stage, juvenile meadow pipits are more buff coloured than the adults, with fewer streaks and pinker legs.

▲ **WARM RECEPTION**

As soon as a parent meadow pipit returns to its nest, it is met by a piping chorus from its open-mouthed chicks, pleading squeakily for food.

Moor Cheepers

A female meadow pipit usually lays her first clutch of three to five brown to reddish eggs, heavily speckled or finely streaked with dark grey, in April. On hatching after 11 to 15 days, the chicks are covered in browny-grey down but blind and helpless. Their gaping mouths have a crimson lining, outlined in yellow. Their squeaking in the nest earned them nicknames of Moor Cheepers or Moor Peeps. Both parents feed and care for them for 10 to 14 days until they are fledged.

The Peregrine

The peregrine is the fastest animal on the planet: when coming in for the kill in its legendary 'stoop' on its prey, its body is a living bullet, travelling at over 150 mph

Watching a peregrine bear down on its prey from a great height at breakneck speed is a breathtaking sight. Blink and you might miss it.

RUGGED SCENERY

In general, the peregrine favours open country with plenty of birds to eat and steep rock faces with ledges on which to roost and nest. It is often associated with cliffs near sea-bird colonies and rocky crags on moorland, particularly in Wales, the Pennines and the Highlands. They are also colonising urban sites: many cities, including London, Bristol and Brighton, are now home to nesting peregrines. Battersea Power Station and Tate Modern at Bankside on the River Thames are their latest haunts.

▶ **MAJESTIC FALCON**
The elegant peregrine is a superlative bird of prey, combining power and energy with beauty and grace.

Aerial Supremo

To appreciate the speed and power of the peregrine, you have to see it in the sky. In leisurely flight, the falcon alternates gentle flapping with spells of gliding on outstretched wings or soaring on updrafts. In level pursuit flight, it uses rapid shallow beats of its long pointed wings, twisting and turning at speeds up to 60 mph. But that is sluggish compared with the acceleration and speed that a diving peregrine achieves through a combination of gravity, supreme control over every wing feather and split-second co-ordination. While still a streaky brown juvenile with a blue-grey eye-ring and base to its beak, the peregrine is adapted for being a dive-bomber. Its broad shoulders and deep chest absorb the impact of hitting its prey like a thunderbolt and the immense g-forces generated by pulling out of its steep dive at top speed. Each nostril leads into a spiral tube which reduces the pressure of the air rushing through it in the meteoric dive.

Annual Cliffhanger

EVEN THOUGH PEREGRINES often pair for life, each spring the male performs some dare-devil aerobatics to arouse his mate's interest in breeding. He picks out several narrow shelves on a steep rocky sea-cliff, upland crag or quarry wall, even on a building, as nesting sites, and scratches out a fresh scrape in the thin soil on each.

Then he takes to the air with a repeated creaky *wichew* call, which sounds like an old gate swinging on rusty hinges, hoping to attract the female's attention. He flies along the cliff face to coax her to view his chosen nest sites. If all goes well, both birds are soon perching and roosting side by side on the same ledge.

In the morning, the pair may go hunting, working together to catch the first food of the day. Duly fortified, the male puts on a truly spectacular courtship display: diving, zigzagging, rolling over and looping the loop to impress his mate. Both peregrines are soon chasing and dive-bombing one another at speed. Back on the ledge, they ritually bow to each other over the scrape, and the male may bring food for the female, before mating.

IN THE NURSERY

From then on the female spends most of her time on the nesting ledge, or eyrie as it is known, guarding the space, and later her eggs and chicks, from all-comers. Meanwhile the male goes hunting for them all. She only leaves when called off to meet him returning with food.

While the chicks are tiny, the female tears off strips of flesh from his catches to feed them. By the time the young falcons, or eyases as they are called, are four weeks old they can rip up prey for themselves, so both parents are free to hunt.

From the third week, the chicks start to look a bit moth-eaten as they lose their white down and brown

feathers start showing through. Soon the chicks are shuffling, then running about on the ledge, often only just avoiding toppling off, and vigorously flapping their stumpy wings.

▲ SOLICITOUS PARENTING
For two or three weeks the female stays with her chicks to shelter them from cold, rain, sunshine and predators, only leaving them to collect food from her partner.

' *There is, sir, an aiery of children, little eyases, that cry out* '

from *Hamlet, Act II, Scene 2* by **William Shakespeare** (1564-1616)

Humble Beginnings

The female lays three or four reddish-brown eggs into a shallow scrape on the ledge and starts incubating full-time when her clutch is complete. She does most of the sitting and all the chicks hatch in 28 to 32 days. The helpless hatchlings grow from drowsy bundles of white fluff into flying fledglings in 38 to 45 days. Young females tend to stay on the ledge longer than the males because they are much larger and need more time to build up their flight muscles by exercising their wings.

Pirate of the Air

ALTHOUGH THE PEREGRINE falcon has a reputation for preferring to attack rock doves and woodpigeons – and, most notoriously, racing and carrier pigeons – its victims generally reflect the local bird population.

Mostly, peregrines feed on small to medium-sized birds, ranging from blue tits to meadow pipits, starlings, fieldfares and skylarks, up to grouse, lapwings and ducks. In coastal areas, they plunder the well-stocked cliff-face larder of puffins, rock doves, kittiwakes, fulmars and guillemots on their doorstep.

The largest bird ever seen taken out by a peregrine was a greylag goose, which was belted into the sea over the Solway Firth. In falconry, trained female peregrines used to be flown at grey herons and red kites.

(The females are particularly heavy for their size and can be as much as a third bigger than the male.)

KEEN SIGHT

Being able to see a long way and judge distances accurately are crucial attributes for a peregrine. Its huge dark brown eyes play a vital role in its hunting prowess. Importantly, they face front, which gives the peregrine sharp three-dimensional vision and acute depth perception.

HUNTING STYLES

A hunting peregrine often perches on a cliff-ledge or rocky crag until it spies a likely victim flying nearby. Then it takes off to intercept it. When a peregrine simply chases its prey, it usually seizes its victim

male

female

> ' *I mark the falcons wing their airy way,*
> *And soon to seize, and, stooping,*
> *strike their prey* '

from *Eclogues* by **Thomas Parnell** (1679-1718)

▲ **IN-FLIGHT REFUELLING**
During courtship and while the female is incubating the eggs or caring for the chicks, the smaller, more agile male does most of the hunting. Often he passes his catch to his mate while she is flying upside down beneath him in an amazing demonstration of aerial athleticism.

on spying its prey, a peregrine soars swiftly before diving

The Famous Stoop

When a peregrine spots its prey flying along, it climbs steeply and rapidly to gain a good height advantage. Then it folds back its wings, rolls over and plunges headlong, ramming its prey from above at speeds of over 150 mph. In slow motion, the peregrine appears to level out just before striking its prey with its clenched feet, knocking it out and ripping its back open with its razor sharp rear talons. The prey then either plummets earthwards in a cloud of feathers, from where the peregrine retrieves it, or it tracks back to grab its quarry from the air before it hits the ground.

If the prey is still alive the falcon kills it with a clean snip at the base of the skull to sever the spinal cord. If it misjudges its aim and misses, it quickly pulls out of the dive and climbs again to have another go before its target gets away.

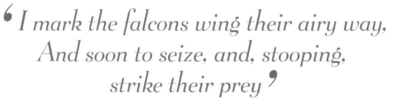

in its huge feet. The long toes are armed with rapier-sharp talons to grip the prey. But in a straight race across the sky, a pigeon can escape from a peregrine by jinking about or dropping suddenly to the ground.

On clear days, a peregrine may adopt the more high-risk strategy of stooping. It drifts about in the sky, waiting for some prey to happen past before dive-bombing it, but may only be successful in one out of ten times.

The peregrine either deals with its victim where it was struck down or, more usually, carries the corpse to a plucking rock to eat it. During the breeding season, prey is taken back to the nesting ledge to feed the family.

LEARNING TO HUNT

For a while after fledgling peregrines start flying, their parents still catch food for them but use their catches to teach the youngsters how to hunt.

At first, the adult calls a youngster to collect the

female peregrine

female goshawk

female sparrowhawk

▲ FALCON OR HAWK?

As a falcon, the peregrine's wings are more pointed than either the goshawk's or sparrowhawk's. Inch for inch, the female peregrine has longer wings, packs more weight and reaches a higher speed than the larger female goshawk.

prey in its talons and passes it from foot to foot. Later the older bird lets go of the prey so that a young falcon can swoop on it as it falls. Soon the youngsters are making mock attacks on passing birds and insects before hunting in earnest and making their first kill, often with parental support.

▲ MENACING SILHOUETTE

The predatory peregrine casts a formidable shadow on the ground that is instantly recognised by all the other birds in the area. It makes flocks of wildfowl or waders take to the air, ground nesting birds run for cover and chicks cower in their nest.

Guarding Prey

After catching a grouse, a peregrine has brought it to a plucking stone to eat it. Like many birds of prey, it is 'mantling' the corpse by spreading its wings to screen it from prying eyes. Then, holding the body down with its feet, it will pluck the breast and tear off shreds of flesh with its hooked beak: a peregrine often only eats the breast meat, leaving the wings and legs intact, still attached to the skeleton. If you stumble across a fresh carcass in this condition, with lots of feathers around it, look and listen out for peregrines. Often a harsh *kak-kak-kak* alarm call is the first sign that they are in the area.

The Blue Hawk

ONE COMMON NAME for the peregrine used to be Blue Hawk, in honour of its blue-grey back and wings, which make it hard to spot against the rocks and shadows among which it flies, perches and nests.

The peregrine is also entitled to feel rather blue about the way it has been treated by many people over the years. Having survived decades of ruthless persecution and pesticide abuse, the peregrine has clawed its way back against all the odds.

Despite a brutal onslaught from gamekeepers, egg collectors and taxidermists in the 19th century, the peregrine's breeding population in Britain held steady at about 800 pairs for about 400 years from the 17th century to the Second World War. Then peregrines were seen as a threat to national security because they intercepted carrier pigeons bringing SOS messages from airmen who'd had to ditch in the sea.

Under emergency war-time powers the Secretary of State for Air brought in the Destruction of Peregrine Falcons Order in July 1940. It authorised agents to kill peregrines and destroy their nests and eggs around the coast. Roughly 600 peregrines were shot and numerous chicks and eggs destroyed between 1940 and February 1946.

> ' *To sit on rocks, to muse o'er flood and fell*
> *To slowly trace the forest's shady scene,*
> *Where things that own not man's*
> *dominion dwell* '

from *Childe Harold* by **Lord Byron** (1788-1824)

▼ **LOFTY LOOKOUT**
A peregrine surveys its domain from a rocky perch on a steep crag with views across a vast expanse of rough open moorland over which it hunts.

By Many Names

- The peregrine's long, pointed wings mark it out as a falcon, a fact endorsed by its scientific name, *Falco peregrinus*. *Falco* comes from the Latin word *falx*, meaning sickle-shaped. This could equally well refer to the crescent arch of the wings or its scything talons and beak. *Peregrinus* relates to the rovings of the peregrine and stems from a combination of *per* for through, and *ager* that means field in Latin.

- It used to be said that the male peregrine was known as a tiercel because he was a third smaller than the female, which became known as the falcon. An alternative explanation is that of three young falcons in the nest, two were usually females and the third was the male.

- In falconry, the female peregrine was always known as the falcon gentle and the male was the tiercel gentle to distinguish them from the heavier

goshawks, which were also called falcon and tiercel. *Gentle* is thought to be an anglicised version of the French word, *gentil*, which meant neat or pretty.

- Sometimes tiercel or tercel is written tassel, as in Shakespeare's *Romeo and Juliet Act ii, Scene 2*

    O, for a falconer's voice,
    To lure this tassel-gentle back again!

- The peregrine's cliff-ledge haunts are enshrined in names such as Stone Hawk, Rock Hawk and Cliff Hawk.

- The hunting peregrine's guided-missile like strikes won it the accolade of Bullet Hawk.

The luckless peregrine was virtually exterminated in parts of the country.

PESTICIDE POISONING

Numbers were only just recovering when they slumped again during the 1950s and 1960s. Peregrines were nearly wiped out by eating lethal doses of DDT and dieldrin that built up in its prey after eating seeds dressed with organophosphate pesticides. The peregrine's plight became a driving force behind the campaign against pollution and the use of DDT was eventually banned.

CURRENT ATTITUDES

Today, the peregrine and its nest are protected by law but many people still seem to bear a grudge against it. Gamekeepers on moorland shoots regard it as an enemy of their grouse. Rightly or wrongly, pigeon-fanciers blame the peregrine when their prize birds fail to return to the coop after a race. Reputedly, pigeon aficionados release pigeons with feathers or legs sprayed with strychnine to poison the peregrines.

' Though that her jesses* were my dear heart strings '

from *Othello, Act iii, Scene 3* by **William Shakespeare** (1564-1616)

Trappings of Falconry

- Falconry was popular in William Shakespeare's time and the bard made extensive use of its terminology in his plays.

- A jess* was a narrow strip of leather fastened to each leg of the peregrine at one end and to a swivel attached to a leash at the other.

- To help locate it, a trained peregrine wore a small spherical silver or brass

bell on each leg, attached by a strip of leather called a *bewit*. In *Lucrece*

Harmless Lucretia, marking what he tells
With trembling fear, as fowl hears
falcon's bells.

- The head of a trained falcon was covered by a leather hood (above) to stop it bating (fluttering excitedly) and flying after its quarry too soon. From *Romeo and Juliet, Act iii, Scene 2*

Hood my unmann'd blood,
bating in my cheeks.

The Mallard

With his resplendent bottle-green head, the mallard drake may be more eyecatching than the modest brown duck, but only she can utter the classic hoarse quark-quark *sound*

Mallards are most familiar as the tame duck-pond ducks that gobble up stale bread in parks and on village greens. They are also probably to blame for toddlers speaking fluent duck. In the more remote country areas, where mallards were frequent targets of guns and wildfowlers, they are still much shyer and quick to take flight.

WATERY ADDRESS

Most stretches of water are home to at least one pair of mallards during the year. In the winter they gather in noisy flocks on lakes and ponds, reservoirs and flooded quarries, canals, rivers and streams.

▶ **TRIBAL GATHERINGS**
As a tribe, mallards like the company of their own kind. Over the winter months they often congregate on ponds in a dabbling, clacking rabble.

male in eclipse plumage

Eclipse Plumage

The mallard drake is a law unto himself. After mating, instead of staying around to help incubate his eggs and rear his ducklings, he retreats to a secluded site to undergo a double moult. Initially he loses his flight feathers, which leaves him grounded and vulnerable. His old feathers are replaced with a fresh coat of drab brown feathers, known as his eclipse plumage, which makes him less conspicuous as he stays in hiding while his main wing feathers are regrowing.

The most difficult months for identifying mallards are July and August, when the drakes, ducks and juveniles are all wearing drab brown feathers. Until his green head feathers regrow, a mallard drake in full eclipse plumage can only be distinguished from the duck because he still has a slightly deeper brown breast and a yellower beak.

Dabbling Ducks

WITH ITS WEBBED feet, broad flattened beak and high buoyancy, the mallard is very well adapted to a life spent paddling, feeding, breeding and even sleeping on water. It can take flight from water or land: springing straight up into the wind with a burst of rapid wingbeats that generates a swishing, whistling sound.

LIFE IN THE WATER

Outside of the breeding season, mallards usually spend their days on quiet open backwaters, then at dusk fly to mudflats, marshes and fields to feed overnight. They eat mainly water plants but also take frogs, insects, shellfish, slugs, snails and worms from the water, plus berries and acorns from woods and grain from stubble fields.

Mallards are mainly surface feeders, sifting small plants and

▲ **STRAINING THE WATER**
A mallard drake dibbles his flat bill on the surface of the water, skimming off tiny animals and plants to eat.

◄ **BLUE FLASHES**
Both ducks and drakes wear purple-blue wing patches. When visible, these badges are the mallard's clearest identifying features but they often get folded away in the wing and can be very hard to see.

animals from water and mud. A row of fine comb-like teeth along the edge of the upper bill slots between two more combs around the rim of the lower bill. The mallard takes up a billful of water and, with a clearly audible splishy-splashy sound, squeezes it out through these plates, trapping food particles. The beak is also used to tear off vegetation.

mallard duck

mallard drake

Head Down

In shallow water, the mallard can up-end itself and search the bottom for food without having to dive. (Ducklings often have to dive down to reach the bottom but adults rarely do.) While it is topsy-turvy, dabbling its beak in the mud on the river bed or bottom of the pond, finding plenty of grubs, worms and snails to eat, on the surface its tail is left high and dry and its feet are flailing in the air. The mallard's legs are positioned well back on its body for stability when it is paddling along in the water but this limits it to a clumsy waddle on land.

Ducking the Issue

TRADITIONALLY, THE FEMALE mallard selects her nesting site in thick vegetation near water, often among nettles, brambles, bracken or heather. There she scrapes out a shallow hollow in the ground and lines it with waterside plants, leaves and grass. While she is laying her eggs, she plucks down from her breast to form a soft, warm lining for the nest.

Sometimes the duck nests in rather more precarious places: in tree-holes or the crowns of pollarded willows. One mallard famously stayed put on her nest in a window-box on the balcony of the house next door to the Iranian Embassy in London, facing Hyde Park, throughout the dramatic siege in 1980.

SINGLE PARENT

After mating, the drake watches his partner closely until all her eggs are laid to make sure she does not mate with another male. (If he gets the opportunity, he may mate with other ducks.) Then he retires to moult, leaving her to do all the incubating. After hatching about 28 days later, the precocious ducklings can run, swim and feed themselves within a couple of hours, as soon as their

▲ LYING LOW
Thanks to her markings and incredible stillness, it is almost impossible to see a mallard duck sitting on her eggs – and even harder to make her leave them.

▶ TEMPORARILY COUPLED
Although a pair of mallards goes everywhere together in the winter and spring, the drake bunks off at the crucial moment, when it comes to incubating the eggs and taking care of the ducklings.

mal[...]
duc[...]

mal[...]
dra[...]

rocking

duck

mock preening

water flicking

Courtship Displays

On mild autumn and winter days, ponds alive with mallard drakes wooing their m[...] for the next breeding season. Several dra[...] circle around a duck, flicking the water w[...] their bills while issuing low grunts followe[...] clear whistles. There is lots of mock pree[...] stretching and rocking as well so that she[...] see the colours on their heads, breasts a[...] wings clearly. The duck remains impassive[...] during the displays until she eventually cho[...] the drake that evidently impressed her mo[...]

Dabbling Ducks

WITH ITS WEBBED feet, broad flattened beak and high buoyancy, the mallard is very well adapted to a life spent paddling, feeding, breeding and even sleeping on water. It can take flight from water or land: springing straight up into the wind with a burst of rapid wingbeats that generates a swishing, whistling sound.

LIFE IN THE WATER

Outside of the breeding season, mallards usually spend their days on quiet open backwaters, then at dusk fly to mudflats, marshes and fields to feed overnight. They eat mainly water plants but also take frogs, insects, shellfish, slugs, snails and worms from the water, plus berries and acorns from woods and grain from stubble fields.

Mallards are mainly surface feeders, sifting small plants and

▲ STRAINING THE WATER
A mallard drake dibbles his flat bill on the surface of the water, skimming off tiny animals and plants to eat.

◄ BLUE FLASHES
Both ducks and drakes wear purple-blue wing patches. When visible, these badges are the mallard's clearest identifying features but they often get folded away in the wing and can be very hard to see.

animals from water and mud. A row of fine comb-like teeth along the edge of the upper bill slots between two more combs around the rim of the lower bill. The mallard takes up a billful of water and, with a clearly audible splishy-splashy sound, squeezes it out through these plates, trapping food particles. The beak is also used to tear off vegetation.

mallard duck

mallard drake

Head Down

In shallow water, the mallard can up-end itself and search the bottom for food without having to dive. (Ducklings often have to dive down to reach the bottom but adults rarely do.) While it is topsy-turvy, dabbling its beak in the mud on the river bed or bottom of the pond, finding plenty of grubs, worms and snails to eat, on the surface its tail is left high and dry and its feet are flailing in the air. The mallard's legs are positioned well back on its body for stability when it is paddling along in the water but this limits it to a clumsy waddle on land.

Ducking the Issue

TRADITIONALLY, THE FEMALE mallard selects her nesting site in thick vegetation near water, often among nettles, brambles, bracken or heather. There she scrapes out a shallow hollow in the ground and lines it with waterside plants, leaves and grass. While she is laying her eggs, she plucks down from her breast to form a soft, warm lining for the nest.

Sometimes the duck nests in rather more precarious places: in tree-holes or the crowns of pollarded willows. One mallard famously stayed put on her nest in a window-box on the balcony of the house next door to the Iranian Embassy in London, facing Hyde Park, throughout the dramatic siege in 1980.

SINGLE PARENT

After mating, the drake watches his partner closely until all her eggs are laid to make sure she does not mate with another male. (If he gets the opportunity, he may mate with other ducks.) Then he retires to moult, leaving her to do all the incubating. After hatching about 28 days later, the precocious ducklings can run, swim and feed themselves within a couple of hours, as soon as their

▲ LYING LOW
Thanks to her markings and incredible stillness, it is almost impossible to see a mallard duck sitting on her eggs – and even harder to make her leave them.

▶ TEMPORARILY COUPLED
Although a pair of mallards goes everywhere together in the winter and spring, the drake bunks off at the crucial moment, when it comes to incubating the eggs and taking care of the ducklings.

mallard duck

mallard drake

rocking

duck

mock preening

water flicking

Courtship Displays

On mild autumn and winter days, ponds are alive with mallard drakes wooing their mates for the next breeding season. Several drakes circle around a duck, flicking the water with their bills while issuing low grunts followed by clear whistles. There is lots of mock preening, stretching and rocking as well so that she can see the colours on their heads, breasts and wings clearly. The duck remains impassive during the displays until she eventually chooses the drake that evidently impressed her most.

► **CLOSELY CHAPERONED**

A lively troupe of mallard ducklings follows their mother down to the water's edge where they will paddle about and feed under her watchful eye.

down has dried and can trap air to keep them warm and buoyant. At that stage, a duckling looks very cute in its khaki-brown and olive-yellow down, with a bold brown streak through each eye.

MOTHER KNOWS BEST

The world is full of curiosities and dangers for inquisitive ducklings. Fortunately, they seem to have an inborn recognition of their mother's *quahg, gegegegeg, quahg, gegegegeg* calls and follow her anywhere.

A mother duck is renowned for protecting her brood with great courage. One call from her and the ducklings dive for cover while she attempts to distract the enemy by pretending to have a broken wing.

Sadly, young mallards have many enemies: on the water they may be eaten by herons, swans and coots, dragged under by a pike or sucked away by strong currents; on land they are attacked by cats, foxes, rats and tawny owls. The survivors are fledged and flying about seven and a half weeks after hatching.

Starting a Family

Mallards generally only produce one large brood a year. The duck lays one pale blue-green egg a day and only starts incubating when her clutch of 10 to 12 eggs is complete, so all the ducklings hatch out within 24 hours. When she leaves to feed or drink, she covers her eggs with a downy quilt to keep them warm while she is away.

'*And warm beneath Are eggs of cloudy green*'

from *Ducks* by **Frederick William Harvey** (1888-1957)

Wild Duck

UNTIL THE BEGINNING of the 20th century, mallards were better known as wild ducks. It is no coincidence that the name mallard was chosen to rhyme with the boastful braggart. The suffix *-art* or *-ard* was added to an Old French word for male, *mâle*, to emphasise the maleness of the drake wild duck. Originally it applied just to him and not to the female wild duck but eventually all wild ducks become known as mallards.

The mallard's scientific name, *Anas platyrhyncos*, also suits it well: *anas* is Latin for a duck; *platyrhyncos* is the Latinised form of the Greek *platurrhunkhos* meaning broad-billed.

FUNNY BIRDS

Somehow, it is hard to take ducks too seriously: the ducks you meet on park and village ponds are friendly, their antics and niggles amusing. Over the years there have been numerous caricatures of ducks: Beatrix Potter's *Jemima Puddleduck*, Walt Disney's *Donald Duck* and

Indian Runner

Rouen

Khaki Campbell

Domesticated Ducks

● The wild mallard is the ancestor of most breeds of farmyard and domestic ducks reared today, including the white Aylesbury, Khaki Campbell, Indian Runner and Rouen. All the drakes of these tame breeds wear their forebear's curled tail feathers as an ancestral badge of honour.

● In China, mallards were farmed on rivers and used to be kept in boats at night. The ducklings were fostered by wise old ducks, which led their charges out on to the river to feed each day. There they mixed with other flocks but each night the nanny ducks would round up their charges and return them to their correct boats.

Daffy Duck to name but three. As the Gloucestershire poet Frederick William Harvey (1888-1957) observed in his ode to *Ducks*

> *O ducks are beautiful things!*
> *But ducks are comical things:*
> *As comical as you.*
> *Quack!*
> *They waddle round, they do.*
> *They eat all sorts of things,*
> *And then they quack!*

William Allingham (1824-1889) fondly recalled a simple image of ducks in his poem *A Memory*.

> *Four ducks on a pond,*
> *A grass bank beyond,*
> *A blue sky of spring,*
> *White clouds on the wing;*
> *What a little thing*
> *To remember for years.*

◀ **FEET FIRST**

As a female mallard comes into land on water she whiffles her wings: separates her flight feathers to lose height quickly. Near the surface, she sticks out her neck while holding her body vertical. Her feet and tail hit the water first with a splash, then she raises her wings as wind brakes.

▶ **SIGN OF THINGS TO COME**

Legend has it that if the ice on a pond is thick enough to bear the weight of a duck at Martinmas (on 11 November), nothing but sludge and muck will follow.

WINGING IT

In full flight, mallards are among the fastest of all birds. The anonymous author of *With the Mallard Drake* felt the excitement of the amazing speed the mallard achieves by beating its wings fast but shallowly.

To share the mallard's stroke of power,
The electric spark in the tip of his beak,
And flying a hundred miles an hour!

DECOYING DUCKS

For others, wild duck hunting was a popular rural sport. A decoy pool was dug with narrow channels radiating from its centre. Then a tame mallard which had had its wings clipped to stop it flying was released on the water as a call duck to lure in a crowd of wild ducks. A trained dog led the inquisitive ducks up a channel where they were funnelled into large nets.

In *The Wild Duck*, the poet John Masefield (1878-1967) agonised over the fate of mallards in these traps:

A cry of the long pain
In the reeds of a steel lagoon.

Part of the Vocabulary

● The duck is well and truly ingrained in the language: there are a surprising number of familiar old sayings linked with ducks and their watery lives.

Like water off a duck's back

To take to something like a duck to water

Fine weather for ducks
(ironically when it is pouring with rain)

Can a duck swim?
(meaning there is no doubt about it)

A lame duck is a bit of a no-hoper.

● In Holland, when ducks and geese splash and plunge about in the water there is said to be a chance of rain.

● There is a north country saying about the weather:

When ducks are driving through the burn,
That night the weather takes a turn.

● The mallard is a swift flier but not as fast as the steam train named after it. On 3 July 1938 a blue streamlined A4 Gresley Pacific LNER locomotive called Mallard set the world speed record for a steam train at 126 mph.

● Mallard Day used to be celebrated each year on 14 January at All Souls' College, Oxford. Members of the college were involved in a rowdy midnight hunt for a mythical giant mallard. The ritual originated when a large mallard flew up from the foundations of the college while it was being built in 1437.

● Ducks and drakes is a game of skimming a flat pebble across the surface of a pond.

The Moorhen

An early name for the moorhen was the Water Hen, because it reminded people of an aquatic chicken as it pecked around the margins of a pond or skedaddled across it

Moorhens are those rather nervous, blue-black birds with red beaks found on stretches of sluggish, still or even stagnant water in lowland Britain. As long as the banks are well-lined with reeds, flags or willows where the moorhen can hide, feed and nest, there is hardly a slow-moving river or stream, pond, lake or reservoir, canal or dyke that does not boast a pair of moorhens in residence at some time during the year.

COURAGEOUS SIDE

Although moorhens always look rather timid and jittery, they display great aggression and bravery when defending their territories and protecting their chicks from danger.

▶ TWITCHY PROGRESS

With barely a ripple, a moorhen glides between the lily pads on a pond. In an action shot, its head would be nodding in and out and tail flicking up and down.

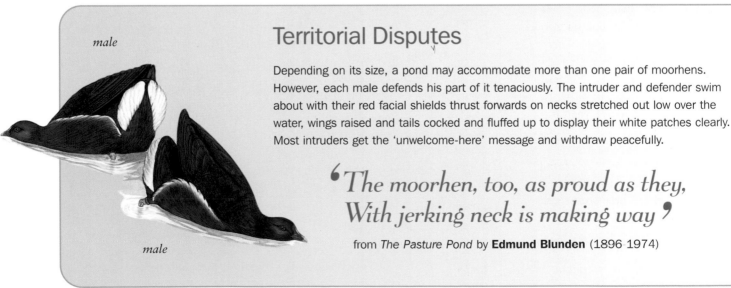

male

male

Territorial Disputes

Depending on its size, a pond may accommodate more than one pair of moorhens. However, each male defends his part of it tenaciously. The intruder and defender swim about with their red facial shields thrust forwards on necks stretched out low over the water, wings raised and tails cocked and fluffed up to display their white patches clearly. Most intruders get the 'unwelcome-here' message and withdraw peacefully.

> *'The moorhen, too, as proud as they,*
> *With jerking neck is making way'*

from *The Pasture Pond* by **Edmund Blunden** (1896-1974)

Waterside Family

ONE OF THE MOST charming features of a pond or canal in spring and summer is the sight of a family of moorhens going about their daily activities. The moorhen's breeding season lasts from April to August. Early on, a male builds several rafts from dead leaves, rushes and other water plants in a number of secluded locations near or on shallow water.

As an amphibious bird, he may wedge his nesting platform on the bank or in an overhanging bough – even climb up to reach an old squirrel drey or woodpigeon nest which he commandeers as the foundation of his own nest – but he often just leaves it floating in the water, anchored to nearby reeds. Once the male has chosen a mate, she selects which raft they convert into a full nest together by building a deep basin in the centre and lining it with grasses and sedge.

WATER BABIES

In each clutch, a moorhen lays from 6 to 11 pale buff eggs flecked with brown. As well as laying eggs in her own nest, a hen moorhen may hunt around for unattended moorhens' nests in which to lay a few more eggs. Nests containing up to 20 eggs probably house eggs deposited there by several different hens.

Both adults share the incubation of the eggs for 19 to 22 days. There is a quick changing of the guard ceremony every time the birds swap places on the nest: both of them raise the feathers on their necks, then lift and shake their wings and exchange throaty croaks.

When danger threatens, if a family of passing swans or a prowling stoat shows an unhealthy interest in their nest or chicks, a pair of moorhens defends their family very fiercely. Both birds bravely stand up to their foe and often succeed in driving it away before any harm is done.

▶ **ON A LIFERAFT**
This moorhen is sitting on its eggs safely tucked away in a well-concealed and inaccessible nest built of dried stems and leaves among the flags at the water's edge.

▼ **FAMILY TRADEMARK**
The newly-hatched fluffy black chicks temporarily have miniature red facial shields and red beaks with yellow tips.

' *The water-hen has nested by a pond Weaving dry flags into a beaten floor* '

from *The Birds* by **Sir John Squire** (1884-1958)

Sparring Partners

● Look and listen out for some noisy rough and tumble in ponds, especially during the breeding season. With territories to defend, male moorhens become remarkably pugnacious.

● If territorial disputes are not settled with a display of markings and aggressive posturing, fighting ensues. The birds approach each other closely, breast to breast, then rear up on their tails to strike out at each other with their big feet. Occasionally, the females join in the mêlée and get into scraps of their own.

● Sometimes, their long toes interlock and the two birds tumble over and over together, making a lot of noise and splashing. Fatalities are rare but defeated males are seen limping away with broken toes and dislocated legs.

Extended Families

NEWLY-HATCHED MOORHEN chicks are precocious little bundles of black down with comically long legs and huge feet. Within hours of hatching, the lively chicks are swimming and bobbing about like small fluffy dark bubbles. The chicks stay close to the nest for the first two weeks, going back to it each night to be sheltered and protected by their parents.

PARENTAL PROTECTION

Unlike ducks, which lead their chicks to the food and let them get on with eating it, moorhens feed their chicks for up to a month. The bright red on the chick's head is a target area for the parents when they are delivering the food. As the youngsters grow and begin to feed themselves, the head colour slowly fades.

When danger threatens, a pair of moorhens minimise the risk to their brood by dividing the chicks between them. The female usually continues to use the nest while the male has to go to one of his old nesting platforms with his band of chicks.

HIDDEN DANGERS

Even though water is a relatively safe habitat for the moorhen, there are still hazards lurking above and below the surface. Mink, otters, foxes and rats lie in wait or raid the nest. Even grass snakes can swim well and are capable of swallowing a moorhen's eggs. Predatory fish, such as pike, may pull the chicks under the water as they swim along.

If they survive all these dangers, the youngsters are fledged and able to fly in 40 to 50 days. The juveniles only get driven away when the adults become territorial again for the next breeding season.

> *And soon the sutty brood from fear elopes*
> *Where bulrush-forrests give*
> *them sweeter hope*
>
> from *The Moorhen's Nest* by **John Clare** (1793-1864)

▲ **FAMILY OUTING**
A parent moorhen takes its bald-headed, sooty brood with it on a paddle through the shallows to find food to feed them all. The chick dipping down right in front of the adult is begging to be fed.

adult

juvenile

chick

Three Generations

A moorhen hatches as a downy sooty black chick with a red beak and bald red head but this colour gradually fades as it grows up. By the time it is fledged, a juvenile moorhen's plumage is two-tone pale greyish-brown in colour with a dull green frontal head plate and beak. It develops the blue-black plumage and striking bright red facial shield of an adult and regains the red beak with its yellow tip over its first winter.

a moorhen has enormous feet, which allow it to walk across soft mud, floating water-lily pads and other aquatic foliage without sinking

Moorhen's Menu

Moorhens feed among waterside vegetation or on dry land, frequently venturing on to grassland and into gardens near a pond. They eat a wide variety of leaves, stems and seeds, as well as snails, worms and insects. They take surface titbits, dip their heads underwater and sometimes upend to catch tiddlers and tadpoles, but rarely dive for food. On land, they occasionally raid duck and pheasant nests for eggs.

Family Helpers

A pair of moorhens often manages to rear two, and sometimes three, large broods a year, but only with the help of juveniles from the first brood. Occasionally the young moorhens help their parents to incubate the eggs but more often they assist in finding food for the chicks after they hatch.

In the picture below, a juvenile from an earlier brood is feeding one of its tiny siblings. The parents have been seen finding food and passing it on to an older offspring, which in turn feeds it to their younger siblings. It is a huge advantage for the adult moorhens to have such nursery assistance but it does mean that the original territory has to be large and strongly defended to support several generations of the same family.

◄ ISLAND SANCTUARY
Long after the eggs have hatched, the nest remains a safe haven for a moorhen family in foul weather and at night.

▲ TAKING FLIGHT
For the moorhen, getting airborne often involves a lengthy, ungainly run-up. Once in the air, its feet hang down like an unretracted undercarriage.

More Hen

FOR A BIRD THAT often looks too timid and scatty to say Boo! to a gosling, let alone a goose, the moorhen can be amazingly aggressive and intrepid at times. Mostly, you see moorhens swimming on ponds or tiptoeing awkwardly about on dry land, as if struggling to control their huge feet, like a diver walking down to the water's edge in large flippers.

CLIMBING TREES

It may come as a surprise to learn that moorhens are also strong tree climbers. Their large feet give them a good grip on fine branches and twigs. In winter, when the water is very cold, groups of moorhens often clamber into low branches over water to roost at dusk. They even scramble up to squirrel dreys or pigeon nests to use them as the base of their nests.

BOBBING CORKS

Moorhens look more comfortable in the water, where they ride very high and look extremely buoyant. Like

The Little Grebe (Tachybaptus ruficollis)

In the moorhen's watery haunts, you may come across another dark little water-bird, the little grebe – once better known as the dabchick. Summer or winter, you can pick it out by its rotund body and blunt 'powder puff' rear end. Bright chestnut cheeks and throat and yellowish patches of bare skin at the base of the beak are its most eye-catching features during the breeding season.

When little grebe chicks are tiny, they often clamber on to their parent's back, where they are safe and warm, and hitch a ride across the water.

in flight

▲ TAKE OFF
When needs must, a little grebe launches itself into the air by skittering across the surface of the water. Its short narrow wings beat furiously as it gets airborne and flutters fast and low for a little way with its neck extended and legs trailing through the water.

Timid and wary by nature, little grebes are elusive and exasperating to watch. No sooner have you spotted one than, in the blink of an eye, it has dived out of sight and you have lost track of it. The chances are that it has bobbed up again among reeds and rushes growing in the water. Although easy to lose sight of, a little grebe is likely to give its presence away by its surprisingly loud, shrill call – a snickering sound that rises and falls in volume and pitch rather like the neighing of a horse or the sound of a stick being run along iron railings.

◄ SAFE HAVEN
A moorhen balancing in a willow tree is a strange and uncommon sight. It may have landed or clambered up there looking for a nesting site or a place to roost.

many aquatic birds, a moorhen has a thick layer of down to trap air, which insulates it against the cold, like a puffa jacket, and also helps to keep it afloat. This down is covered by longer, overlapping feathers that stop water penetrating to the skin and chilling the body.

To keep these feathers waterproof, a moorhen must oil them regularly from a special oil gland situated at the base of its tail. It wipes its beak over the gland then rubs the oil into its feathers while preening.

HIDDEN DEPTHS

At the first hint of danger moorhens scurry back to the nearest water and perform a neat disappearing trick. Although they rarely, if ever, dive for food, when threatened they hide under water, holding themselves down with their feet. Just their beaks poke above the surface so that they can breathe while submerged.

FAIR GAME

In times past, moorhens' nests were frequently molested by prying hands. If they couldn't reach a nest easily, children would tie spoons to long sticks and use them to scoop out the eggs. Easy to catch and good eating, moorhens and their eggs were also traditional fare for travellers.

> ' *On hanging sallow's farthest stretch,*
> *A moorhen 'gins her nest of sedge,*
> *Safe from the destroying schoolboy's reach* '

from *The Shepherd's Calendar: March* by **John Clare** (1793-1864)

Moor Names

● Rather than referring to high moorland, when the moorhen is found in lowland areas, the *moor* in its name could have been derived from the Anglo-Saxon word *mor* meaning bog or marsh. This is just the sort of wetland moorhens like to inhabit. Mor-hen and More-hen were early alternative spellings for moorhen.

● Long ago, large English houses and castles were defended by moats, occupied by Mot-hens or Moat-hens.

● The most commonly accepted explanation for the moorhen's present name is that it was a corruption of merehen, where *mere* meant lake.

● The moorhen's scientific name is *Gallinula chloropus*, the green-footed chicken. In Latin, *gallina* is a poultry hen; adding *-ulus* as a suffix indicates smallness. The *chloropus* part of the name is made up of two Greek words: *chloros* meaning yellow-green and *pous* for foot.

moorhen

coot

THE COOT (*Fulica atra*)
The moorhen and the coot often get mistaken for one another, because they are both 'black' birds sharing the same stretches of water. The most obvious difference is that a moorhen has a red facial guard and beak, while a coot's are white. Moorhens are also smaller, with a white line along each side and a sticky-up tail in the water. It is harder to see that a moorhen has long, thin toes while the coot has large, lobed feet.

The Kingfisher

Even though the kingfisher is dressed in the most dazzling plumage, its low arrow-like flight and stillness when watching for fish to catch make it remarkably hard to spot

The kingfisher is one of the most vibrantly coloured birds in the country. But, unless you are lucky, the only sighting you are likely to get of it is a streak of electric blue as it whizzes by. Before you can say 'Was that a kingfisher?' it has vanished into a hole in the bank or taken shelter in an overhanging tree.

COLOURFUL ILLUSION

The colours of a kingfisher change constantly, depending on the strength and direction of the light. Viewed from above, its dappled iridescent blues and greens blend invisibly with the ever-shifting pattern of reflections on the surface of the water.

▶ JEWEL OF THE STREAM
When photographed in bright sunshine, it is almost impossible to believe that a kingfisher's shimmering brilliance can be invisible in the shadows of the river-bank.

a kingfisher can hover briefly before diving into the water to catch a fish

Spotting Kingfishers

As a kingfisher's plumage and stillness help to make it so inconspicuous, the best chance of sighting one is when it moves. As you walk quietly beside a peaceful stream or river, or along a canal towpath, listen out for the shrill whistling call a kingfisher makes when disturbed.

Then watch for a flash of electric blue as a kingfisher flies past, like a paper dart, straight and unswerving. In flight, the pale turquoise streak down its back from neck to tail is particularly eye-catching. You may even be close enough to hear the whirring of its short wings flapping very quickly as it passes.

...

Experts at Fishing

THE KINGFISHER'S PATIENT approach to fishing is very effective. Perched on a low overhanging branch or fishing post, it gazes intently into the water, on the alert for any little fish swimming within diving range.

When it spots some prey and is on the verge of diving, a kingfisher raises its head, stretches its neck and visibly flattens its feathers before launching itself off its perch into the dive. Its aim is usually uncannily accurate. The kingfisher's eyes are able to filter out any glare and reflections from the ripples on the surface and make split-second adjustments for the way light bends and distorts the precise position of its prey underwater.

◄ WELL HELD
With astounding alacrity and precision, a kingfisher dives and clamps a fish in its beak, then flies out of the water and back to its perch in one seamless manoeuvre.

▲ TRANQUIL SETTING
A kingfisher's ideal hunting ground is a peaceful stretch of clear shallow stream, with overhanging branches from where it can study the water below for small fish.

TAKING THE FISH

As a kingfisher enters the water with a quiet plop, its long, strong beak is thrust forward until it closes around the fish. At the same time, on hitting the water, the kingfisher immediately arches its back and uses its short tail as a rudder to turn itself up towards the surface again.

With a final downward thrust of its wings, the kingfisher bursts free of the water and flies back to its perch in a shower of droplets. The whole dive is over in about two seconds.

Swallowing the Catch

After catching a fish in its beak, the kingfisher flies back to an overhanging branch. There, it either swallows small fish whole, while they are still wriggling about, or bashes larger ones on the branch to stun them first. Fish are always swallowed head first, so the fins, scales and spines won't catch in its throat.

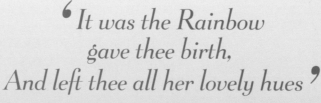

'*It was the Rainbow gave thee birth, And left thee all her lovely hues*'
from *The Kingfisher* by **W H Davies** (1871-1940)

River-bank Family

A KINGFISHER'S WORLD revolves around its own peaceful stretch of fresh water where it can catch fish and build its nesting tunnel in the steep sandy banks.

During the nesting season, which starts in late April, neighbouring male and female kingfishers combine their territories. They split up again in July when breeding is over and return to a solitary existence.

FIRST ENCOUNTER

When they meet up for the first time, a male and female kingfisher get quite agitated. They whistle and chase each other up and down the water, sometimes flying high above the tree tops. The excitement wanes when the male catches a fish and presents it to the female for the first time. This seals their engagement and the pair settle down to excavating a nesting hole in the river-bank.

DIGGING OUT THE NEST

The male starts off the tunnelling by flying at the bank and chipping out a small hole, which both birds then enlarge with their beaks and kick the sand out with their feet. Two toes on each foot are partially fused to

male

female

▲ TEMPTING TITBIT

As part of his courtship ritual, the male teases the female with a fish. He offers it to her head first, then pulls it away again before she can take it. Only when they are ready to mate does he let her take the morsel to reinforce their pair bond.

'There came
Swift as a meteor's shining flame
A kingfisher from out the brake
And almost seemed to leave a wake
Of brilliant hues behind'

from *The Cherwell Waterlily* by **Frederick William Faber** (1814-1863)

Nesting Chamber

the tunnel slopes upwards from the entrance to stop the nest getting flooded and to let the nestlings' waste drain out

A pair of kingfishers excavates a tunnel up to 1m (3¼ft) long in a sandy river-bank. It has a 5cm (2in) diameter entrance hole and a nesting chamber at the far end. They cover the chamber floor with regurgitated fish bones and lay six to eight round white eggs on top. Both birds incubate the clutch for 19 to 21 days.

The chicks grow rapidly in the stinking nesting chamber, supplied with up to 100 fish a day by their busy parents. The youngsters take it in turns to face the entrance to the nest and be the first to greet a parent returning with food, so they all get fair shares.

Digging out the nesting tunnel, and then crawling along it every time they bring food to their chicks, is dirty work for the kingfishers. They often dive into the water just to clean their feathers.

◄ **FEEDING THE FAMILY**
With a family of chicks to feed, a kingfisher's choice of nesting site and its fishing skills are put to the sternest test. It cannot afford to wait long on its fishing stump for prey to happen past and every dive needs to be rewarded with a catch that it can take back to its nesting tunnel.

▲ **GROOMING SESSIONS**
After two or three hunting dives, a kingfisher can spend up to 30 minutes preening its plumage. It must re-oil its feathers often to keep them waterproof so that it can rise out of the water after taking a plunge and fly straight off. Otherwise it will drown because it cannot swim!

strengthen them for this. The legs are very short, which is fine for perching and crawling along narrow tunnels.

In a good year, a pair of kingfishers may rear two or three broods. They usually dig a fresh tunnel for each, because the previous one becomes such a smelly mess after rearing a family of chicks in it.

THE FUTURE IS BRIGHT

Worldwide, kingfisher numbers are falling, but in Britain, the population may be on the increase. In recent years, tighter pollution controls have led to cleaner rivers and streams for kingfishers to inhabit and more fish for them to eat. A series of mild winters has also improved their survival rate, as many have died in prolonged spells of icy weather.

▲ **GREEDY FLEDGLINGS**
When fledged, about 24 days after hatching, the young look similar to their parents, with slightly duller plumage and white tips to their beaks. Immediately after leaving the nest, they stay hidden on the banks, making feeble attempts to fish while relying on their parents to feed them.

The Sand Martin

Sand martins are likely to be the first birds you see chasing insects across the sky each spring as they make it back from Africa earlier than swallows or house martins

The sand martin is a summer visitor to Britain, coming here to breed and catch insects. It starts arriving back in March – the British Trust for Ornithology's web site reported the first sighting of 2003 on 3 March in Shropshire.

Sand martins are less familiar than swallows or house martins because they nest in isolated sand pits and gravel quarries, along river-banks or on sea cliffs around the coast.

COMMUNAL SPIRIT

Sand martins never tire of each other's company: they feed together, breed in colonies and roost in flocks before flying off in September to spend the winter together in Africa.

▶ **NEST IN PEACE**
A sand martin is rarely still: this one is momentarily distracted from digging out its nesting tunnel or feeding its chicks.

house martin

sand martin

swallow

Telling the Difference

In the swirling mass of martins and swallows that assemble in large flocks before departing for Africa in the autumn, the sand martins are the ones with the brown back and underwings and a distinctive brown band across their white chests; house martins have all-white underparts, throat and rump with a blue-black back; swallows have white underparts too, but their throat is red with a blue-black chest-band and rump. They are also larger, with longer tail streamers, and generally fly lower with greater grace and assurance than the martins.

'I've seen thee far away from all thy tribe Flirting about the unfrequented sky'

from *The Sand-Martin* by **John Clare** (1793-1864)

Fly Fishing

SAND MARTINS FLOCK to stretches of water to feed on the masses of insects that are breeding there or hatching from their aquatic larval forms during the summer.

The sand martin feeds on the wing, snapping up flying insects in mid-air. Some years sand martins get back from Africa too early for their own good, before the weather has warmed up enough for many insects to be active. Then it is only damp areas around sewage farms, marshes and sand dunes, where temperatures are milder and insects abound, that save them from starvation.

PROBLEMS IN AFRICA

Sand martins fly south for the winter, to an area called the Sahel in West Africa, south of the Sahara Desert. Over the lush wetlands there they rely on finding flying insects to eat. Close to Burkina Faso's northern border there is a freshwater lake, the Mare d'Oursi, which is fringed by sand dunes.

The lake is a magnet to many species of bird, including sand martins, that risk migrating across the Sahara twice a year, to breed in Europe and overwinter in Africa.

Recent droughts in this region have been disastrous for the sand martins and other birds. Between the 1968 and 1969 breeding seasons, and again in 1983 to 1984, there was a catastrophic slump in the numbers of sand martins returning to breed in Britain. Nearly a million nested here before the droughts but, by the 1990s, only about 200,000 were turning up each spring.

▲ FLYING SQUAD
Flooded quarries, reservoirs, freshwater lakes and rivers are all happy hunting grounds for flocks of sand martins. Large numbers of them are often seen swooping over the surface of the water, busily snapping up insects.

Sweeping Up

Although agile in the air, a sand martin never flies very high and rarely glides. It can look quite moth-like, unsteady and fluttery, because the wings make a very full beat, closing to to the sides of the body on each stroke. Like the swallow, the sand martin flies low enough over the water to dip its beak into the surface and take a sip or grab a fly. Sometimes it lands beside a pool then shuffles awkwardly down to the water's edge on its short legs and small feet to take a drink.

'And rapid skim the surface of the lake
With eager bill their insect prey to take'

from *Spring* by **Heinrich von Kleist** (1777-1811)

Cliff Colonies

MANY TRIBES OF sand martins loyally return to nest in the same quarries, pits and cliffs every year. When they get back, some settle for making quick repairs to existing tunnels and reuse them as nests. If the weather is still cold, they often huddle in their old tunnels to keep warm.

CAVE DWELLERS

More often, the quarry face has been disturbed or collapsed while they were away, or the old entrance holes have got too wide, so they set about excavating fresh tunnels. The little birds work with great speed and energy, using just their stubby beaks and small feet to shift masses of sand and pebbles. If the digging bird comes up against a large pebble or band of rock, the pair abandon that tunnel and start again elsewhere. They work in the mornings and feed in the afternoons.

When the excavation is complete, the male starts hovering at the tunnel entrance, singing his twittery, chirpy song, to encourage his partner to join him. He defends a small territory around the nest-hole to avoid being cuckolded by another male mating with his partner. Occasionally, opportunistic starlings and house

◄ FEATHER LINING
A sand martin returns with a precious feather to add to the lining of its nest chamber. If one bird in the colony sheds a feather, other members make great play of chasing after it.

Excavating a Tunnel

To start a new nesting hole, a sand martin has to cling to the face of the cliff and chip out a round hole with its beak. It enlarges this by moving around, gradually nibbling away at it until eventually there is a slight lip to stand on. Both the male and female share the digging. which gets easier when they can perch in the hole and work horizontally along the tunnel. The nesting tunnel goes about 65cm (26in) into the bank – usually just farther than an arm's reach. A small nest chamber opens out at the end, which the sand martins line with feathers and grass.

in a colony, many nest-holes are dug on a single cliff face

a sand martin has to shuffle along the tunnel between its nest and the entrance hole

sparrows dispossess the industrious sand martins and set up home in their nest tunnels instead.

CAVE DWELLERS

The hen lays four or five matt pure white eggs in the nest and both birds share the incubation for around 14 days. On hatching, the nestlings are covered in pale grey down. The lining to their mouths is pale yellow so that their parents can see where to deliver the insects they feed them in the dark nesting chamber.

Both parents keep up a prodigious supply of insects for their young for between 19 and 24 days until the chicks fledge. Towards the end of the fledging phase, the nestlings escape from the dark, cramped confines of the nest chamber and gather at the entrance of the tunnel, waiting for their parents to return with food.

UNASSAILABLE POSITION

Young sand martins are usually safe in their inaccessible nests. Built into precipitous cliffs, the entrance holes

and tunnels look unreachable. But a wily stoat was once seen creeping along a sandy bank where sand martins were nesting and raiding the tunnels for chicks.

Generally, the sand martin has few enemies. One small bird of prey, the hobby does fly fast enough to snatch it out of the air and patrolling sparrowhawks can sometimes take them by surprise as well.

EARLY INDEPENDENCE

The sand martin's first clutch of eggs is usually laid by the end of April, so most find time to raise two broods a year, especially in warm summers when there are plenty of insects flying about.

While a second brood is being raised, the first clutch of juveniles flies off to a new feeding area. There they roost each night with other young sand martins and non-breeding adults among the reeds or willow trees in marshland, on the banks of rivers or along estuaries.

Distinctly Young

At close range, juvenile sand martins have pale bronze, silver or gold fringes to their flight feathers, which distinguish them from the adults. For a few days after its first flight, a fledgling returns to the family burrow to roost. After that, all the youngsters start gathering in a nursery, where their parents continue to feed them, apparently recognising their own offspring by their individual calls amid the chattering horde.

juveniles

◄ **COMINGS AND GOINGS**
At the height of the breeding season, a sand-martin colony is a lively, noisy place. It can be quite dizzying to watch hundreds of sand martins whizzing back and forth to their nest-holes all day long.

'Where frequent quarries give thee dwelling place With strangest taste and labour undeterred Drilling small holes along the quarry side'

from *The Sand-Martin* by **John Clare** (1793-1864)

the tunnel tilts slightly uphill so water seeping through the sand and waste from the nest can drain away

► **PERSONAL HYGIENE**
The nest chamber crawls with fleas and lice – adults preen themselves frequently to get rid of these parasites

At the Cliff Face

THESE DAYS, SAND martins have a wider choice of suitable vertical sand and gravel banks in which to nest than ever before, due to an increase in quarrying to supply the expanding house- and road-building industries.

For hundreds of years, sand martins have relied on quarry owners allowing them to nest in their pits. Traditionally, quarrymen have always had a great respect for the industrious sand martin and used to be very protective of the birds' nests. Work on the sand martin's side of the quarry was usually suspended during the breeding season. After the birds left later in the summer, work was resumed and by the time they returned the following spring, a freshly cleared face awaited them.

There has been more conflict of interests in recent times as expensive heavy-duty diggers have to be kept busy to pay their way. But the law is on the sand martin's side: under the Wildlife and Countryside Act 1981 it is an offence to intentionally take, damage, destroy or disturb the eggs or nest of a sand martin while it is being built or in use. Sadly, sand martins haven't got a leg to stand on when a sand pit is closed down, because it is no longer economically viable, and then re-landscaped.

HELPING HAND

In the light of the problems encountered by sand martins in Africa during the winter and the catastrophic fall in their numbers, special efforts have been made to create more breeding sites for them. During the construction of the

◄ **EXCAVATORS TO THE RESCUE**
In a sand pit, the sand martins' nesting holes are usually arranged in neat rows. The birds often reuse the tunnels but the cliff eventually crumbles. Quarrying exposes fresh sand faces for them to mine.

Farewell Gatherings

When nesting is over for another year, sand martins start gathering in flocks. During the day, they feed greedily on swarms of late-summer insects flying over water or around warm roof tiles. Before leaving, sand martins need to lay down fat reserves to fuel their 3000 mile flight to West Africa for the winter. They also spend a lot of their time preening to get their feathers into tip-top condition for their long journey. Prior to departure, large flocks start congregating on telephone wires and overhead cables. At dusk, all the birds go noisily to roost together in reedbeds and willows along estuaries, river-banks and coastal marshes.

Most sand martins make a beeline for their tribal nesting quarters year after year for generations. Then, one year, out of the blue, a tribe may fail to turn up in their traditional haunts. It is possible that in the previous year, their breeding was disturbed by digging, predators or parasites, which put the sand martins off coming back to their usual nesting location.

magnificent glass domes for the Eden Project, the green theme park in Cornwall, in the late 1990s, a new sand cliff was exposed especially for sand martins – and was soon adopted by a colony of them.

PRE-FAB ACCOMMODATION

In the past, some enterprising sand martins have saved precious time and effort by using drainpipes as ready-made nesting holes instead of digging nesting holes for themselves. Small colonies used to nest in the dry drainage pipes in a railway cutting near Clapham Junction in London and beside the River Cam near King's College in Cambridge.

Knowing this, in some places, artificial holes have been created to accommodate sand martins. In the Ribble Valley in Lancashire, plastic and concrete tunnels were installed as temporary nesting places for the sand martin while work on creating a new canal link and fresh sand banks for them was in progress. The birds seemed happy to adopt these pre-fabricated tunnels as convenient and secure nesting sites.

'Warn'd of approaching winter, gathered, play
The swallow-people; and tossed wide around
O'er the calm sky, in convolution swift,
The feathered eddy floats'

from *Migration* by **James Thomson** (1700-1748)

Lore and Legend

• The sand martin's scientific name, *Riparia riparia*, describes it perfectly as a bank-nesting bank nester. *Riparia* means one who haunts the river-bank and comes from the Latin for river-bank, *ripa*.

• The sand martin has been a Sand Martin for a very long time. Other names, such as Bank Martin or Pit Martin, generally refer to its habit of nesting in banks or quarries.

• Other appropriate adjectives have been added to swallow to describe the sand martin and its nesting habits: Bank Swallow, Sand Swallow or River Swallow.

• In Scotland, sand martins used to be called Bitter Banks or Bitteries, where bitter described the birds' habit of biting at the sand in a bank, cliff or quarry wall with their beaks as they started to excavate their nesting tunnels.

The Reed Bunting

In summer, a walk along the banks of a reed-lined waterway is often brightened by a glimpse of a handsome cock reed bunting weaving his way through the vegetation

At first sight, a cock reed bunting does look rather like a very smart cock sparrow: both have a black bib and streaky brown and black back. But the male reed bunting's markings are generally brighter and stronger, topped off with a natty black hood.

AMONG THE RUSHES

By and large, the reed bunting is a wetland bird. It frequents reeds, sedges, rushes and willows growing around ponds and rivers, in estuaries and along canals. Reed buntings are also partial to coastal flats where meadows are divided up by dykes and tangled hedges. A few choose to live more inland on farmland.

▶ DASHING SUITOR
In his spring finery, the male reed bunting is sartorially splendid, with his smart jet-black head set off in style by a crisp white collar and strong moustache stripes.

male in winter

male in summer

Seasonal Plumage

After the breeding season is over for another year, reed buntings undergo their annual moult. The males emerge with pale brown tips to their black feathers which completely camouflage the blackness of their heads in the autumn. These tips gradually get worn away over the winter until, by the following spring, the cock birds can show off their magnificent black hoods again.

'Where the reeds whisper when the zephyrs blow'

from *The Borough* by **George Crabbe** (1754-1832)

The Water Sparrow

THE REED BUNTING mainly plunders reedbeds and water meadows for its food. During the summer, it eats the insects that feed on the leaves of reeds and sedges: butterfly and moth caterpillars, flies, bees and wasps, beetles, bugs and aphids and mites. It may also take small snails and shrimps from the water.

In the winter, reed buntings forage in small groups over open, rough ground in search of seeds and grains of marsh plants and grasses. They sometimes join up with yellowhammers and finches to search the grassland and roost together, particularly during very cold weather.

TOUGH TIMES

Like many grain- and seed-eating birds that feed their chicks on insects, the number of reed buntings declined alarmingly in the 1970s. Between 1968 and 1985, the pattern of land drainage changed drastically, leading to the loss of the reed bunting's natural wetland habitats. Clearance of river-bank vegetation also deprived them of their traditional nesting sites and feeding grounds.

At the same time, many agricultural practices and time-tables were being revolutionised: for the reed buntings the effects of heavy pesticide and fertiliser use were exacerbated by a switch from spring to autumn sown cereal crops which left fewer stubble fields and less spare grain for them to feed on over the winter.

▲ **GREEN GRASS OF HOME**
After a successful insect hunt, this perky cock reed bunting clings to a grass stem and takes stock of his surroundings before carrying his booty back to feed a nestful of demanding chicks nearby.

Every Grain Counts

A grass seedhead bends under the weight of a female reed bunting as she inches her way along, determined to pluck out as many precious seeds as she can reach before the stem leans right over. (In comparison to the snazzy cock bird, her plumage is plain and brown, with darker streaks on her flanks and breast. Her head has clear stripy markings, with dark cheeks, pale 'eyebrows' and a double pale-and-black moustache on either side of her beak. Juveniles look like even streakier versions of the female.)

In autumn, reed buntings, especially the youngsters, roam about in search of seeds in grassland and on farmland farther inland, often a long way from water. During the winter, some may visit urban gardens where there are bird-feeders; if you see a sparrow-like bird that stands out in a crowd of house sparrows, eating seeds in your garden, the conspicuous interloper may be a reed bunting.

Reedbed Family

MALE REED BUNTINGS start returning to the reedbeds and setting up territories as early as February. A cock reed bunting is hard to miss when he perches high up on a reed stem or darts up from cover, throws back his head and sings his tinkling song, *plink-plink-plink-tséeri*, over and over again.

LITTLE SHOW-OFF

When the females arrive back in March, the males chase them around enthusiastically; pursuits often end with both birds rolling about in mock fights. In his courtship displays the male fluffs up his white collar, raises his crown feathers and inflates his throat to show off his black bib.

Then he partly opens his wings and flutters his fanned tail in front of the female. If he succeeds in impressing her, she remains in his territory.

MORE THAN ONE BASKET

Some cheeky males successfully perform their courtship routine to more than one female and run a small harem of hens, each with her own nest and brood of chicks, within his territory.

After building a nest and laying her eggs, the female does most of the incubating, which lasts for up to 14 days. In recent years, for all the hens' vigilance, as many as a third of reed-bunting eggs have failed to hatch for some unknown reason.

male in summer

female in summer

▲ WORKING RELATIONSHIP
In a reed-bunting partnership, the male has all the flashy feathers and brags about them incessantly, while his dowdier mate gets on with the practicalities of nest-building and egg-laying.

' *The reed sparrow's nest it was close to the sallows* '

from *The Round Oak* by **John Clare** (1793-1864)

Locating the Nest

The reed bunting usually nests near fresh water, often in marshy places and vegetation along river-banks and around lakes but not necessarily in reedbeds. In recent years, there has been an unexpected expansion of nesting into drier places such as young conifer plantations and fields of rape. Nearly as many as three-quarters of rape fields now seem to hold a reed-bunting family.

The female builds her nest low down in the reeds, in the stump of a willow tree or on the ground in a tussock of grass. The nest is usually well concealed and you have to watch closely to see the adults coming and going to find it. Reed buntings are territorial but, depending on space and food supply, they may occasionally nest quite close together in small loose colonies.

PARENTAL DEDICATION

On hatching, the helpless chicks are covered in long black fluff. They have a dark pink lining to their mouths with yellowish flanges and a pale tip to their tongues.

Both parents work tirelessly to care for their family. On sunny days, the female stands astride the nest with her wings slightly spread to shade the chicks from the heat of the sun. Meanwhile, the male finds most of the food, bringing insects back to the nest and passing them to his mate for her to feed the nestlings.

PERSONAL SACRIFICE

The nest is easiest to locate when the chicks are being fed because of the frequent visits of the adult birds and the noise the youngsters make when

▶ **PROTECTIVE COLOURING**

Independence is a bewildering experience for most fledglings. This young reed bunting will need all the camouflage afforded by its dull, streaky plumage while it learns to cope with finding food and shelter for itself.

▼ **IN A WICKER BASKET**

While her mate sings to proclaim their territory, the female reed bunting gets on with weaving an untidy cup of dry reeds and grasses lined with hair, finer grass and old reed tops and willow fluff. Into her nest she lays four or five olive-brown or pale green eggs marked with black squiggles, the bunting's signature.

> ' *Mounted on a bending reed,*
> *Chanting as my fancies lead,*
> *Tender tales I oft repeat,*
> *Clear, harmonious, soft and sweet* '
>
> from *The Song of the Reed Sparrow* by **Anon** (19th century)

their parents return with food. If their nest is threatened, both the male and female reed bunting may feign injury by shuffling along the ground with wings half spread to distract a predator's attention. All being well, the chicks are ready to leave the nest in 10 to 12 days.

EARLY DAYS

Life for newly-fledged reed buntings is also fraught with danger. Research suggests that fewer than ever are surviving their first year, maybe due to a shortage of food after fledging and in the winter. Farmers are being encouraged to plant seed-rich crops on set-aside land to create buffer zones that will provide food for the winter, good cover and nesting sites for birds such as the reed bunting.

Disappearing Reedbeds

Some of the reed bunting's favourite stomping grounds among waterlogged reedbeds are under serious threat. Dominated by the common reed, *Phragmites australis,* a reedbed is a high maintenance habitat. In the old days, the reeds were cropped regularly by reed cutters who supplied reeds to roof thatchers. Harvesting the reed stems promoted fresh growth and stopped other plants getting established. But since reed-cutting has fallen into decline, boggy woodland plants have started to encroach and displace the reeds.

On a positive note, all major reedbeds are now under nature conservation control. New reedbeds are being planted as a natural way of treating domestic sewage, industrial effluent and dirty run off from farmland. The underground roots and stems of the reeds trap and oxygenate the sediment while micro-organisms living in the silt break down waste and purify the water. When established, these reedbeds are also expected to support a variety of endangered birdlife, including reed buntings.

The Lapwing

*Famous the world over for its oft-repeated, melancholy
pee-wit call and wispy crest, the lapwing used to be
a striking and popular symbol of country life*

Once a common bird of the open countryside, lapwings are currently facing a crisis, as suitable nesting sites and food for their chicks become scarcer.

CURRENT HAUNTS

Lapwings are still found in depleted numbers on damp open farmland, moorland, wet grassland, marshes and saltmarshes all over the country. They may turn up on golf courses, playing fields and racecourses too. In autumn, many lapwings move to the coast for the winter. There they congregate in large flocks to feed on mudflats at low tide. The rest of the time they stand hunched up in close groups in moist fields and pastures.

▶ CRESTED WADER

When a lapwing feeds in flooded pastures, it only picks food from the surface of the water. On mudflats exposed at low tide it digs for worms, crabs and snails.

female

male

Recognising Lapwings

With its jaunty crest and broad wings, a lapwing is fairly easy to pick out. In the air, lapwings are transformed from neat little waders into large, broad-winged birds with a distinctive floppy wing beat and slow-motion irregular flapping. The lapwing's famous contact call, a harsh wheezy *pee-wit*, is one of the most haunting and evocative sounds heard in the countryside.

'*Under the after-sunset sky
Two pewits sport and cry* '

from *Two Pewits* by **Edward Thomas** (1878-1917)

Troubled Times

FARMERS AND LAPWINGS used to live in harmony when the farming cycle suited the lapwing's nesting habits, but modern farming has had dire consequences for the birds.

Since the early 1960s, lapwing numbers have fallen by a staggering 80 per cent in England and Wales – between 1987 and 1998 alone the population halved. In recent years, chick survival has been particularly poor, often with fewer than a quarter fledging in many broods. Shortages of food and wet weather are always bad news for these tiny fluffballs: their down is not waterproof and they must avoid getting their feet caked with mud, as this impedes their mobility and could stop them feeding.

LOSS OF NESTING SITES

The main culprit for the general decline of lapwings is the reduction of mixed farming, which provided them with an ideal combination of arable fields and rough pastures on which they could feed and nest.

One serious problem is the switch from spring-sown cereal crops to autumn planting, so that shoots are too tall when the lapwing is looking for open nest sites on the ground. When the field margins are ploughed up too, to maximise productivity, the lapwing has nowhere to go.

The dearth of suitable breeding sites leaves eggs and chicks more exposed and vulnerable to predation. Often the only apparently suitable nesting area in a field is right in the tractor's wheel tracks, where the crop stays shorter, but these are easily patrolled by foxes.

LOSS OF FEEDING GROUNDS

On many farms, soggy pastures have been drained to create better grazing, leaving fewer waterlogged marshy areas, wetlands, ponds and ditches. This makes the ground harder, and the worms and grubs more difficult for the lapwings to extract.

Even on wild remote moorland, the use of strong sheep-dip and worming chemicals has killed off large numbers of dung beetles and flies that used to breed on the sheep droppings, depriving the lapwings of their local food supply.

▼ PRIZE PICKINGS
The lapwing prefers to feed on damp grassland or bare earth where the soil is soft and easy to probe with its beak. This one has hit the jackpot: an earthworm to tug out of the ground.

Good Ground

Although lapwings eat mainly earthworms, they also take plenty of pests, such as wireworms and leatherjackets, which live close to the surface of the soil. They scratch about in grassy and rushy tussocks to disturb other insects such as beetles, flies and caterpillars as well as to find spiders, slugs and snails.

' *Why dost thou not fly among the corn fields?* **'**

from *O Lapwing!* by **William Blake** (1757-1827)

beetle

earthworm

caterpillar

Parents United

LAPWINGS MAY BE in difficulties, but not for want of parental dedication. Breeding success calls for some gold-medal aerobatics, Oscar-worthy acting and fearless teamwork.

Lapwings nest early: in March, April and May. The males are keenly territorial; each one picks out an acre or so of open farmland, marsh or moorland, where patches of bare soil are dotted with short grass. Ideally, the nesting area is extensive enough for a number of pairs to form a loose colony for their mutual protection. In poor habitats, when only a few can nest together, each egg and chick is less well protected and more likely to be attacked by predators.

PREPARING THE GROUND

Before his nuptial flight, the male lapwing scratches out several shallow hollows in the bare earth, often on slightly raised ground to avoid flooding and to give a good view of the surrounding area. Later, his mate tries out each scrape for size, then chooses one to be used as their nest. Sometimes she lines it with a few strands of grass. Into this saucer, the hen lapwing lays a clutch of four pear-shaped eggs. They are buff to olive in colour and covered in dark splotches. The well-camouflaged eggs are pointed so that they fit neatly together and roll back into the nest if disturbed.

FOR THE FAMILY

The female lapwing does most of the incubating of her eggs for 21 to 28 days. When sheep or cattle trample dangerously close to her nest, she leaps up, flapping her outspread wings to shoo them away. Newly-hatched lapwings are active at once:

male

▲ ON WATCH
As long as there are eggs in the nest or chicks on the ground, a parent lapwing is always on the alert for predators and intruders trespassing on its territory.

male

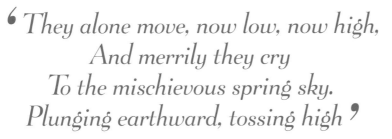

' *They alone move, now low, now high,*
And merrily they cry
To the mischievous spring sky.
Plunging earthward, tossing high '

from *Two Pewits* by **Edward Thomas** (1878-1917)

male

Passionate Courtship Display

In spring, one of the most memorable sights to behold over marshland and farmland is the male lapwing's spectacular aerial courtship display. It is his great claim to fame, which brings birdwatchers from all over the world to witness his spectacularly uninhibited performance. Swooping over his nesting territory, he performs a reckless dance across the sky. His broad wings flap wildly as he towers steeply and wheels around before plunging earthward again, rolling and tumbling, somersaulting and corkscrewing as he dives. At times, a male lapwing can look as though he is totally out of control. When he passes overhead, the humming of his beating wings is clearly audible. While executing his bewildering aerial manoeuvres, the male lapwing sings a haunting song – a plaintive whistling *peerrweet, weet, weet peerweet* or *willock-a-weet*.

as tiny chicks they can even swim, a wise precaution if they were to fall into a deep pool. As soon as their down has dried, their mother leads them away from the exposed nest to grassy feeding grounds where there is more cover.

COURAGEOUS CHAPERONES

Defenceless young lapwings can find most of their own food but rely on their parents for protection. Both do their utmost to keep their family safe for 35 to 40 days until the youngsters are fledged and flying.

On rainy days, a mother lapwing's wide wings make good umbrellas to shelter her tiny chicks. And she is prepared to put her life on the line to lure predators, such as foxes and badgers, away from the nest by dragging herself along the ground, pretending to have a broken wing.

Meanwhile, the male lapwing provides aerial cover for his family: he joins forces with other males to mob crows, gulls and birds of prey or to dive bomb intruders on the ground. On hearing their parents' warning calls, the chicks squat and freeze until the all-clear is sounded.

▲ SITTING PRETTY
Sitting on her eggs in the middle of a ploughed field, a female lapwing may look overexposed. But at least she is surrounded by a good source of food and has a clear view all around her.

◄ JUST A FEW HOURS OLD
Less than 24 hours ago, this lapwing chick was curled up inside an eggshell. Now its down is all fluffy and it is already exercising its spindly legs to explore its waterlogged surroundings.

Winter Movements

In July, many lapwings start heading for the coast where they gather in vast flocks. There they are joined by squadrons of lapwings escaping the deep freeze of an eastern European winter. Crowds of lapwings spend their days arrayed in serried ranks, huddled up against a bitter head wind, and feed on the worms, shrimps and crabs creeping over the mud at low tide.

A lapwing suffers in harsh winters because it cannot forage properly when the ground is frozen or covered in snow. As cold weather closes in, lapwings swiftly move on to milder climes in Ireland or France and Spain.

Peewit and Flopwing

THE LAPWING IS ingrained in country folklore but it has not always been a very popular bird. Its dramatic aerial displays led country folk to believe that Peewits were spirits of the departed that were destined to haunt the earth restlessly.

Lapwings were also despised for mocking Christ at his Crucifixion. For such spitefulness, they were condemned to be homeless for ever and to wander with a sorrowful cry.

UNTRUSTWORTHY BIRD

From early times, the lapwing had a reputation for being a deceitful bird because of its desperate attempts to lead predators or hunters away from its well-concealed nest by feigning injury. In *The Parlement of Foules*, the poet Geoffrey Chaucer (c.1345-1400) described '*the false lapwing, ful of trecherye*'.

Lapwing became a simile for a distracting ploy. In his play *Campaspe*, John Lyly (c.1554-1606) referred to deceit when he wrote

You resemble the lapwing, who crieth most where her nest is not.

NOISY TRAITORS

According to Scottish tradition, agitated lapwings screeching and flying over their nests among the heather frequently betrayed banned meetings of the Covenanters to the soldiers. In the 17th century, these Presbyterian rebels refused to recognise King Charles ll as head of the church. Writing about the revolt over a hundred years later, John Leyden (1775-1811) recorded in his poem *Wandering Covenanter*

The lapwing's clamorous whoop attends their flight,
Pursues their steps where'er the wanderers go,
Till the shrill scream betrays them to the foe.

' *The white-winged plover wheels*
Her sounding flight, and then directly on
In long excursion skims the level lawn
To tempt him from her nest '

from *The Seasons: Spring* by **James Thomson** (1700-1748)

Also Known As

- The name lapwing originates from an Anglo-Saxon description of the lapwing as *hleapewince*, which meant 'one who turns about in flight'. Over the years, *hleapewince* evolved into Lapwing via Lapwinch and Lapwink.

- The lapwing's scientific name is *Vanellus vanellus* – a double helping of 'little fan' from *vannus*, the Latin for a fan used for winnowing grain. It refers to the slow flapping of the lapwing's wings.

- At one time the lapwing was better known as the Peewit after its *pee-wit* call. In the northwest it was the Teewit, in Scotland and the northeast it was a Chewsit, Tewhit, Tewfit or Teuchit.

- A Scottish name for the lapwing was Peesweep, as in *The Transformation*, a poem written by Walter Wingate (1865-1918).

An atmosphere of sobbing wings –
And lo! An arrant peesweep swings
Against the sky!

- Adding an 'f' to lapwing made Flapwing. From there, it was only another single letter change to the equally appropriate Flopwing. As the agricultural poet, John Clare (1793-1864), saw it

The pewet hollos chewsit as she flyes
And flops about the shepherd.

- Another evocative West Country name for the lapwing was Lymptwigg, again based on its limp wing beat.

- In the 15th and 16th centuries lapwings were recorded in household account books as Wypes, a name that imitates their piercing call.

◄ **TOO MANY CHANGES**
Many of the lapwing's current woes are summed up here: a female lapwing bravely sits tight on her nest among well-sprouted cereal even though a plough looms nearby.

'*From the grey moor, on feeble wing,*
The screaming plovers idly spring'

from *The First of April* by **Thomas Warton** (1728-1790)

Country Folklore

- In ancient pagan folklore, Eostre, the goddess of spring, was often depicted with a hare's head. The story goes that she saved a wounded lapwing by turning it into a hare. From then on it was believed that lapwing eggs were laid by hares: a myth most likely rooted in the similarity between the lapwing's shallow nest and a hare's form, its resting place.

- The festival of Eostre was celebrated around the spring equinox at the end of March. People would hunt for lapwing eggs as offerings for the goddess. Long after Christian Easter celebrations had superseded pagan rites, these traditional symbols are still part of the festivities, although now the eggs are chocolate rather than real and the mad March hare has become the cuter Easter bunny.

- In the 19th century, lapwing eggs were collected as a sought-after culinary delicacy. It took the Lapwing Act of 1926 to save and protect them.

adult black-headed gull in winter plumage

black-headed gull in first winter plumage

golden plover

▲ **MIXED FLOCKS**
In the winter, mixed flocks of lapwings, starlings, golden plovers and black-headed gulls often appear around estuaries, flood plains and gravel pits, especially on the east coast. The others take advantage of the lapwings: the gulls steal their food and, in breezy weather, starlings use them as windshields.

The Dipper

The dipper is a novelty on two counts: it is a water bird that sings like a thrush and a songbird that frequently and deliberately immerses itself in the water to find food

I f the dipper is an unfamiliar bird, imagine a giant black wren with the same stumpy tail, then give it a large, silvery bib and stand it on a rock in a stream. That is the dipper in a nutshell. It resembles the wren in other ways too: it is restless, sings all the time and builds a domed nest.

BROOK BOUND

The dipper is closely associated with shallow, swift-running streams, often in secluded mountainous or hilly countryside, with boulders in the middle of the water and trees along the banks. It takes a very harsh winter to freeze rivers and drive dippers downstream, sometimes as far as estuaries and the coast.

▶ DASHING DIPPER
One way of telling if there is a dipper in residence on a stretch of stream is to look for an accumulation of white droppings on the boulders in the water.

Taking a Bow

The dipper gets its name from the way in which it bobs up and down all the time. Whenever it lands on a rock, it does a few press ups, flexing its strong legs in a series of pert bows and curtsies while jerking its tail down at the same time. By moving continuously, it may well make itself less visible against the water rushing past it on all sides.

'Must you fly through mad waters where the heaped up granite breaks them up?'

from *The Water Ouzel* by **Harriet Monroe** (1860-1936)

Aquatic Athlete

THE DIPPER IS completely at home in water: it can wade through the shallows, float on top or swim beneath the surface and walk along the stream bed.

GETTING WET

Occasionally a dipper dives into the water from a boulder or overhanging branch, but more usually it simply walks confidently off a rock into the stream and disappears below the surface. Once submerged, it may swim through the water, using its wings to propel itself along.

But generally the dipper is more likely to walk or run along the bottom, flicking over pebbles with its beak and snapping up any morsels it disturbs before they get swept away in the current. The smaller prey is swallowed at once but larger items are taken back to the surface to be dealt with there or on a rock.

WATERPROOFING

The dipper is well adapted to its aquatic lifestyle. Its unusually thick plumage helps to keep its body dry and warm in the water. There is an extra-large preen gland on its rump,

supplying the oily secretion that a dipper regularly applies to its feathers to waterproof them.

ON THE MENU

Dippers eat a variety of water insects and their larvae, including beetles, water boatmen and dragonfly larvae, as well as freshwater snails, shrimps and worms. In summer, they take mainly caddis-fly larvae and stonefly nymphs, along with some mayfly

▲ PURPOSEFUL FLIGHT
Often the first you see of a dipper is its white breast as it flies swiftly towards you, with typically fast, deep wing beats, along a river or stream.

nymphs and blackfly larvae. In the spring, a dipper may take tadpoles and small fish such as minnows. It also looks for food among the rocks, gravelly patches and plants along the banks of a stream.

Running under Water

When walking underwater a dipper looks quite silvery because of the tiny air bubbles clinging to its feathers. This trapped air stops it getting too cold but also increases its buoyancy. It has to cling on to the pebbles on the stream bed with its strong feet to stop itself rising. The dipper heads into the current, using the flow of water over its back, tail and wings to hold it down as well. Fine-tuning the angle of its wings makes it very agile. On average, a dipper can stay submerged for as long as 23 seconds before coming up for air.

Waterside Family

EARLY IN THE year, male and female dippers are busy pairing up and sorting out their territories along a stream. Soon couples start singing and posturing vigorously to defend their exclusive claim to a stretch of water; it may be up to 2 miles or as little as 165 yards, depending on the richness of the habitat.

A lot of bobbing, blinking, chest puffing and singing goes on when territorial rivals meet. Disputes over water are much fiercer than over land. Once breeding sites have been claimed, territories are defended less vehemently. Neighbouring dippers seem to respect each other's borders and rarely trespass.

▶ **DRY SANCTUARY**
Although a pair of dippers builds its nest low down near the water, the chicks inside stay remarkably dry, sheltered from any splashing by a thick mossy canopy.

Nesting Apartment Block

It appears that the population density of dippers on a stream is often limited by the number of nest sites available. On some stretches, territories do not abut one another because of a lack of suitable nesting places.

Dippers frequently lodge their nests in chinks in the stonework of old bridges and walls beside small streams or even under bridges in towns if the river is suitable. To help more dippers find somewhere safe to build their nests, nest-boxes have been fixed on bridge supports along some rivers in Wales and northern England. The dippers were quick to adopt the new sheltered cubbyholes as alternative sites in which to nest and raise their families.

'Maybe she dreamed a nest, so safe, so dear, Where the keen spray leaps whitely to the weir; And smooth warm eggs that hold a mystery'

from *The Water Ousel* by **Mary Webb** (1881-1927)

Dipperling

Although dipper chicks hatch at the same time, they develop at different rates. The first may fledge in 20 days and the last up to four days later. If forced to quit the nest before fledging, the chicks can drop into the water and swim to safety. After fledging, their parents feed them for another week. They become fully independent 11 to 18 days after leaving the nest.

juvenile

◀ **PIECE BY PIECE**
A dipper is out and about along the stream collecting a few strands of grass to weave into its shaggy domed nest. It is always remarkably sure-footed on slippery wet rocks on the banks and in the water.

On upland streams, nesting dippers and grey wagtails can be neighbours. Sometimes, dippers adopt an old grey wagtail's nest as the foundation for their nest and grey wagtails do the reverse.

CONSTRUCTION WORK

The nest is always built over or close to water, often among the rocks in the bank protected by an overhang; on a ledge behind a waterfall; or in the roots of a waterside tree.

Working from the inside, both birds construct a bulky canopy of moss, dry grasses, lichens, bracken and ferns with a low, downward-facing entrance. The female then creates a neater cup-shaped nest inside and lines it with dry leaves.

It takes the dippers up to four weeks to build their domed nest.

Generally there is no attempt to hide it but, although the nest is clearly visible on the bank, it could easily be mistaken for a clump of flood debris caught up in the rocks or roots.

The female usually lays four or five plain white eggs, although up to eight have been recorded. She does most of the incubating for about 16 days. The male sometimes relieves her in the morning after she has done the overnight stint. Dippers sit closely but are likely to abandon the nest if disturbed.

IN THE BEGINNING

On hatching, the chicks are covered in grey down and the bright orange linings to their mouths are outlined in yellow. Given the cool, damp location of the nest, the female stays with her chicks for up to 12 days to keep them warm. As soon as they are strong enough, the fastidious young dippers start coming to the entrance of the nest and squeezing out their droppings, wrapped in a faecal sack, on to the bank below. The parent birds quickly remove the little white packages to avoid giving the location of the nest away.

ANOTHER FAMILY

Normally, a pair of dippers raises two broods a year, sometimes three. The parents start a second brood about 10 days after the first family has left the nest. After a bit of spring cleaning, the old nest is usually relined with fresh leaves and reused. However, at the beginning of each breeding season, any old nests are always dismantled and completely new ones built.

Spirit of the Foam

THE DIPPER'S LOYALTY to its home stream and supreme confidence in tumbling white water is legendary, as is its ability to keep on singing regardless of the harshest weather.

The dipper's scientific name, *Cinclus cinclus*, harks back to another bobbing bird, maybe a wagtail of some kind, that Aristotle called *kinklos*. The dipper that lives in this country is sometimes referred to as the white-throated dipper, *Cinclus cinclus gularis*, to draw attention to its dazzling white bib: the Latin for throat is *gula*.

ANGLERS' ANGER

In the 19th century, dippers were unpopular with fishermen who blamed them for eating trout and salmon spawn and reducing fish stocks in the river for future years.

Winter Wonderland

Even in the iciest winters, as long as there is some running water, a dipper stays on its home stream. Writing in *The Charm of Birds*, Viscount Grey of Fallodon (1862-1933) recalled how, one bitterly cold day he was wading slowly through deep snow drifts above a frozen river when suddenly he was heartened by the sound of a dipper's song: *from an unfrozen stream below there came up to us the sound of a dipper, singing its full song, undeterred by the conditions that were distressing all other life, unaffected by the cold, undismayed by the desolation.*

Some angling associations even offered a bounty for dipper corpses. In fact, as the dipper mostly eats aquatic insect larvae, it was never likely to have been the main culprit.

INTOLERANT NEIGHBOURS

In turn, dippers do not welcome the grey wagtail or kingfisher on their stretch of stream and can be quite aggressive if either attempts to set up a wholly overlapping territory. Sometimes, wrens and song thrushes get pushed out too.

SIGN OF WATER PURITY

The dipper favours apparently hazardous white-water habitats, because its preferred prey, aquatic insect larvae, abound in these clean, well-oxygenated torrents. It can also see its prey in the clear water.

Extensive pine reafforestation in upland Wales in the latter part of the 20th century raised the acidity levels

◄ **THROUGH THE CURTAIN**
When a dipper builds its nest behind a waterfall it has to fly through the cascade to reach it. Amazingly, it doesn't miss a wingbeat as it flies straight at the watery curtain and disappears.

of some of the streams where dippers traditionally live. Stonefly nymphs and caddisfly larvae are particularly intolerant of raised acidity. Studies showed that when stream waters become more acid, dippers are affected badly. They start breeding later, lay smaller clutches of eggs with thinner shells due to reduced calcium availability, and each brood takes longer to fledge.

OUTLOOK IS FINE

Although local dipper populations have wavered over the past 30 years, overall numbers are fairly stable. Reassuringly, dippers have been quick to colonise the old mining valleys in South Wales where water quality has improved greatly since mining ceased.

General measures to control pollution and manage the water flow on rivers and streams better are sure to be beneficial for the dipper. The only real cloud on the horizon is an ugly rumour that the predatory mink is expanding its range and has begun to catch dippers.

'Little brown surf-bather of the mountains! Spirit of foam, lover of cataracts, shaking your wings in falling waters!'

from *The Water Ouzel* by **Harriet Monroe** (1860-1936)

Lore and Legend

- Given the dipper's affinity for water, not surprisingly the word water figured in many of its local nicknames. For a long time its alternative common name was the Water Ousel or Water Blackbird, because ousel was an old-fashioned name for the blackbird. In some places, Water Ousel was contracted to the rather delightful Wizzel.

- Along with water, blackness was commonly featured in the dipper's country names: Water Crow is self-explanatory; in Water Colly, colly meant as black as coal in mining districts.

- It was also called the Water Piet, the little water pie, on account of its 'black-and-white' plumage. Piet was an old-fashioned way of writing pied. To the Irish, the dipper was the River Pie.

- In Gaelic the dipper is called *an gobha dubh nan allt*, meaning the blacksmith of the stream.

- In Welsh it is *trochwyr*. Appropriately enough, this translates into 'the immerser in water'.

- In the north of England, the dipper was better known as Bessy Ducker. This came from the Norse word *dukke* which means to dip or dive. The addition of a popular first name such as Bessy implies a special fondness for and familiarity with the bird. In Yorkshire the dipper was called Willy Fisher by fellow anglers.

The Grey Wagtail

The grey wagtail earned its nickname of Rocky Wagtail twice over by being a wobbly bird, whose tail sways up and down incessantly, and by living in rocky watery places

If you only know the grey wagtail by name, then this pretty bird with its yellow breast and ash-grey back is going to come as a pleasant surprise. It has all the charming skittishness of the pied wagtail but you are more likely to find this one flitting around streams while you are out hill-walking than see it dashing across your lawn.

WHITE WATER

The grey wagtail's favoured haunts are beside clear, fast-flowing rocky hill streams and rivers with tree-lined banks and small gravelly beaches on the bends. During the summer, it is more common in northern England and Wales than it is in central and southern England or Scotland.

▶ **FINE FATHER**
It is early summer and this male grey wagtail is standing on a rock in the middle of a stream, collecting a beakful of insects for his chicks in a nest nearby.

female

male in winter plumage

male in summer plumage

Facial Awareness

In spring and summer, an adult male wagtail has bold markings on his head: a flashy white stripe above each eye and a white moustache-like flourish on either side of his beak. He also has a bold black bib and a yellow breast, while the female's throat is pale. In winter, they are more difficult to tell apart: both have whitish throats and pale buff breasts, with any yellow confined to a vivid patch under the tail.

*'The wagtail gazed, but faltered not
In dip and sip and prinking'*

from *Wagtail and Baby* by **Thomas Hardy** (1840-1928)

Dashing Fly-chaser

DURING THE SPRING and summer, grey wagtails dash nimbly over rocks and pebbles, feasting on the swarms of gnats, midges, damselflies and other small flies that buzz and dance over the running water in upland streams.

In shallow water near the banks, a grey wagtail may get its feet wet catching stonefly and caddisfly larvae, tiny freshwater shrimps, tadpoles and small fish, such as minnows, and picking river limpets and snails off the rocks. When feeding chicks in the nest, grey wagtails may catch up to 20,000 items of food a day.

UNWAGTAIL-LIKE BEHAVIOUR

Unlike other wagtails, a grey wagtail may perch in trees during the day and catch tree-based insects and spiders as well. It takes caterpillars and sawflies living on the leaves and in the bark of such trees as alder and birch growing along the banks.

WINTERTIME

Cold snaps that are chilly enough to freeze a stream are dicey times for grey wagtails. Then they have to move downstream, to more lowland

areas. There they converge on mill-races, watercress beds, reservoir run-offs and canal locks, wherever the water gets churned up like the waters of an upland stream.

Many head for the coast, where salt water does not freeze as readily as fresh water; here they dash along the beach in crazy wagtail fashion, picking flies from seaweed.

▲ WAGTAIL COUNTRY

A stream rushing over a small waterfall or weir suits the grey wagtail. The clean, well-oxygenated water down stream supports a rich variety of aquatic insect larvae that hatch into flying insects.

Ways of Catching Flies

Generally, a grey wagtail lunges at flying insects from a rock in the middle of a stream or runs across gravel and floating water plants in hot pursuit. Occasionally, it may leap up and flutter gracefully over the water, hovering momentarily to catch a fly in mid-air. Such 'leaps' may carry the grey wagtail nearly 6 metres (20 feet) into the air to snatch insects. Watching a grey wagtail pick off a mass of mayflies emerging from the water on a summer's evening is like witnessing an aerial ballet.

fluttery fly-catching leap in the air

'*The brooklet rings its tinkling bells The swarming insects drone and hum* '

from *Midsummer* by **John Townsend Trowbridge** (1827-1916)

Waterside Nursery

AFTER A MILD winter or in a warm spring, grey wagtails may start nesting as early as mid March but generally most egg-laying takes place at the end of April.

Often the first indication of a grey wagtail's presence is its short metallic *tzi-tzi* call heard above the gushing of the stream. The male grey wagtail is not much of a singer. His song is a twittery melody which he sings from mid March to mid May as a musical backing to his courtship display.

In a spectacular song-flight, the male flutters up off his perch and slowly parachutes down, singing all the while, to show off his breeding colours at their best. Regardless of age or sex, all grey wagtails have a striking lemon-yellow patch under their tail. In spring, this yellowness floods over the male's breast in a glorious wash of sunny colour.

He fans his tail, so that its white and black feathers are clearly visible. After landing on top of a tree, he shivers his wings and takes off again. On the ground, he rushes towards the female and throws back his head to show off his black bib.

SETTING UP HOME

Grey wagtails nearly always build a nest and raise their families close to running water to be near a good source of food. A pair of grey wagtails claims a territory along the banks of a fast-flowing stream, and chases away other grey wagtails that are caught trespassing. The female usually builds her nest on a rocky ledge or in a crevice in a dry-stone wall or bank with a good overhang to shelter it from spray. Occasionally, she uses a dipper's old nest, a sand martin's tunnel or nooks in bridge supports and canal sides instead.

NEW LIFE

Grey wagtail hatchlings are covered in a golden-buff down and have

▲ **WELL TUCKED AWAY**
This male grey wagtail's mate chose a nicely sheltered but sunny spot, well screened by vegetation, in which to build her nest. Between them, the parents have reared their healthy looking brood to the threshold of fledging and flying.

Egg Cup

The female grey wagtail builds a neatly cupped nest of moss, grass and roots and gives it a snug lining of feathers, wool and hair. Into this cosy cradle in April or early May she lays four to six pale yellowish-grey eggs, which are thickly mottled with light brown. Then the female shares the incubation of her clutch with her mate for 11 to 14 days.

▶ WING BAR
The adult male grey wagtail has a conspicuous white wing bar above and below his wing.

male

◀ MATES FOR A SEASON
A male and female grey wagtail pair up and are faithful to each other for just one breeding season. In that time, they may rear two or three families together.

Roof-top Wagtails

Breeding over for another year, some grey wagtails head for towns, mainly to lakes and ponds in parks and gardens. A few make the puddles on flat roofs and in guttering their hunting grounds. Grey wagtails are seen strutting along the ridge of a roof, with their heads dipping forward at every stride. There they plunder the insects attracted to the warmth of the tiles and dig around in the gutters for food. Grey wagtails used to frequent the roofs of the stands at Lords cricket ground and Edgware tube station in London.

an orange lining to their mouths, with their beaks outlined in pale yellow flanges. The chicks spend 13 to 14 days in the nest, gobbling down thousands of insects delivered by their parents. At fledging time, when their chicks are practising their flying skills, the adults are very protective of their vulnerable young and may bravely pretend to be injured to lure predators away.

> ❛ *'Mid fall of waters, you reside,*
> *'Mid broken rocks, a rugged scene,*
> *With green and grassy dales between* ❜
>
> from *Ode to Fancy* by **Joseph Warton** (1722-1800)

yellow wagtail

Winter Watery Roosts

After the breeding season is over for another year, grey wagtails shift their areas of operation from upland watercourses and become more visible in milder lowland regions over the winter. While in transit, in July and August and again in March, grey wagtails may be seen feeding in watery haunts outside their normal range. Although grey wagtails are not sociable birds for most of the year, during the winter they do roost together in trees and reedbeds – a winter roost in Hampshire once accommodated 180 grey wagtails. Even so, they like to maintain more personal space than pied or yellow wagtails. Depending on food supply, loose feeding flocks may form in winter but each bird still defends an area to call its own.

THE YELLOW WAGTAIL (Motacilla flava)
Grey wagtails and yellow wagtails are often confused, as both are quite yellow. If you see a yellow-coloured wagtail beside a stream it is likely to be a grey wagtail, because the yellow wagtail lives mainly in damp meadows and marshes. A yellowy wagtail seen anywhere in winter is certainly a grey wagtail because yellow wagtails are only summer visitors.

CHAPTER 5 · FACTFILES

The Barn Owl

Distribution

Barn owls are patchily but broadly distributed across the British Isles. In fact, they are one of the most widely spread birds in the world, found on every continent and large island, apart from Antarctica. Usually they avoid living in mountainous regions where the weather is too harsh and are rarely found in tropical forests or desert areas.

Apart from regional differences in colour – a dark-breasted form inhabits Central Europe to the Ukraine for example – the same night-hunting bird with the heart-shaped face is familiar around the world.

Very rarely, barn owls from mainland Europe fly over to join British residents for the winter.

☐ areas where the bird stays all year

NAMES

SCIENTIFIC NAME: *Tyto alba*
NICKNAMES: White Owl, Screech Owl, Hissing Owl, Billy Wix, Jenny Owl

IDENTIFICATION

APPEARANCE: adult's wings and back are golden, speckled with silvery grey; male has pure white underparts and underwings; female's are more buff and flecked with black; juvenile has golden, silver-flecked back with buff underparts
SIZE: 33-35cm (13-14in) from beak to tail; female is larger than male
WINGSPAN: 85-93cm (34-37in)
WEIGHT: 330-400g (12-14oz)
VOICE: ranging from a rasping *hissss* to a blood-curdling shriek, which sounds like a shrill *kee-yak*, and an eerie snore

FOOD

Eats small mammals, particularly short-tailed voles, common shrews and field mice; also takes frogs and fledglings

BEHAVIOUR

Largely nocturnal, hunting in the dark; nest sites are vigorously defended
ENEMIES: cold and wet weather, modern farming methods, pesticides, particularly rodent poisons, and cars

BREEDING

PAIRING UP: in early spring, the male and female find a sheltered roost together in an abandoned building or hollow tree
NEST: the female scrapes out a slight hollow in a tree-hole or on a dark ledge or beam in a barn or outbuilding
EGGS: In April or May, 4-7 matt white, oval eggs, 38-46mm (1½-1¾in) long, are laid at 2-3 day intervals on a bed of regurgitated waste pellets
INCUBATION: the female incubates from the first egg; each one hatches 32-34 days after it is laid, resulting in a brood of different ages and sizes
YOUNG: on hatching, each chick is scantily covered in a white fluffy down; the female stays with the chicks for 2-3 weeks, to keep them warm and feed them food the male brings her; then she goes hunting too, until the chicks are fledged in 2-3 months
MOULT: gradual replacement of major wing and tail feathers over 3-4 years
LIFE EXPECTANCY: average lifespan is 18 months; few live longer than 5 years

POPULATION IN BRITAIN

Fewer than 4000 pairs breed each year

HABITAT

Favours open grassland, especially on coastal marshes, farmland, hedge banks and verges, to hunt over at night, with sheltered roosts in deserted farm buildings, church towers or hollow trees nearby

NATURE WATCH

● In early spring, listen out for male barn owls screeching at night. Their shrieks are much eerier than the tawny owl's hooting: a drawn-out *kee-yak*.
● Any barn owl spied in the headlights in late spring, early summer is likely to be a male. If you get a good look, you'll see that his white breast is unmarked.

The Bullfinch

NAMES

SCIENTIFIC NAME: *Pyrrhula pyrrhula*
NICKNAMES: Bully, Alpe, Coal Hood, Budpicker, Budfinch, Blood Hoop

IDENTIFICATION

APPEARANCE: adult male has startling pink-vermilion underparts and a grey back; adult females have muted greyish-pink underparts and a brown back; both have heavy black beaks, black skullcaps and tails, obvious white rumps and black wings with a single white wing bar; juvenile is browny and lacks black head
SIZE: 14-16cm (5½-6½in) long
WINGSPAN: 16-18cm (6½-7in)
WEIGHT: 21-27g (⅔-1oz)
FLIGHT: low, slow and undulating
VOICE: low whistling *deu-deu* call; in spring male sings a quiet, hesitant medley of wheezes, creaks and whistles

FOOD

Consumes seeds and fruits; when food is short in late winter, early spring eats buds on fruit trees and shrubs in the garden or visits bird-tables; young fed on insects, spiders and snails as well

BEHAVIOUR

Never ventures far from cover; very stealthy at breeding time when trying not to draw attention to its nest
ENEMIES: nests are preyed on by all the usual suspects: jays, magpies, weasels and stoats, squirrels and cats

BREEDING

PAIRING UP: from late April to July or August; forms lifelong pair bonds; generally raises 2 families each year
NESTING: female builds a platform of interlaced twigs with a shallow cup lined with rootlets and hair in the centre in thick cover; male may help to gather material
EGGS: lays 4-6 green-blue eggs with purplish-brown streaks and spots
INCUBATION: female sits fast for 12-14 days, attended by male
YOUNG: nestlings have long grey down; inside of mouth is pink with yellow flanges; fed by both parents, who usually visit the nest together; fed on a porridge of seeds and insects, regurgitated from food pouches in cheeks; gradually weaned on to seeds; fledged in 2 weeks
MOULT: after the breeding season
LIFE EXPECTANCY: 2-4 years

POPULATION IN BRITAIN

Fewer than 200,000 breed each year

Distribution

The bullfinch is an increasingly rare resident throughout most of the British Isles. It was always scarcer in northern parts of Scotland.

It is widely distributed in Europe, although notably absent from much of southern Spain and Portugal, and in northern Scandinavia. The European bullfinch's range extends east through Asia to Japan.

British residents rarely roam far from their birthplace. In Scotland and northeast England, resident bullfinches may be joined by visitors from Scandinavia for the winter. Scandinavian bullfinches are larger; the cock birds have brighter pink breasts and the hen birds are generally paler.

☐ areas where the bird stays all year
☐ areas where the bird is a summer visitor
☐ areas where the bird is a winter visitor

HABITAT

Resides in woodland, hedgerows, parks, orchards, churchyards and gardens

NATURE WATCH

● The bullfinch's chunky physique, with its big head and thick neck, and square patch of dazzling white rump above the black tail feathers are defining features.
● Planting seed-headed flowers and berry-bearing shrubs and climbers in gardens and parks can help bullfinches get through the winter.

The Cuckoo

NAMES
SCIENTIFIC NAME: *Cuculus canorus*
NICKNAMES: Gowk, Gawky, Geck

IDENTIFICATION
APPEARANCE: adult male and female are indistinguishable in the wild: ash-grey head, breast and upperparts; long narrow pointed wings; underparts barred grey with black lines; long tail with white spots and tip, barred below; small head with yellow eyes and downturned beak; yellow legs and feet, two toes forwards, two back; juvenile plumage is a rich brown with white edges
SIZE: 32-34cm (12⅔-13½in) long
WINGSPAN: 55-65cm (22-26in)
WEIGHT: 100-130g (4-5¼oz)
FLIGHT: flies low with its head held high; wings carried below midline of body
VOICE: male utters *cuc-koo, cuc-koo* call; female makes a bubbling call

FOOD
Especially fond of eating hairy caterpillars; also takes other insects, such as beetles and grasshoppers, and worms

BEHAVIOUR
It is a brood parasite, commandeering the nests of small, insect-eating birds to lay its eggs in and leaving its chicks to be raised by foster parents (the hosts)
MIGRATION: summer visitor to Britain; spends the winter in sub-Saharan Africa

BREEDING
PAIRING UP: promiscuous rather than paired; female attracts males with her bubbling calls; after mating she seeks nests to lay her eggs in, but does not stop to brood her eggs or rear her chicks
NESTING: does not build a nest; uses nests belonging to other birds; a female usually targets the same type of bird
EGGS: relatively small; lays up to a total of 25, each one in a different nest; eggs are usually streaky and sometimes mimic the host's
INCUBATION: leaves incubation to foster parents; hatches in 12 days
YOUNG: chick bare, with strong wing stumps and hollow in back which it uses to heave other eggs or nestlings out of the nest; huge orange gape and hissing spur foster parents to feed it; fledged in 17-21 days; fed for another week or so
MOULT: adults moult when back in Africa
LIFE EXPECTANCY: probably 4-5 years

POPULATION IN BRITAIN
About 24,000 breed each year

Distribution
After spending the winter in Africa, south of the Sahara Desert, the cuckoo is a common and widely distributed summer visitor to Britain. On their return journey, cuckoos reach southern Europe early in spring and generally arrive in southern England by 14 April and in Yorkshire by 21 April.

In July or early August, after breeding, the adults head back to sunny Africa for the winter again. Young cuckoos follow in late August or September. How they navigate the journey of roughly 3000 miles for the first time is still a mystery. They probably have an in-built awareness about heading south and learn their route back on the way.

☐ areas where the bird is a summer visitor
▨ migration route to Africa for the winter

HABITAT
Lives on farmland, heathland and moorland, in reedbeds and woodland

NATURE WATCH
● With its grey upperparts, long tail, barred breast and downcurved beak, the cuckoo can be mistaken for a sparrowhawk in flight. Although they both fly low, the cuckoo's wings are pointed, whereas the sparrowhawk's are rounded.
● At first glance, the cuckoo's thin, pointed wings, especially those of a red-brown juvenile, may be confused with a kestrel's in the air.

The Dartford Warbler

Distribution

The dry lowland heathland in southern England lies at the northern limit of the Dartford warbler's range. Even so, Dartford warblers stay in Britain for the winter: in extended snowy spells, they may come close to being wiped out.

In recent years, the Dartford warbler has been expanding its range north and east from its strongholds in Dorset, the New Forest in Hampshire and Surrey. There are growing colonies in Cornwall, Devon, Sussex, Kent and Suffolk.

The global population of Dartford warblers fluctuates between 2 and 4 million pairs. Most breed in Spain and France, a few in Portugal and Italy. Some migrate from Spain to spend the winter in North Africa.

☐ areas where the bird stays all year
☐ areas where the bird is a winter visitor

NAMES
SCIENTIFIC NAME: *Sylvia undata*
NICKNAME: Furze Wren

IDENTIFICATION
APPEARANCE: the male has a dark brown-grey back, dark grey head and wine-coloured underparts with white speckles on a rusty-brown throat; he has a bright orange eye and red eye-ring; the female is paler and browner; the juvenile is paler and duller still; all have a long dark tail, short rounded wings, spiky beak and dull yellow legs and feet
SIZE: 12.5cm (5in) long
WINGSPAN: 13-18.5cm (5¼-7½in)
WEIGHT: 9-12g (⅓-½oz)
FLIGHT: wobbly and bouncy
VOICE: song is a scratchy warble; call is a distinctive low buzzing *chrrr*

FOOD
Finds insects and spiders on gorse, heather and bracken

BEHAVIOUR
Shy and elusive during the breeding season; adults form into small flocks in the autumn and stay on their nesting grounds all year round; a few drift from east to west over the winter

ENEMIES: foxes, cats and dogs, crows and snakes; loss of habitat; heathland fires; snowy weather

BREEDING
PAIRING UP: between March and July; rears 2, maybe 3 broods a year
NESTING: female builds a nest of stems, roots, grass and moss and lines it with horsehair, wool and plant down, close to the ground in clumps of gorse or heather
EGGS: usually lays 3-5 pale eggs marked with grey or brown
INCUBATION: mainly by the female for 11-13 days
YOUNG: hatchlings are naked; mouth lining is orange-yellow marked by two brown spots, outlined in yellow flanges; fed by both parents; leave the nest after 14 days with short tails, which grow to full length in about 10 days; disperse to new locations in autumn
MOULT: undergoes a late summer moult
LIFE EXPECTANCY: up to 5 years

POPULATION IN BRITAIN
Between 1500 and 2000 pairs breed in southern England every year; numbers fluctuate, depending on the severity of the winter chill, but are increasing

HABITAT
Favours sandy lowland heathland, which had been shrinking fast but is now protected in nature reserves; needs well-managed gorse and heather bushes for shelter, food and nesting

NATURE WATCH
● In spring, look out for an excitable pixie-like bird that suddenly appears amid the gorse to deliver a burst of song. The constant wagging and pumping of his extraordinarily long tail is most conspicuous. When he flies off, it trails after him like a streamer.

The Dipper

Distribution

Dippers are largely found on the fast flowing streams in upland regions of northern England, Wales, Scotland and Ireland. They also live on moorland streams in the West Country but are rarely seen in southeast England. In mountainous areas, where the rivers drop steeply down to the sea, dippers may be found not far from the coast.

Most British dippers are resident throughout their range, except during severe winters or heavy flooding. Dippers from Scandinavia do wander south for the winter and may turn up on the east coast of the British Isles.

The dipper occurs on hill-streams from Spain across Europe through Turkey to the Himalayas and Siberia.

☐ areas where the bird stays all year
☐ areas where the bird is a summer visitor
☐ areas where the bird is a winter visitor

NAMES
SCIENTIFIC NAME: *Cinclus cinclus*
NICKNAMES: Water Ouzel, Bessy Ducker

IDENTIFICATION
APPEARANCE: the adult male and female both look like a large, dark wren with a white bib; the crown is chocolate-brown and the back is dark slate-grey with touches of black; a snowy white throat and chest merge into a chestnut band across the belly which gradually darkens towards the stumpy tail; juveniles are much greyer and their bibs are less obvious
SIZE: 18cm (7in) long
WINGSPAN: 25-30cm (10-12in)
WEIGHT: 55-75g (2-2¾oz)
FLIGHT: short wings beat very fast as it flies up and down, low over the stream
VOICE: male and female sing brightly for most of the year; call is a loud *zit-zit-zit*

FOOD
Has a novel way of finding food by submerging itself in fast-flowing upland streams and walking along the bottom, turning over pebbles to dislodge aquatic insect larvae, worms, freshwater shrimps and snails; also looks for insects in the vegetation along the banks

BEHAVIOUR
Largely solitary, territorial bird, except during the breeding season; bobs and bows restlessly when it lands on rocks in the middle of a stream
ENEMIES: pollution and possibly mink

BREEDING
PAIRING UP: in mild springs, nests early, from February or March to July; usually raises 2, sometimes 3 broods a year
NESTING: both male and female stuff a bulky ball-shaped nest of moss, dry grass and lichens lined with dry leaves into a crevice between waterside rocks or tree roots, under bridges or behind a waterfall; there is a downward-facing entrance near the bottom
EGGS: lays 4 or 5 plain white eggs
INCUBATION: the female does most of the incubating for 16 days
YOUNG: nestlings are covered with grey down and have orange linings to their mouths outlined with yellow flanges; chicks are fledged in 20-24 days
MOULT: feathers renewed after breeding
LIFE EXPECTANCY: up to 5 years

POPULATION IN BRITAIN
Roughly 18,000 pairs breed each year

HABITAT
Restricted to clear, fast-flowing streams, mainly in upland regions; mostly stays on the same stretch of stream all year

NATURE WATCH
● The combination of the dipper's size, colouring, habits and habitat makes it unique. Possibly, a glimpse of a ring ouzel (a blackbird-like bird with a white breast-band), especially the browner female, beside an upland stream in summer could be mistaken for a dipper.

The Fieldfare

Distribution

Fieldfares are regular and common winter visitors to the British Isles, arriving in October and leaving again in April. There are usually rather more of them in the north and east of England than in the south and west, although they do roam in search of food.

Fieldfares are resident in central and eastern Europe. Most of the fieldfares that visit Britain during the winter spend their summer breeding or being reared across northern Europe, in Scandinavia and Russia.

The fieldfare's breeding range extends eastwards across most of Asia and westwards through Holland into eastern France, southwards through Germany and the forest belt to Switzerland.

☐ areas where the bird stays all year
☐ areas where the bird is a summer visitor
▨ areas where the bird is a winter visitor

NAMES
SCIENTIFIC NAME: *Turdus pilaris*
NICKNAMES: Blue Back, Grey Thrush

IDENTIFICATION
APPEARANCE: the male and female look similar: both have a grey head, pale chestnut breast with dark spots, rich chestnut back and wings, a grey rump and long black tail; the beak is yellow with a black tip; juveniles are spottier
SIZE: 25.5cm (10in) long
WINGSPAN: 39-42cm (15½-16¾in)
WEIGHT: 80-130g (2¾-4½oz)
FLIGHT: bursts of wingbeats interrupted by brief open- and closed-wing glides
VOICE: song is a tuneless medley of whistles, squeaks and chuckles, rarely heard in this country; a harsh *cha-cha-chak* call as it takes flight and is flying

FOOD
As a winter visitor, it feasts on autumn berries and windfall apples; also probes ploughed fields and pastures for worms, snails and slugs, insects and spiders; only visits gardens in harsh weather

BEHAVIOUR
Highly sociable thrushes, nesting in small colonies and feeding in winter flocks of 30 to 200 birds, often with redwings, blackbirds and starlings
ENEMIES: bad weather, migration flights, gulls, hawks, owls, crows and martens

BREEDING
PAIRING UP: fieldfares from Britain breed in northern Europe from June to August; most rear 1 brood a year, some 2
NESTING: nest built in the fork of a tree from woven grasses, moss and twigs held together with mud and lined with fine grass
EGGS: lays 4-7 pale blue eggs lightly dusted with reddish brown
INCUBATION: unusually, the female starts incubating about halfway through laying her clutch and sits for 10-12 days
YOUNG: hatchlings are covered in buff down; fed copious worms, slugs and snails; often leave the nest unfledged, 12 days after hatching and fly in 16 days
MOULT: in Scandinavia from July to September before migrating; adults have a full moult but youngsters just moult their head and body feathers
LIFESPAN: 5-10 years

POPULATION IN BRITAIN
Up to 1 million spend the winter here, arriving in October, leaving again in April

HABITAT
Lives in woodland fringes and hedges; feeds in ploughed fields and pastures

NATURE WATCH
● There is no obvious reason why fieldfares should not breed in Britain but probably fewer than 25 pairs regularly fledge young here. As colonial nesters, it may be this very scarcity that is holding them back. Fieldfares are breeding in northern France; if enough vagrants hop over the English Channel they may set up a viable breeding colony in the south.

The Green Woodpecker

Distribution

Green woodpeckers are widely distributed residents over England and Wales, but scarcer in Scotland and absent from Ireland and the Isle of Man. Their range is shrinking from the west, where numbers have been falling in the West Country and parts of Wales.

The green woodpecker is widespread in Europe, although it is not found on Iceland, in northern Scandinavia or on islands in the Mediterranean.

Over much of France, Germany and southern Scandinavia there is another slightly smaller greenish woodpecker, the grey-headed woodpecker. The male has a red forehead but is dull grey rather than pale green and yellow like the green woodpecker.

☐ areas where the bird stays all year

NAMES
SCIENTIFIC NAME: *Picus viridis*
NICKNAMES: Yaffle, Highhoe, Rain Bird, Wood Spite, Wood Awl and many others

IDENTIFICATION
APPEARANCE: sexes look similar, except the male has red moustachial markings while the female's are black; both have a scarlet crown, grass green back and wings, paler green underparts and golden rump; pale eyes and long pointed beak; juvenile has a red cap but dark streaked underside, white spotted upperparts and no black around the eyes
SIZE: 30-33cm (12-13in) long
WINGSPAN: 40-42cm (16-16½in)
WEIGHT: 180-220g (6-8oz)
FLIGHT: extremely undulating
VOICE: instantly recognisable *kleu-kleu-kleu* laugh; harsh *keu-keu-kook* flight call; male occasionally drums on hollow branches to broadcast his presence

FOOD
Does hunt for insects on trees but feeds mainly on the ground; is particularly partial to ants and uses its long sticky tongue to scoop them out of the nest; also consumes nuts, fruit and acorns in the winter

BEHAVIOUR
Solitary, except during the breeding season; easily recognised from loud cackling cries and switchback flight
ENEMIES: starlings pirate their nest holes; squirrels steal their eggs

BREEDING
PAIRING UP: from April to the first half of July; noisy courtship involves aerial chases; rears only 1 brood per year
NESTING: prefers to adopt a ready-made tree-hole but, if necessary, both birds excavate a large hole in a dead or rotting tree; floor of nesting chamber is lined with wood chippings
EGGS: lays 5-7 pure white eggs
INCUBATION: both male and female sit for 18-19 days
YOUNG: hatchlings are helpless and naked; both parents feed their chicks on insects; fledglings leave the nest after 23-26 days; for another 3-7 weeks they accompany their parents everywhere
MOULT: changes feathers in the autumn
LIFE EXPECTANCY: from 5-10 years

POPULATION IN BRITAIN
Up to 15,000 breed each year (there are no green woodpeckers in Ireland)

HABITAT
A bird of open woodland and parkland with mature deciduous trees and grassy areas; visits gardens to probe the lawn for insects and ants

NATURE WATCH
● Its 'laughing' call on take-off is an early-warning sign that there is a green woodpecker in the locality. A sighting of its undulating flight and, with any luck, a view of its yellow rump confirms it.
● The green woodpecker or golden oriole question almost always has to come down in favour of the woodpecker, which is a much more common bird.

The Grey Partridge

Distribution

Grey partridges were once very common and widespread on arable farmland and short grassland in lowland Britain – most abundant in East Anglia and rarer in Wales and Scotland. However, changes in farming methods have made life much tougher for them and numbers have fallen alarmingly.

Partridges are hardy birds that never wander far from home or migrate. They are found from northern Spain, across Europe, as far as Finland in the north and central Asia in the east. The grey partridge has also been introduced into Canada and the United States, where it is often known as the Hungarian partridge because many of the original birds came from eastern Europe.

NAMES
SCIENTIFIC NAME: *Perdix perdix*
NICKNAMES: Common or English Partridge

IDENTIFICATION
APPEARANCE: male and female are neat, round birds with grey underparts, streaked brown backs and wings and short chestnut tails; a mature male has a brown horseshoe-shaped patch on his belly and an orange face; the female is duller, with a smaller or no breast mark; juveniles are browner and streakier
SIZE: 28-32cm (11¼-12¾in) long
WINGSPAN: 45-48cm (18-19¼in)
WEIGHT: 350-400g (12½-14oz)
FLIGHT: whirring wings and bowed wing glides; usually flies under 500m (550yd), rarely farther than 1¼ miles
VOICE: creaky *keev-it, keev-it* call; frantic *it-it-it* in flight; sharp rallying *fi-sack*

FOOD
Adults feed mainly on shoots, leaves, grain, weed seeds and berries and a few slugs and worms; chicks need a plentiful supply of small insects for first 10 days

BEHAVIOUR
Territorial during the breeding season; otherwise a sociable bird, living in a small flock known as a covey

ENEMIES: intensive farming methods, loss of hedges, pesticides; hooves and farm machinery; nest-robbing predators

BREEDING
PAIRING UP: in January or February; rears only 1 brood a year
NESTING: hen scratches out a shallow hollow in the ground and lines it with dry grass and leaves; well-concealed under a hedge or among a cereal crop
EGGS: lays 10-25 olive-buff eggs, the largest clutch of any land bird in the UK
INCUBATION: female sits for 24-25 days
YOUNG: as soon as the chicks' buff and brown streaked down is dry, they are up and running; both parents are extremely attentive; youngsters are fledged and flying by day 15 but do not reach their adult weight until they are 100 days old
MOULT: generally in the summer, but often moulting for much of the year
LIFE EXPECTANCY: up to 5 years

POPULATION IN BRITAIN
Fewer than 150,000 pairs now breed each year; due to loss and degradation of its habitat, numbers fell by 90 per cent in the last quarter of 20th century

☐ areas where the bird stays all year

HABITAT
Found mainly on well-managed arable farmland but also on sand dunes

NATURE WATCH
● Although adult pheasants and partridges look very different, their small, brown juveniles are harder to tell apart.
● Conservation groups, landowners and farmers are collaborating to halt the grey partridge's decline. They aim to control predators, create more nesting cover and a reliable food supply, especially during the breeding season, as well as delay spraying and grass-cutting until the chicks are fledged.

The Grey Wagtail

Distribution

The grey wagtail is widely distributed over Britain. There are generally more grey wagtails in northern and western areas in the summer, when it is scarce in or absent from the lowland eastern and Midland counties.

In winter, most grey wagtails move south to be near moving water or sewage farms, watercress beds and coastal marshes; some settle around garden ponds and on rooftops. Grey wagtails from other parts of Europe may go as far as Africa for the winter.

Grey wagtails breed throughout most of Europe, although are surprisingly absent from much of Scandinavia. Their range extends through Turkey, Iran and Kashmir as far east as Japan and China.

☐ areas where the bird stays all year
☐ areas where the bird is a summer visitor
☐ areas where the bird is a winter visitor

HABITAT
Lives beside fast-flowing streams and rivers during the summer; moves south to lowland waters for the winter

NAMES
SCIENTIFIC NAME: *Motacilla cinerea*
NICKNAMES: Grey Wagster, Rocky Wagtail

IDENTIFICATION
APPEARANCE: all have a bright yellow patch under a long black tail with white trim and a grey back and head; in the summer, the male has a yellow breast and black bib while the female's underside is paler; in winter males and females are both pale; juveniles are even paler and more buff
SIZE: 18-20cm (7-8in) long
WINGSPAN: 25-27cm (10-10¾in)
WEIGHT: 14-22g (½-¾oz)
FLIGHT: very undulating with the long tail exaggerating the waviness
VOICE: sharp metallic *tzi-tzi* call heard on streams; twittery song in courtship

FOOD
Hunts for insects flying beside and over water, in trees and on roofs; picks up aquatic insect larvae, small freshwater shrimps and snails from the water

BEHAVIOUR
Usually seen in ones or twos, flitting and bobbing about near water; forms loose roosting and feeding flocks in winter
ENEMIES: freezing weather; pollution and habitat destruction

BREEDING
PAIRING UP: from mid March to June; rears 2, maybe 3 broods a year; male performs a splendid courtship display, fluttering up and parachuting down with tail fanned to impress female
NESTING: female builds a nest cup from moss and grass and lines it with wool and hair; usually on a rocky ledge or crevice in a bank, cliff or wall near running water
EGGS: lays 4-6 yellowy-grey eggs mottled with brown
INCUBATION: shared by both sexes for 11-14 days
YOUNG: hatchlings are covered in a buffish down with an orange lining to their mouths rimmed with a pale yellow flange; both parents hunt insects to feed them; youngsters fledge in 13-14 days
MOULT: in the summer after breeding
LIFE EXPECTANCY: up to 5 years

POPULATION IN BRITAIN
Roughly 50,000 pairs breed each year; population fell in 1970s but is now stable

NATURE WATCH
● To avoid mistaking a grey wagtail for a yellow one, look at the bird's back: it is grey in a grey wagtail and olive-green in a yellow wagtail. The grey wagtail also has brown rather than black legs, a much longer, black tail and a broad pale bar, visible on each wing in flight, that the yellow wagtail lacks.

The Kestrel

Distribution

Kestrels are common and familiar over a wide range of habitats throughout the British Isles and in much of Europe, Africa and Asia. They benefited from woodland clearance to create grazing for sheep and cattle: the grass is home to the rodents they hunt.

Family groups disperse in late summer, but the juvenile kestrels rarely roam far, at least for the first year. In autumn there is a general drift from north to south. Ireland is a winter refuge for kestrels based in northern England and Scotland. Food shortages and bad weather may produce a localised movement to lower ground. On the northeast coast of England the kestrel is a regular winter migrant from Scandinavia.

☐ areas where the bird stays all year
☐ areas where the bird is a summer visitor

NAMES
SCIENTIFIC NAME: *Falco tinnunculus*
NICKNAMES: Windhover, Cress Hawk and Stanniel are three of many

IDENTIFICATION
APPEARANCE: male is smaller than female with a blue-grey head, nape and rump; grey tail has a broad black band near white tip; buff underparts flecked with black and a russet brown back and wings spotted with black; juvenile looks like adult female (above) – brown with black bars and flecks
SIZE: 32-35cm (12-14in) long
WINGSPAN: 71-80cm (28-32in)
WEIGHT: 136-314g (5-11oz)
FLIGHT: shows incredible control while hovering and diving
VOICE: generally quite quiet, except in the breeding season when the pair use noisy *keelie-keelie-kee-kee-kee* calls

FOOD
Hunts for small mammals, especially rodents, mainly voles, birds, frogs, lizards, insects and worms, by hovering in the air, from a perch or on the ground

BEHAVIOUR
Frequently hovers, as if suspended in mid-air, with raised wings and fanned tail for hunting; largely solitary, except during the breeding season; may mate for life
ENEMIES: changes in farming methods, birds of prey, bad weather and traffic

BREEDING
PAIRING UP: breeds from mid April to July; rears just 1 brood a year
NESTING: adopts an old magpie, crow or squirrel nest, or uses a tree-hole, ledge or crevice on a cliff or building
EGGS: lays 4 or 5 whitish eggs densely spattered with rusty brown
INCUBATION: chiefly by the female for about 28 days
YOUNG: hatchlings are covered in wispy white down which becomes darker; male brings food to nest at first, while the hen broods the nestlings; when the chicks are bigger, both parents hunt; fledglings are ready to fly the nest in 27-34 days
MOULT: feather replacement is spread over several months from May to October so the ability to fly is never lost
LIFE EXPECTANCY: up to 15 years

POPULATION IN BRITAIN
Currently about 60,000 pairs breed each year but numbers are declining rapidly

HABITAT
Lives in a wide range of open habitats, from seaside cliffs to moorland, farmland to city parks, gardens and wasteland

NATURE WATCH
● Look out for nest-boxes attached to posts beside motorways, which solved the problem of kestrel chicks being swept from nests under motorway bridges on to the road below.
● Hunting along motorways has paid off for the kestrel, which has become a favourite with people who admire its flying skills and want to protect it.

The Kingfisher

Distribution

The European or common kingfisher is widely but patchily distributed along lowland streams, rivers and canals, on ponds, lakes and flooded quarries all over the British Isles, although absent in the north of Scotland.

Farther afield, the kingfisher's range extends throughout most of Europe and southern Asia, as far east as Japan. There are 86 different species of kingfisher worldwide, including the kookaburra in Australia.

In Britain during harsh winters, many kingfishers make their way to the coast, where the salty water is less likely to freeze than the shallow freshwater in their regular haunts. If the water surface ices over, the kingfisher cannot fish.

☐ areas where the bird stays all year
☐ areas where the bird is a summer visitor
☐ areas where the bird is a winter visitor

NAMES
SCIENTIFIC NAME: *Alcedo atthis*
NICKNAMES: Dipper in Shropshire, Fisher in Yorkshire

IDENTIFICATION
APPEARANCE: adult has chestnut-orange breast and iridescent blue-green back, wings and head; the feet are bright red; the male's beak is all black, the female has a reddish lower bill; juvenile is duller with a white tip to its black beak
SIZE: unique silhouette with dagger-like beak and stumpy tail; 15-17cm (6-6½in) long, including 4cm (1½in) beak
WINGSPAN: 25cm (10in)
WEIGHT: 27-30g (1oz)
FLIGHT: straight, swift and low over the water; rapidly beating wings generate a whirring sound
VOICE: distinctive short shrill piping call of *chee* repeated two or three times; *shrit-it-it* is used as a warning call

FOOD
Dives for small fish, particularly minnows and sticklebacks, but also takes frogs, snails and insects, mainly dragonflies

BEHAVIOUR
Roosts in cover near water; except during the breeding season, kingfishers are loners
ENEMIES: not many, as the colourful plumage warns predators that its flesh tastes vile; icy conditions are a killer

BREEDING
PAIRING UP: male and female get together in the middle to end of February; raises 2-3 broods a year, depending on the weather, from late March to July
NESTING: male and female excavate a 60cm (2ft) long upward-angled nesting tunnel in sandy or muddy banks beside the water
EGGS: lays 6-8 shiny white roundish eggs on a spiky platform of regurgitated fish bones and scales in a chamber at the end of the nesting tunnel
INCUBATION: both parents share the sitting for 19-21 days
YOUNG: hatch featherless; fed by both parents, they leave the nest 23-27 days later; soon have to fend for themselves
MOULT: after the breeding season, adults lose and replace their old feathers
LIFE EXPECTANCY: on average 2 years

POPULATION
Roughly 6000 pairs breed each year

HABITAT
Lives on stretches of clear slow-moving or still fresh water – tree-lined streams and rivers, canals and flooded gravel pits

NATURE WATCH
● As more worked-out gravel and sand pits are left to flood, kingfishers are finding new places to live.
● Fortunately, kingfishers are prolific breeders and, given a few favourable summers, can restore the population losses following a severe winter.

The Lapwing

Distribution

Although the lapwing is still the most common and widespread wader in the British Isles, its numbers have declined drastically in the past 30 years, due largely to changes in farming methods.

Most British lapwings stay here all year round. Even so, over the winter the population is in a constant state of flux as lapwings come and go: many arrive from northern Europe; ice and snow drives others south and west, to Ireland, France, as far as Spain. Most return soon after a thaw.

Lapwings breed across northern and eastern Europe, from the Arctic Circle to the Black Sea. Winter movements take them south to the Mediterranean and North Africa, India and east to Japan.

☐ areas where the bird stays all year
☐ areas where the bird is a summer visitor
☐ areas where the bird is a winter visitor

NAMES
SCIENTIFIC NAME: *Vanellus vanellus*
NICKNAMES: Green Plover, Peewit

IDENTIFICATION
APPEARANCE: the male and female look similar, with an iridescent green back, white underparts and a cinnamon patch under the tail; he has a black throat, she has more white on her neck; his wispy crest is longer than hers; juvenile looks like a scaly adult with buff fringes to its dark feathers and a shorter crest
SIZE: 28-31cm (11¼-12½in) long
WINGSPAN: 82-87cm (32¾-34¾in)
WEIGHT: 140-320g (5-11½oz)
FLIGHT: erratic, floppy wing beats flicker black and white; speedy in direct flight; male has a spectacular nuptial display
VOICE: strongly associated with its melancholy whistling *pee-wit* call

FOOD
Seeks earthworms, insects, spiders, centipedes, slugs and snails in soft soil, mud and grassland; also eats small frogs, fish, crabs and the odd berry

BEHAVIOUR
Territorial during the breeding season but forms large mobile flocks in autumn; in icy winters, moves south and west to Ireland and western Europe
ENEMIES: gulls, crows, badgers, foxes, dogs, hedgehogs, modern farming

BREEDING
PAIRING UP: male performs an exciting aerial courtship display in March and April; usually rears only 1 brood a year
NESTING: male scratches out shallow hollows on top of slight mounds on open ground; his mate lines one with grass
EGGS: lays 4 pear-shaped buff-to-olive eggs with dark speckles and blotches
INCUBATION: by female for 21-28 days
YOUNG: as soon as the chicks' mottled brown-and-black down is dry, their mother leads them into cover to feed; they squat and freeze on hearing a parental alarm call; parents guard the chicks bravely for 35-40 days until they are fledged and can fly
MOULT: post-breeding; pale edges on new feathers wear off over the winter, revealing a glossy iridescence by spring
LIFE EXPECTANCY: up to 10 years

POPULATION IN BRITAIN
From 190,000 to 240,000 pairs breed each year; up to 2 million winter here

HABITAT
Widespread on open farmland, marshes and saltmarshes throughout the year; gathers on estuaries and along coasts in the winter; prefers expanses of patchy bare earth and tufty grass for breeding

NATURE WATCH
● Even at long range, the slow, steady flapping action of the broad, rounded wings is very distinctive, especially when seen as a flickering mass of seemingly black and white in a large flock.

The Mallard

Distribution

Mallards are the most common and widespread duck on stretches of fresh water across the northern hemisphere: in the British Isles, over mainland Europe, Asia and North America. They have also been introduced to Australia and New Zealand.

Those that breed in Britain rarely move far to feed. In harsh winters some may gravitate to estuaries and saltmarshes around the coast to avoid frozen pools. There they are joined by numerous incomers from Scandinavia and eastern Europe that overwinter in Britain. The visitors stay until the following March, then move north again in a series of short hops to reach their breeding quarters by the end of April.

☐ areas where the bird stays all year
☐ areas where the bird is a summer visitor
☐ areas where the bird is a winter visitor

HABITAT
Lives near any kind of water from lakes, ponds and canals to rivers, streams, estuaries and saltmarshes

NATURE WATCH
● Mallards are often found with other ducks. One way to distinguish between the drakes is to look at their heads: the mallard's is bottle-green, the pintail's dark brown with a white stripe, the teal's chestnut with green stripes outlined in yellow and the gadwall's dull brown.

NAMES
SCIENTIFIC NAME: *Anas platyrhynchos*
NICKNAMES: Wild or Common Duck

IDENTIFICATION
APPEARANCE: for breeding, drake has green head, purple-brown breast and white dog-collar (above); in his 'eclipse plumage' during a double summer moult he looks like a drab female with mottled brown plumage; juveniles look like females; all have violet-blue wing flashes
SIZE: 50-65cm (20-25in)
WINGSPAN: 81-95cm (32-37in)
WEIGHT: 0.75-1.5kg (1¾-3¼lb)
FLIGHT: swift, strong and agile; rises straight off the water or ground
VOICE: female utters a loud *quack-quack*; males have a huskier *queck* and whistle during courtship; ducklings *peep*

FOOD
Mainly a surface feeder, filtering small plants, insects, slugs, snails and worms from water and mud through its beak; sometimes up-ends to dabble on the bottom; gobbles up stale bread in parks

BEHAVIOUR
Gregarious for most of the year, feeding and travelling in flocks

ENEMIES: foxes, rats, cats, pike, hawks, coots, swans, herons and shoots

BREEDING
PAIRING UP: courtship starts the previous autumn; nests from March to July; usually rears just 1 brood a year; the whole burden of nest-building and chick-rearing falls to the female as the male withdraws to moult
NESTING: female selects a quiet place in thick vegetation where she scratches out a shallow hollow which she fills with grass and leaves and lines with feathers plucked from her own breast
EGGS: lays 10-12 greenish-blue eggs
INCUBATION: female sits for 28-29 days
YOUNG: clad in khaki and yellow down with a dark eye-stripe, ducklings are ready for action only hours after hatching; closely chaperoned by their mother; fledged and flying in 7-8 weeks
MOULT: drake's double moult starts in June and lasts until September; the duck moults after rearing her ducklings
LIFE EXPECTANCY: 15-25 years

POPULATION IN BRITAIN
About 150,000 pairs breed each year; numbers are on the increase

The Meadow Pipit

NAMES

SCIENTIFIC NAME: *Anthus pratensis*
NICKNAMES: Mipit, Titlark

IDENTIFICATION

APPEARANCE: both male and female look like robin-sized song thrushes, with dark brown upper parts on which each feather is beautifully fringed in paler brown; underparts are paler with dark streaks and spots; outer tail feathers are white and show up best in flight; juveniles are paler
SIZE: 14.5cm (5¾in) long
WINGSPAN: 22-25cm (8¾-10in)
WEIGHT: 16-25g (⅔-⅞oz)
FLIGHT: weak and stuttery
VOICE: gives a squeaky *tseep* call when disturbed; song is an accelerating *pheet-pheet-pheet* on the way up and sweeter on the way down, ending on a swift trill

FOOD

Eats mainly insects found on the ground, including beetles, caterpillars, crickets; also takes spiders, worms, small snails and slugs

BEHAVIOUR

Lark-like in its song-flights; wagtail-like in its dashing about; after breeding, forms loose flocks, often with larks and wagtails
ENEMIES: birds of prey such as the merlin and hen harrier; hard winters and wet summers; change of land use

BREEDING

PAIRING UP: from April to July; male has a low-level song-flight, singing as he parachutes back to the ground; usually rears 2 broods a year
NESTING: the female weaves a neat cup of grasses and moss, lined with fine grass and hair, buried in the base of a grassy tussock or under a clump of heather; nests are often hijacked by cuckoos
EGGS: lays 3-5 brown to reddish eggs spattered or streaked with dark grey
INCUBATION: female does the sitting; chicks hatch in 11-15 days
YOUNG: chicks are covered in brownish-grey down; mouths are lined with crimson and outlined in pale yellow; both parents are kept busy feeding the nestlings; fledged in 14-16 days
MOULT: in late summer, after breeding
LIFE EXPECTANCY: up to 5 years

POPULATION IN BRITAIN

Up to 3 million pairs breed each year

Distribution

The meadow pipit is the most common songbird in hilly countryside during the summer months. It is found on heath and moorland in northern and southwest England, mid Wales, Scotland and western Ireland.

In autumn, northern birds start moving south to spend the winter along the coast in Ireland and south and southwest England. Meanwhile, the southern birds head off to sunnier climes in Spain, Portugal, southern France and North Africa for the winter.

During the winter, the outgoers are replaced several times over by flocks of meadow pipits arriving from Iceland and northern Europe, either in transit or as overwintering visitors.

☐ areas where the bird stays all year
☐ areas where the bird is a summer visitor
☐ areas where the bird is a winter visitor

HABITAT

Spends the summer breeding on open spaces – hill pastures, moors and heaths, dunes and saltmarshes; winters on farmland, estuaries and beaches

NATURE WATCH

● Severe weather in the meadow pipits' winter quarters in Spain and Portugal may have contributed to a fall in their numbers since the 1970s.
● Meadow pipits thrive in young conifer plantations, before the trees grow too tall and spreading.

The Moorhen

NAMES
SCIENTIFIC NAME: *Gallinula chloropus*
NICKNAMES: Water Hen, Marsh-hen

IDENTIFICATION
APPEARANCE: sexes are alike – bluish-black with a dark olive back and wings, a white line along the flanks and upside-down white V under tail; adults have a red frontal plate and beak with yellow tip; long greeny-yellow legs, with scarlet garters at the top, and huge feet with long toes; juveniles are grey-brown with off-white chin and throat
SIZE: 32-35cm (12½-14in) long
WINGSPAN: 50-55cm (20-22in)
WEIGHT: males 250-420g (9-15oz); females 260-375g (9¼-13½oz)
FLIGHT: weak, with dangling legs
VOICE: variety of loud and harsh clucking and gurgling contact calls; noisy alarm calls of *kurruk* and *kittik*

FOOD
Eats leaves, seeds and berries, snails, insects, worms, fish and tadpoles found in waterside vegetation and in water meadows, fields and gardens

BEHAVIOUR
Often found in loose flocks for feeding and roosting; identified by the jerky movement of its head when walking or swimming and the flicking of its tail
ENEMIES: fish, rats, snakes, mink, foxes, otters, stoats and crows; land drainage

BREEDING
PAIRING UP: from April to August; each pair rears 1-3 broods a year
NESTING: both birds build a platform of reeds with central cup on or near water
EGGS: lays 6-11 creamy-buff eggs flecked with reddish-brown and dark grey
INCUBATION: both sexes incubate the eggs for 19-22 days
YOUNG: covered in blackish down with red beaks, the chicks can walk and swim a few hours after hatching; take 40-50 days to fledge; unusually, juveniles help to rear their younger siblings
MOULT: adults have a complete post-breeding moult in late summer and some moult their body plumage again in March; youngsters only moult their body feathers in their first autumn
LIFESPAN: up to 11 years

POPULATION IN BRITAIN
Over 300,000 pairs breed; in excess of 1 million may overwinter here

Distribution

The moorhen is a widespread, common and familiar water bird: there is barely a stretch of fresh water across lowland Britain without its resident moorhen at some stage in the year. They are absent from the higher ground of northwest Scotland and mid-Wales.

Moorhens in the British Isles stay put, rarely roaming farther than 10 to 15 miles. In eastern Europe and Scandinavia, where the winters are much colder, moorhens are forced to move south to find warmer areas. Many reach Britain, swelling the population to upwards of one million in the winter.

The moorhen is distributed almost all over the world, except in Australasia and Antarctica.

☐ areas where the bird stays all year
☐ areas where the bird is a summer visitor

HABITAT
Turns up on stretches of still or sluggish water, from local ponds to canals, ditches and rivers, wherever there is dense fringe vegetation to provide cover

NATURE WATCH
● Moorhens usually panic when disturbed. They swim quickly into cover or run back into the water, with their heads down and wings flapping, emitting a loud sharp squawking *kittik* or *kurruk*. You often have only a few seconds to look for a defining red beak and a band of white feathers along each blue-black flank.

The Nightingale

Distribution

After spending the winter in tropical Africa, nightingales arrive back in England during the middle of April. They leave again towards the end of August or the beginning of September. In the meantime they occupy the southeast corner of England, south of a line from the Humber to the Severn estuaries. They never nest at more than 180m (600ft) above sea level.

The nightingale's breeding range extends as far west as Portugal, south to northwest Africa and eastward through central Asia to Mongolia. Southern Denmark represents its northern limit, England its westerly limit. In England, their range has been contracting eastwards since the mid-20th century.

☐ areas where the bird breeds in summer
▨ migration routes to Africa for the winter

NAMES

SCIENTIFIC NAME: *Luscinia megarhynchos*

NICKNAMES: Philomel or Philomela

IDENTIFICATION

APPEARANCE: adult males and females look identical, with sober brown plumage; chestnut upperparts, pale buff underparts with brighter rusty chestnut tail feathers; large dark eyes with indistinct pale eye-rings; juveniles are more speckly

SIZE: 15-16.5cm (6-6½in) long

WINGSPAN: 23-26cm (9-10½in)

WEIGHT: 18-27g (½-1oz)

FLIGHT: strong at low level for short distances between patches of cover

VOICE: a legendary songster with brilliant complex song frequently sung during the night as well as by day; soft *hweet* contact call; harsh *tchaa-tchaa* alarm

FOOD

Searches leaf litter for insects, spiders and worms; eats berries in late summer

BEHAVIOUR

Secretive life spent skulking in the undergrowth; sings for 6 weeks only, before chicks hatch

MIGRATION: breeds in England each summer between mid April and August; winters in tropical West Africa

BREEDING

PAIRING UP: from mid April to July; females seduced by the males' superb singing and energetic display; each pair has time to rear only 1 brood a year

NESTING: female builds an untidy nest of dried leaves, a little moss and grass lined with fine roots, hair and wool which is well camouflaged in the undergrowth

EGGS: 4 or 5 eggs look olive-brown but on closer inspection have a blue-green background densely freckled with brown

INCUBATION: female sits for 13 days

YOUNG: chicks are covered in grey down, with orange lining to mouths outlined in pale yellow flanges; fed by both parents, leave nest in about 12-13 days

MOULT: complete moult takes place during the winter after they get to Africa

LIFE EXPECTANCY: 3-5 years

POPULATION IN BRITAIN

Between 2000-5000 breed in the southeast of England each year; numbers have dropped since coppicing was abandoned in the mid-20th century

HABITAT

Lives where there are thickets and dense scrub, in copses, on commons and heaths and in hedgerows among tangled brambles, honeysuckle and nettles

NATURE WATCH

● For the best chance of hearing a male nightingale sing, you really need to stake out open woodland and coppices in southeast England after dark in spring and early summer. Although he does sing during the day, it is easier to listen to his fabulous solo performance at night, when few other birds are singing.

The Nightjar

Distribution

The nightjar is scattered in suitable breeding sites over England and Wales but is now rare in Scotland and Ireland. The numbers coming here each summer are small; its range has been contracting and numbers falling since about 1930. Recent efforts to save heathland and conifer plantation sites for nightjars to breed on have been rewarded with signs of a recovery in the past 10 years.

Nightjars breed from Ireland east to Russia and China, south to the Middle East and North Africa and as far north as southern Scandinavia. They return to Britain from their winter quarters in Africa in May and are gone again by October, flying south to winter below the equator as far as the Cape.

☐ areas where the bird is a summer visitor

☐ migration routes to southern Africa

NAMES
SCIENTIFIC NAME: *Caprimulgus europaeus*
NICKNAMES: Goatsucker, Fern Owl, Nighthawk, Churn Owl

IDENTIFICATION
APPEARANCE: male and female are covered in a mosaic of buff, brown and grey spots and bars; only the adult male has white flashes near his wingtips and at the tips of his tail; head is flattened, with a stubby beak and large dark eyes; long wings and tail but short legs; juveniles look like the female
SIZE: 26-28cm (10-11in) long
WINGSPAN: 54-60cm (21½-23½in)
WEIGHT: 75-100g (2⅝-3⅝oz)
FLIGHT: zigzaggy, drifting or bounding
VOICE: song is a fantastic, prolonged purring *churrrr* that comes out of the darkness; contact call is a deep *coo-ic*

FOOD
Eats flying insects, particularly large moths and beetles, caught on the wing after dark over pastures, heathland, woodland clearings and near water

BEHAVIOUR
Nests in Britain as a summer visitor and spends the winter in southern Africa; establishes a large nesting territory; otherwise solitary
ENEMIES: loss of habitat, lack of insects, bad weather, disturbance at the nest and predators that take eggs and chicks

BREEDING
PAIRING UP: from May to July; male performs a flamboyant courtship flight to display white flashes on wings and tail
NESTING: nest is an unlined dimple on the bare ground
EGGS: 2 grey-white eggs marbled grey
INCUBATION: female does most of the sitting; chicks hatch in 17-19 days
YOUNG: chicks are covered in a grey-brown down; fed by both parents for the first 12 days, then female concentrates on a second brood while the male looks after the first; fly in 16-17 days but not independent for another 4 weeks
MOULT: quickly after breeding before going; has a wing and tail moult in Africa to replace worn flight feathers on adults and acquire white spots in young males
LIFE EXPECTANCY: up to 11 years

POPULATION IN BRITAIN
Up to 4000 pairs breed here each year

HABITAT
Nests on bare, open heath and moorland, sand dunes and clear-felled pine plantations before regeneration

NATURE WATCH
● A nightjar may be mistaken for a kestrel hunting at dusk: the long barred tails look similar, but only at a distance.
● Stick to the designated paths across heathland and always keep dogs on a lead during the birds' breeding season to avoid disturbing sitting nightjars or, worse still, trampling on their eggs and chicks.

The Nuthatch

Distribution

Nuthatches are widespread but locally concentrated in Wales, the Midlands and southern England, south of a line from the Mersey to the Wash. There are pockets of population in northeast England, with reports of a few pairs breeding in Scotland. Nuthatches are absent from Ireland and the Isle of Man. A limited flight range restricts their distribution, with most birds spending their entire lives within a few miles of where they hatched.

The nuthatch is found in deciduous and coniferous woodland all over Europe, through the Middle East to China and Japan. There is even an isolated population in the Atlas Mountains of Morocco.

☐ areas where the bird stays all year

NAMES
SCIENTIFIC NAME: *Sitta europaea*
NICKNAMES: Woodcracker, Mud Stopper

IDENTIFICATION
APPEARANCE: male slightly larger than female; sexes look alike, with blue-grey upperparts, black eyestripe, white cheeks, cinnamon-tinted breast and chestnut flanks (male has wider and richer rusty colour); juveniles are duller versions of the adults
SIZE: 14cm (5½in) long
WINGSPAN: 22.5-27cm (9-10⅔in)
WEIGHT: 20-25g (⅔-1oz)
FLIGHT: direct, fast and undulating
VOICE: large repertoire of calls and songs; excited *twit* or *twit-twit-twit* when disturbed; sharp, hissing *tsi-si-si* alarm call; uses *tsit-tsit* contact call just before taking off; songs are variations on a long repeated boyish whistle *pwee-ah, pwee-ah, pwee-ah*

FOOD
Eats mainly insects and their grubs found on trees during spring and summer; in autumn and winter, adds seeds and nuts, such as hazelnuts, chestnuts, acorns and beechmast, to its diet; cracks the shells with its powerful beak

BEHAVIOUR
Highly territorial; pairs often stay in their patch of woodland all year; never roam far; nimble inquisitive birds with unique ability to climb down trunks headfirst
ENEMIES: many die in icy winters

BREEDING
PAIRING UP: courtship begins in January, breeding in April and May; males sing noisily before eggs hatch, then fall silent; usually have only one brood each year
NESTING: female selects suitable nesting hole or nest-box and tailors the entrance to fit by plastering it with mud; collects flakes of bark to line the nest-hole
EGGS: 6-9 white eggs with a scattering of reddish specks
INCUBATION: female sits for 13-18 days
YOUNG: hatchlings scantily covered with grey down; mouths lined in pink with cream flanges; fed mostly on insects by both parents; fledged in 20-24 days; dependent on parents for another 8-14 days, then banished from territory
MOULT: adults in late summer
LIFE EXPECTANCY: 8 years maximum

POPULATION IN BRITAIN
About 130,000 breed each year

HABITAT
Very much a woodland bird, although it does live in established parks and neighbouring gardens with large trees

NATURE WATCH
● It is worth taking a pair of field glasses with you on a woodland walk. You may only get a glimpse of a nervous nuthatch, climbing jerkily on a tree trunk, before it flies off to a more distant tree where you can watch it through your binoculars.
● Listen out for the nuthatch's loud metallic *twit-twit-twit* calls which are usually the clearest clue that there is a nuthatch in the area.

The Peregrine

NAMES
SCIENTIFIC NAME: *Falco peregrinus*
NICKNAMES: Blue Hawk, Cliff Hawk

IDENTIFICATION
APPEARANCE: adults have slate-grey backs and wings, pale underparts barred in grey; dark crown and moustache markings; long yellow legs and huge feet with sharp talons; eye-rings and base of beak are yellow; juvenile is browner, with dark-streaked underside and blue eye-rings, legs and feet
SIZE: 36-48cm (14½-19¼in) long; male is up to a third smaller than female
WINGSPAN: 95-115cm (38-46in)
WEIGHT: male 600-750g (21½-26¾oz); female 925-1300g (33-46½oz)
FLIGHT: dives on prey at colossal speed
VOICE: harsh loud *kak-kak-kak* alarm; creaky *wichew* courtship call

FOOD
Hunts a cross-section of the birds in an area, ranging in size from tits to ducks; it bashes them out of the sky in a cloud of feathers; also takes a few rabbits

BEHAVIOUR
Returns to traditional nest sites (eyries); perches for long periods on rocky outcrops, cliff ledges, pylons or buildings
ENEMIES: pesticides, gamekeepers and pigeon fanciers, foxes, pine martens, polecats, owls, birds of prey and fulmars

BREEDING
PAIRING UP: aerial courtship displays take place in March and April; rears only 1 brood a year
NESTING: on a rocky ledge in a shallow saucer scraped in the debris
EGGS: lays 3 or 4 buff eggs with reddish brown markings at 2-3 day intervals
INCUBATION: female starts sitting when her clutch is complete; male helps out; chicks hatch 29-32 days after laying
YOUNG: female protects the downy white hatchlings for up to 17 days while the male hunts alone; after 3 weeks, brown feathers start coming through; then female hunts too; chicks fledge in 35-42 days; both parents continue to feed youngsters for 2 months until they have learned to hunt and kill for themselves
MOULT: from June to September
LIFE EXPECTANCY: up to 15 years

POPULATION IN BRITAIN
About 1500 pairs breed each year; numbers are stable or falling in places

Distribution
Although the peregrine is widely dispersed, and hunts birds on all continents, it is rare throughout its range. Numbers appear to have stabilised: local fluctuations depend on food supply and persecution.

Peregrines return to traditional family eyries to nest each spring. Over the summer, they are mainly found on the cliffs, upland crags and quarries in southwest England, Wales, the Pennines, Lake District and Scotland or nesting on buildings in cities.

When there is plenty of prey, adult peregrines stay in their breeding area all year, only roving if food runs short. In winter, young peregrines roam about looking for fresh hunting grounds.

☐ areas where the bird stays all year
☐ areas where the bird is a summer visitor
☐ areas where the bird is a winter visitor

HABITAT
Craggy mountainous regions and coastal cliffs with ledges for nesting and open countryside to furnish enough prey

NATURE WATCH
● The peregrine leaves few clues behind. As it plucks its prey and eats mainly flesh, only a few regurgitated pellets collect under perches or nesting ledges. When it leaves large prey half eaten, intending to return later, the carcass is picked over by foxes, gulls and crows.

The Pheasant

Distribution

The pheasant's natural range extends from the Caspian Sea to Myanmar and China. It was brought to Europe thousands of years ago, where it is now widespread, except in Spain and Portugal and northern Scandinavia.

When and how pheasants reached Britain is lost in the mists of time but they are now a familiar feature of the countryside all year around. As a poor long-distance flier, the pheasant rarely roams far from its home territory. Sadly, pheasants are often crushed on roads: they seem to spot traffic late, panic and dash out in front of the vehicle.

More recently, the pheasant has become established across North America and in New Zealand.

☐ areas where the bird stays all year

NAMES

SCIENTIFIC NAME: *Phasianus colchicus*
NICKNAMES: Comet, Cock up

IDENTIFICATION

APPEARANCE: cock bird's plumage (above) is a mass of iridescent bottle green, blue, purple, rust, copper, buff and black; he has a bright red patch around each golden eye and a scarlet wattle; female is a mosaic of buff, brown and black; both have a long barred tail juveniles look like tailless females at first
SIZE: 55-90cm (22-36ln) of which half is tail; male is much larger than female
WINGSPAN: 70-90cm (28-36in)
WEIGHT: 1-1.5kg (2-3¼lb)
FLIGHT: fast but brief on whirring wings, mostly followed by a glide to cover
VOICE: male crows *kokorok;* a repeated raucous *kocock, kocock* alarm call

FOOD

Adult forages for grains, seeds, buds and shoots plus a few insects, spiders and earthworms; chicks eat mainly spiders and insects for the first 6 weeks

BEHAVIOUR

Male is polygynous, assembling and fiercely defending a harem of partners within his territory; females are more sociable throughout the year
ENEMIES: eggs and chicks are taken by crows, magpies, jays, hedgehogs, stoats, weasels and birds of prey; road traffic

BREEDING

PAIRING UP: from March until early June; only 1 large brood per year
NESTING: female scrapes out a shallow hollow in the ground and lines it with dead leaves and dried grass, usually under a hedge or in tangled undergrowth
EGGS: 8-15 smooth greeny-brown eggs; several females may lay in same nest
INCUBATION: female sits for 23-28 days
YOUNG: cock bird plays no part in family life; chicks hatch at the same time and are soon running about and feeding themselves; fly on rudimentary wings when about 12 days old, long before fully grown; stay with their mother for 10-11 weeks
MOULT: late summer after breeding
LIFE EXPECTANCY: up to 7 years; most are bred to be shot in their first year

POPULATION IN BRITAIN

Numbers are artificially inflated every autumn by the release of 20-30 million young birds, reared in captivity to be shot

HABITAT

Found everywhere, except on high peaks, from hedgerows and fields to seashore

NATURE WATCH

● Even the ostentatious cock pheasant is put in the shade by two ornamental pheasants introduced from China: small populations of the golden pheasant (*Chrysolophus pictus*) breed in pine plantations as far apart as East Anglia, Hampshire, Anglesey in North Wales and Galloway in Scotland; a few Lady Amherst's pheasant (*Chrysolophus amherstiae*) breed in Hertfordshire, Buckinghamshire and Bedfordshire.

The Reed Bunting

Distribution

At the moment, reed buntings are still quite common and widespread in Britain, favouring waterside habitats.

Many reed buntings stay in the British Isles all year round, although there is a southerly shift in the winter. A few come here just to nest in summer and move on to mainland Europe for the winter; others immigrants come from farther north to overwinter in Britain: over 1 million reed buntings are thought to spend the winter here. Wintering Scandinavian reed buntings have broader beaks than the residents.

In the summer, reed buntings breed across much of northern Europe, including Scandinavia, and spread east over Russia as far as China and Japan.

☐ areas where the bird stays all year
☐ areas where the bird is a summer visitor
☐ areas where the bird is a winter visitor

NAMES
SCIENTIFIC NAME: *Emberiza schoeniclus*
NICKNAMES: Reed Sparrow, Water Sparrow, Black-bonnet

IDENTIFICATION
APPEARANCE: in spring and summer, the male has a striking jet black head, white collar and streaked chestnut and black back; during the winter his plumage is duller; the brown-streaked female is dowdier all year round; juveniles look similar to females but even drabber
SIZE: 15-16cm (6-6½in) long
WINGSPAN: 21-26cm (8½-10½in)
WEIGHT: 17-25g (⅔-⅞oz)
FLIGHT: jerky with irregular bursts of wing beating; long, notched tail is conspicuous
VOICE: calls include a high-pitched *tseeu* and a metallic *chink*; his song is a much-repeated *plink-plink-plink-tséeri*

FOOD
Feeds mainly on insects in the summer; eats seeds, grains and shoots over the winter; visits garden bird-feeders to take grain and seeds in winter

BEHAVIOUR
Territorial during the breeding season but otherwise forages and roosts in small groups with other seed eaters
ENEMIES: cold winters, birds of prey, loss of reedbeds and watery habitats and changes in agricultural practices

BREEDING
PAIRING UP: from mid March to July; usually manages to rear 2, sometimes 3 broods a year
NESTING: female builds a scruffy nest of loosely woven grass and moss, lined with hair, finer grasses and reed or willow fluff, low down in vegetation around watery places
EGGS: lays 4 or 5 olive eggs covered in dark scribbles
INCUBATION: largely by the female alone for 12-14 days
YOUNG: on hatching the chicks are covered in a fine dark down and have pink linings to their mouths, outlined in pale yellow; both parents feed them insects; fledged and ready to leave the nest after 10-12 days
MOULT: sheds and grows new feathers at the end of the breeding season
LIFE EXPECTANCY: from 2-3 years

POPULATION IN BRITAIN
Roughly 350,000 pairs breed each year

HABITAT
In summer lives among the reeds and willows along the margins of rivers, canals, dykes and estuaries; wanders farther afield in the winter to find food

NATURE WATCH
● Although not a high-profile bird, the reed bunting benefits from the protection and creation of wetlands for rarer birds.
● By planting seed-rich crops on set-aside land, farmers are providing winter food and nest sites for the reed bunting.

The Sand Martin

NAMES

SCIENTIFIC NAME: *Riparia riparia*
NICKNAMES: Sand Swallow, Bank Swallow

IDENTIFICATION

APPEARANCE: the male and female look alike – both have brown upperparts and white underparts, broken by a brown band across the chest; wings are brown top and bottom; tail is slightly notched in a shallow fork; the juvenile's flight feathers have pale edges
SIZE: 12cm (4¾in) long
WINGSPAN: 26-29cm (10½-11½in)
WEIGHT: 13-14g (½oz)
FLIGHT: wings are long and pointed, flight is slightly fluttering
VOICE: call to each other all the time while flying with a low, grating *chirrrrup*; song sung by the male at the nesting tunnel is a weak, harsh twitter

FOOD

Hunts for insects on the wing, usually flying low over water; drinks by dipping its beak into the water while flying along

BEHAVIOUR

Highly gregarious bird, nesting, feeding, roosting and travelling together;
a summer visitor, it overwinters in West Africa and returns in March to breed
ENEMIES: cold spells here and droughts in Africa; birds of prey; falling numbers of flying insects

BREEDING

PAIRING UP: from April to July; usually rears 2 broods each year
NESTING: both birds excavate a long tunnel in a steep sandy bank or cliff with a nesting chamber at the far end which is lined with feathers and grass
EGGS: lays 4 or 5 pure white eggs
INCUBATION: both parents take turns to incubate the eggs for 14 days
YOUNG: on hatching, the chicks are covered with pale grey down and have a yellow lining to the mouth; chicks are fed by both parents and ready to fly after about 21 days; gather in noisy flocks before leaving for Africa in late summer
MOULT: most undergo a minor body moult in August and a full body and wing feather moults in their winter quarters
LIFE EXPECTANCY: up to 5 years

POPULATION IN BRITAIN

About 200,000 pairs breed each year; numbers crashed after African droughts in the 1960s and 1980s

Distribution

The sand martin's distribution is largely dictated by the availability of suitable sand and gravel banks and cliffs in which to dig its nesting tunnels. Localised colonies often contain hundreds of birds.

Sand martins gather in waterside reedbeds and willow trees from July and start leaving for West Africa in August. By the end of September, they have gone, until the following March or early April. The winter is spent hunting insects along the southern edge of the Sahara – starting in Senegal and moving east to Burkina Faso.

In the summer, the sand martin is found all over the northern hemisphere, from North America to Japan.

☐ areas where the bird is a summer visitor
☐ migration routes to West Africa for winter

HABITAT

A bird of the air, frequently seen flying over stretches of water as it feeds or nesting in quarries, cliffs or river-banks

NATURE WATCH

● Natural slides create a fresh face on sheer sand banks and cliffs where sand martins can dig new nest tunnels. But sometimes the birds need a little help from their friends to maintain old nest sites: shoring up fragile cliffs or clearing overgrown ones and in-filling sloping canal and river-banks to restore vertical sides for the sand martins to excavate.

The Skylark

NAMES
SCIENTIFIC NAME: *Alauda arvensis*
NICKNAMES: Laverock, Lady Hen

IDENTIFICATION
APPEARANCE: males and females look alike: both have streaky cream, buff and brown plumage with white outer tail feathers and edges to wings; male has erectile crest; long claw on rear toe to control grass; juvenile feathers outlined in white, with no white edge to the wings
SIZE: 18-19cm (7-7½in) long
WINGSPAN: 30-36cm (12-14⅓in)
WEIGHT: 33-45g (1⅓-1¾oz)
FLIGHT: song-flight extraordinarily vertical and controlled; ordinary flight floppy winged and undulating
VOICE: supremely lyrical medley of high-pitched liquid trills and chirrups; *preet* and *priee* contact calls

FOOD
During the summer, eats mainly insects, worms and seeds; in autumn switches to seeds, grains and fresh green shoots

BEHAVIOUR
Lives and nests on the ground, walking and running through the grass; crouches and freezes if in danger

ENEMIES: farm machinery, birds of prey, crows, cats, weasels and people

BREEDING
PAIRING UP: from April to July; male sings an elaborate song while flying high into the sky and back to woo a female and broadcast his territory; usually mates for life; a pair can rear up to 4 broods each year
NESTING: nest created in a shallow depression in the ground, lined with dried grass, protected by a tuft of long grass or overhanging clod of earth
EGGS: lays 3-5 greyish eggs heavily splotched with brown or green
INCUBATION: female sits for 10 days
YOUNG: chicks hatch naked and helpless; fed by both parents; leave nest after 10 days to run around in the grass; fledged and ready to fly 10 days later
MOULT: in the autumn
LIFE EXPECTANCY: as long as they survive their first winter, up to 8 years

POPULATION IN BRITAIN
As many as 1.5 million pairs breeding each year; due to changes in farming practices over the last 30 years, numbers have fallen by three-quarters

Distribution

Despite severe losses in recent years, the skylark is still one of the more widespread and common breeding birds in Britain.

Skylarks are resident throughout the year, although from August until November many start moving south to spend the winter in western and southern Europe. Those that stay are joined by a huge influx from central and northern Europe for the winter. Return journeys are made in spring, between February and mid May.

The skylark is heard singing on a vast stage, from Spain, across Europe and central Asia to the eastern tip of Russia, from the fringes of the Sahara to within the Arctic Circle.

☐ areas where the bird stays all year
☐ areas where the bird is a summer visitor
☐ areas where the bird is a winter visitor

HABITAT
One of the few songbirds that thrives in open countryside – in meadows, pastures, fields, heathland, sand dunes, shingle, saltmarshes and golf courses

NATURE WATCH
● Often heard singing gloriously before it is spied as a distant dot on high.
● Organic farming is good for birds in general, but not for skylarks. Fields are generally small, limiting the number of territories the area can support.

The Sparrowhawk

Distribution

The sparrowhawk is widespread, even common in woodland throughout England, Wales and most of Scotland. Occasionally it comes into gardens to poach small songbirds as they are feeding at bird-tables.

Sparrowhawks breeding in Britain stay put during the winter. In the autumn, they are joined on the east coast by sparrowhawks from farther north, especially juveniles reared in Scandinavia earlier in the year. They start arriving in September and leave again in March or April.

The sparrowhawk breeds in woodland and forest across Europe and Asia, from Ireland to Japan, from northern Scandinavia to North Africa.

- ☐ areas where the bird stays all year
- ☐ areas where the bird is a summer visitor
- ☐ areas where the bird is a winter visitor

NAMES
SCIENTIFIC NAME: *Accipiter nisus*
NICKNAMES: Spar Hawk, Hedge Hawk, Spear Havoc

IDENTIFICATION
APPEARANCE: female (right above) is larger than the male (left above); he has a steely grey back and wings with orange barring underneath; she has browner-grey upperparts and grey barring below; juveniles are browner than their mothers
SIZE: male 28-30cm (11¼-12in) long; female 35-38cm (14-15¼in)
WINGSPAN: 60-80cm (24-32in)
WEIGHT: male 130-160g (4⅓-5⅓oz); female 280-320g (10-11½oz)
FLIGHT: dashing flight with a typical flap-flap-glide use of the wings
VOICE: a sharp *kek-kek-kek-kek-kek* alarm call; soft thin *pii-ih* when breeding

FOOD
Mainly snatches songbirds, such as tits and finches; female also takes larger prey such as thrushes and pigeons

BEHAVIOUR
Largely solitary outside the breeding season; may join communal roosts with other birds of prey during the winter

ENEMIES: goshawks, heavy doses of pesticide and farming practices, such as the uprooting of hedges, that reduce their food supply, illegal persecution from gamekeepers and bad weather

BREEDING
PAIRING UP: from May to July; raises only 1 brood a year
NESTING: constructs a bulky platform of sticks and twigs lined with flakes of bark and down high up in a tree against the trunk, preferably a conifer
EGGS: usually lays 4-5 white eggs splattered with reddish brown
INCUBATION: normally by the female for 32-35 days
YOUNG: hatchlings clad in white down but dark feathers soon start growing through; female stays at the nest to care for the nestlings while the male hunts and brings her food to tear up for them; chicks are flying in 24-30 days
MOULT: both adults and juveniles undergo a full moult in the autumn
LIFE EXPECTANCY: up to 10 years

POPULATION IN BRITAIN
As many as 50,000 pairs may breed each year

HABITAT
Found wherever there are trees from coniferous or deciduous woodland to parks and gardens

NATURE WATCH
● A marauding sparrowhawk soon spots a popular bird-table. In the twinkling of an eye, it can swoop down and snatch a little songbird while it is busy feeding. Placing a bird-table in a sheltered spot in the garden, near accessible cover, can thwart a sparrowhawk's flying attack.

The Stonechat

NAMES
SCIENTIFIC NAME: *Saxicola torquata*
NICKNAMES: Blacky Top, Furze Hacker

IDENTIFICATION
APPEARANCE: in spring, the cock bird is a little bobby-dazzler with his bold black head and chin, white collar and chestnut breast; his autumn-winter plumage is more faded and browner, more like the female's; brown-speckled juveniles look similar to young robins
SIZE: 12.5cm (5in) long
WINGSPAN: 18-21cm (7-8½in)
WEIGHT: 14-17g (½-⅝oz)
FLIGHT: darting and dodging from bush to bush; jerky, butterfly song dance
VOICE: frequently uses an insistent and persistent *tchack, tchack* alarm call; male sings a soft warbling jingle

FOOD
Drops on any insects and spiders it spies from its gorsy perch and can pluck flying insects from the air; also eats a few slugs, snails, worms and the odd small lizard; in winter, resorts to eating seeds

BEHAVIOUR
Perches out in the open to sing, hunt and guard the nest; most stay on their home range all year round but may drift to the coast in harsh winters
ENEMIES: bad weather (especially in winter), snakes, stoats and birds of prey

BREEDING
PAIRING UP: nesting starts as early as March and continues into July; rears up to three, maybe even four broods a year
NESTING: female buries her nest in a clump of grass or heather under a gorse bush, weaving a cup of grass and moss lined with hair, wool and feathers
EGGS: lays 4-6 pale blue eggs with dark brown freckles around the broad end
INCUBATION: female sits for 13-14 days
YOUNG: hatchlings are clad in a brownish-grey down and have yellow linings to their mouths flanged in pale yellow; fed by both parents, the fledglings leave the nest in 12-16 days; both parents continue to feed them for five days or so; then the female starts a second brood while the male copes with the young until the new family hatches
MOULT: as soon as breeding is over
LIFE EXPECTANCY: up to 5 years

POPULATION IN BRITAIN
16,000-40,000 pairs breed each year

Distribution
Stonechats are still quite common on the heaths, moorland, clifftops and dunes along the west coasts of England, Scotland and Ireland and on the Lleyn Peninsula in North Wales.

Hardy little birds, most stonechats stay on their breeding grounds all year round: only a few travel south for a Mediterranean winter.

Most European stonechats breed in the scrublands and vineyards of France, Spain and Italy. Those that nest in Central Europe spend the winter along the north coast of Spain or around the Mediterranean.

Stonechats also breed in Asia, all the way to Japan, and south as far as southern Africa.

☐ areas where the bird stays all year
☐ areas where the bird is a summer visitor
☐ areas where the bird is a winter visitor

HABITAT
Favours gorse, heather, bramble and bracken on heathland, clifftops, dunes and links golf courses

NATURE WATCH
● In summer, stonechats share the gorsy heathland with whinchats. Both have dark brown, orange and buff plumage and are easily confused. To tell the two apart look at the head: a stonechat's head is totally dark while the whinchat has a white stripe above each eye.

The Swallow

Distribution

The swallow is widely distributed over the British Isles from April to September. After rearing two or three broods of chicks, adults and juveniles fly 6250 miles to southern Africa for the southern-hemisphere summer, to avoid winter in the northern hemisphere.

Many swallows marked with rings in Britain have been recovered in Orange Free State, Transvaal or Cape Province in South Africa, although some go no farther than southern Europe. Migration takes a heavy toll – on average, only 50 per cent of adults and 80 per cent of young birds survive the return trip. It has also been shown that swallows return to the barn or area where they were reared or raised an earlier family..

☐ areas where the bird is a summer visitor

▨ routes to southern Africa for the winter

NAMES
SCIENTIFIC NAME: *Hirundo rustica*
NICKNAME: Barn Swallow

IDENTIFICATION
APPEARANCE: adults have iridescent blue-black plumage on crown, back, rump and wings, pale underparts, chestnut-red markings on face and throat and deeply forked tails; male is slightly glossier than female, with ruddier underparts and longer tail streamers; juvenile is duller and paler, with forked tail but no tail streamers
SIZE: 17-21cm (6⅔-8½in) long
WINGSPAN: 32-35cm (12⅔-14in)
WEIGHT: 16-25g (½-1oz)
FLIGHT: fast, powerful and agile
VOICE: sharp *tswit, tswit* call in flight is loud and twittery when excited; song is a warbling melody of twittering notes

FOOD
Catches flying insects on the wing; takes mainly large flies, such as bluebottles, and mosquitoes over water; may snatch hanging caterpillars to feed young

BEHAVIOUR
Spends most of its time flying; nests communally, vigorously defending a small territory around its nest; summer visitor to Britain; spends our winter in southern Africa
ENEMIES: birds of prey, storms and cold weather, fatigue, traffic, cats and rats

BREEDING
PAIRING UP: mid April to September; rears 2, maybe 3 broods a year
NESTING: both male and female build a shallow cup-shaped nest from mud, lined with dry grass, hair and feathers, in barns, outbuildings and warehouses and on girders under bridges
EGGS: 4-6 elongated whitish eggs with red speckling
INCUBATION: female sits for 13-15 days
YOUNG: chicks covered in grey down, with yellow lining to mouth outlined in cream flanges; fed insects by both parents, leave nest after about 18-21 days; fed for another week before forming large flocks
MOULT: in southern Africa
LIFE EXPECTANCY: up to 9 years

POPULATION IN BRITAIN
About 800,000 breed each summer; fewer accessible farm buildings, cleaner farmyards and many barn conversions have led to a sharp population decline

HABITAT
The skies above meadows, rivers, canals, ponds, sewage farms, farmyards and towns

NATURE WATCH
● During a dry spell, when the ground is parched and cracked, water a patch of earth for the swallows so they can find mud for building their nests.
● Swallows are being seen in Britain earlier every year and this is taken as a sign of climate change. In northern and eastern Europe they often arrive back when snow is still on the ground.

The Treecreeper

Distribution

The treecreeper is a widely distributed resident across the British Isles, except in treeless areas in East Anglia and the Isles of Scilly, Orkney and Shetland. Its range is receding in the west of Ireland

The Eurasian treecreeper breeds from Ireland, through eastern Europe and Scandinavia across southern Russia to the Himalayas, China and Japan. It is only patchily distributed in Spain and France, but it has strongholds in the Mediterranean on Corsica and in Greece.

Most treecreepers rarely roam farther than 12 miles from their parent's territory. Sometimes Scandinavian treecreepers, with whiter eyebrows and more white spots on top, end up on this side of the North Sea during the winter.

☐ areas where the bird stays all year

NAMES
SCIENTIFIC NAME: *Certhia familiaris*
NICKNAMES: Tree Mouse, Tree Climber

IDENTIFICATION
APPEARANCE: male and female look alike with pale 'eyebrow', mottled brown backs and wings and silvery white underparts; long, fine down-curved beak; juveniles are more heavily blotched with white on back and have shorter beaks
SIZE: 12.5cm (5in) long
WINGSPAN: 18-21cm (7-8½in)
WEIGHT: 8-12g (¼-½oz)
FLIGHT: weak and low, from high in one tree to the base of another nearby
VOICE: male sings a high-pitched tinkling song *tsee-tsee-tsi-tsi-si-si-si-si-sisisisisisi-tsee*; sharp contact call notes of *tsee* and a slightly softer *tsit*

FOOD
Hunts for insects and spiders on bark, always searching a tree from the bottom upwards; rarely eats seeds but may take chopped nuts and suet from gardens

BEHAVIOUR
Territorial during the breeding season; lives alone for most of the year or tags along with mixed flocks of tits, goldcrests and nuthatches roaming woodland
ENEMIES: freezing or wet weather; few otherwise, due to its camouflaged plumage and well-concealed nest

BREEDING
PAIRING UP: mid March to June; very vocal from February to May, leading to lively chases through and up trees; often rears 2 broods a year
NESTING: builds nest in cavity behind flap of bark or ivy; both birds gather bark, twigs, wood chips, grass, moss and lichen for the nest cup; female lines it with hair, wool and feathers
EGGS: normally lays 5 or 6 white eggs with pink to reddish markings around rounded end (3-8 are possible)
INCUBATION: female sits for 14-15 days
YOUNG: nestlings are covered in dark grey down with yellow lining to mouth; both parents feed them on insects; fledglings leave the nest after 13-18 days; stay in a family group for up to another 14 days
MOULT: late July to late August
LIFE EXPECTANCY: 2-3 years

POPULATION IN BRITAIN
About 245,000 breed each year

HABITAT
Lives in mature deciduous and mixed woodland, well-wooded parks, farmland and gardens

NATURE WATCH
● The only other bird in the woods with a similar tree-hugging lifestyle is the nuthatch, which can climb headfirst down a tree as well as up, while the treecreeper can only go up.
● It suffers when old trees, its prime nest sites, are felled. It benefited from an increase in insect life on dead and dying trees after Dutch elm disease and the 1987 gales in southern England.

The Willow Warbler

Distribution

The willow warbler is common and widespread throughout the British Isles every summer. It is less reliant on finding mature woodland than the chiffchaff: willow warblers can cope with a patch of scrub or a few bushes as long as there are insects to eat and somewhere to nest.

Willow warblers breed across Europe and Asia. Oddly, although they settle farther north than the chiffchaff, they never spend the winter in Britain, whereas a small number of chiffchaffs do stay in southern England each year.

The willow warblers arrive back in Europe from their wintering quarters in West Africa in late March, early April and start leaving again in July. They have all departed by the end of September.

☐ areas where the bird is a summer visitor
▨ migration routes to Africa

NAMES
SCIENTIFIC NAME: *Phylloscopus trochilus*
NICKNAMES: Willow Wren, Tom Thumb

IDENTIFICATION
APPEARANCE: both male and female are slightly built little birds, greenish brown above and pale yellow-buff below; the only distinctive marking is a creamy stripe over each eye; legs and feet are light brown; the juveniles are usually a brighter yellow than their parents
SIZE: 11cm (4¾in) long
WINGSPAN: 16.5-22cm (6½-8¾in)
WEIGHT: 6-10g (¼-⅓oz)
FLIGHT: wings are relatively long for migration flights
VOICE: male sings a lyrical song in descending scale; contact call is a whistling *hoo-eet*; alarm call is *piu-piu*

FOOD
Eats mainly insects, which it picks off leaves and bark or plucks from the air on the wing; includes some soft fruits and early berries in its diet in late summer when building itself up for the long migration flight

BEHAVIOUR
Visits this country each summer to breed; spends our winter months in West Africa; solitary, except during the breeding season
ENEMIES: sparrowhawks and cats; use of insecticides; habitat destruction

BREEDING
PAIRING UP: breeding starts as soon as the females return from Africa in April
NESTING: nest is a loose ball of grass, leaves and moss lined with feathers and hair that is well concealed on the ground
EGGS: lays 6-8 white eggs lightly dusted with faint red
INCUBATION: undertaken mainly by the female for 13 days
YOUNG: hatchlings are scantily clad in whitish down with an orange-yellow gape and yellow flanges; fed caterpillars by both parents; spend about 13 days in the nest before fledging
MOULT: unusually undergoes two moults a year: a quick moult in July before leaving and another longer one while in Africa to keep feathers pristine
LIFE EXPECTANCY: up to 5 years

POPULATION IN BRITAIN
Over 2 million pairs breed each summer; numbers have fallen in recent years

HABITAT
All over the country, wherever there are trees in which to feed and grassy banks where they can conceal their nests

NATURE WATCH
● Three types of leaf warbler breed here each summer: the willow warbler, chiffchaff and wood warbler. All three of these tiny, yellow-green birds are virtually indistinguishable. Only their songs differ significantly: a descending trill from the willow warbler, the chiffy-chaffy of the chiffchaff and a whistle plus *sip, sip, sip, tr-r-r-r-r-r-ree-e-e* from the wood warbler.

INDEX

The entries in **bold type** refer to the main feature on the bird